Consecrated Women?

Jonathan Baker, the editor of this volume, is Principal of Pusey House, Oxford.

Numerous individuals contributed to *Consecrated Women?*, either as members of the theological and legal working parties which were convened to reflect on the issues involved, or as advisers to them. Details of all contributors can be found in Appendix 1.

Consecrated Women?

*A Contribution to the
Women Bishops Debate*

Edited by
Jonathan Baker

CANTERBURY
PRESS
Norwich

FORWARD IN FAITH
WITH A VISION FOR UNITY AND TRUTH

© Forward in Faith 2004

First published in 2004 by the Canterbury Press Norwich
(a publishing imprint of Hymns Ancient & Modern Limited,
a registered charity)
St Mary's Works, St Mary's Plain,
Norwich, Norfolk, NR3 3BH

www.scm-canterburypress.co.uk

British Library Cataloguing in Publication data

A catalogue record for this book is available
from the British Library

ISBN 1-85311-509-6

Contents

Contents

Foreword
By the Archbishop of York,
Dr David Hope

The question of the ordination of women to the Episcopate raises profound and far-reaching issues fundamental to the life of the whole Church. Already within the Anglican Communion, given that a number of Provinces have ordained women to the Episcopate 'the opportunities to participate in each other's ministry are reduced . . . and interdependence and communion thereby suffers some restriction' – so concluded the first Report of the then Archbishop of Canterbury's Commission on Communion and Women in the Episcopate.

Furthermore, it made the point that 'whatever the merits of either case', i.e. for or against this development, 'it is likely that, for the time being, the ordination of women to the priesthood and the Episcopate will remain an area of disagreement'.

I have always argued right from the start that in the matter of the ordination of women the fundamental question must be that of women and the Episcopate. For better or worse the Church of England has embarked on what might be termed the 'incremental' approach, namely beginning first with the Diaconate, currently the presbyterate/priesthood and now facing the issue of women and the Episcopate.

In fact it seemed to me entirely anomalous that the legislation pertaining to the ordination of women to the priesthood should in its very second clause contain a prohibition on the possibility of women being ordained to the Episcopate.

The Report to be published from the Working Party under

the Bishop of Rochester's chairmanship takes very seriously this whole question and presents the arguments for and against with considerable clarity and care. It demonstrates that while some may assume the matter a foregone conclusion, there nevertheless remain some very substantial theological and ecclesiological considerations to be further explored before any final conclusion is reached. Furthermore and no less important is the ecumenical dimension both of the debate itself and of the effect any decision might have on our ecumenical relationships.

This present contribution from a working party sponsored by Forward in Faith seeks further to explicate and develop a number of points of view already to be found in the Rochester Working Party's Report. It is a serious examination of the Biblical and patristic material and also seeks to engage altogether more fully with the arguments deployed in favour of moving forward to ordain women to the Episcopate. There are here some formidable contributions that make for serious theological thinking and reflection which should be a timely signal to the Church of England not to move forward over-hastily towards any legislation, but rather further to ponder and pray.

Serious consideration of course will need to be given to what provision should or ought to be made for those who remain, for whatever reason, unable to accept the ordination of women to the Episcopate.

Already there is the Act of Synod, but in my view this will not in its present form at least bear the weight of moving forward to ordain women as Bishops. Not everyone will agree with the detailed draft Measure set out in the concluding pages of this document, nevertheless it seeks to set out with clarity what some sort of 'provincial' arrangement might look like and how it might operate. Some may wish to revisit the proposals set out by the then 'Eames Commission' – the Archbishop of Canterbury's Commission on Communion and Women in the Episcopate.

But the fact of the matter remains that if the Church of England is seeking, given those continuing disagreements about which the Eames Commission spoke, truly to live with this diversity of view, living together in the highest possible degree of communion, then appropriate provision will need to be made. Paradoxically this may mean a somewhat greater distancing between those opposed and those in favour, albeit anomalous, yet ultimately in the service of the Gospel and in the service of that altogether wider unity for which Christ prayed so fervently – that the world might believe.

✠ David Ebor:

Preface
By the Bishop of Fulham,
John Broadhurst

As the Church of England entered upon the protracted debate about the ordination of women to the priesthood, which lasted through the 1980s and early 1990s, the General Synod realized that it was in an almost impossible position. At the one extreme there were those who believed that the ordination of women was a proper development of the Christian tradition, demanded by Scripture. They claimed that it was an issue of justice and that, unless the Church proceeded, it would be thought irrelevant in the modern world. At the other extreme were those who believed that the ordination of women would be a betrayal of the Christian tradition, based on a false Christology. It was at variance with the Church of England's historic claim to be part of the Catholic Church, with no doctrine or teachings of her own, and her practice of never demanding assent to anything which could not be proved from Scripture. Between the ends of the spectrum, there were large numbers of people holding a wide variety of views.

In the years which have followed, many accounts of that process have been published, naturally including reference to the many reports which General Synod received on the subject in the years before the 1992 debate. What is often omitted is any reference to the parallel debate which took place over that period about the *consequences* of such legislation – the real possibility of major division.

This concern came to a head in 1986, with the publication of *The Ordination of Women to the Priesthood: The Scope of the Legislation* (GS 738) – the report of a group appointed by the Standing Committee of General Synod and chaired by Professor David McClean. It was clear from its report that the group was concerned to protect the interests of opponents to the ordination of women and took the view that whatever safeguards were made for opponents should be both 'specific' and 'entrenched'. The group, though concerned about the need to secure Parliamentary approval and to safeguard constitutional rights, was clear that the Church had to 'address the issues on their merits alone'. Furthermore, it acknowledged the reality that those who rejected the act of a bishop in ordaining a woman 'would feel in conscience bound to refuse the ministrations of such bishops'. It was this understanding which led the group to examine five possibilities:

a the delegation of episcopal ministry;
b exemption from the spiritual jurisdiction of the diocesan bishop;
c the creation of 'non-geographical' dioceses;
d the creation of a separate body in some continuing relationship with the Church of England; and
e complete separation.

The report also went on to suggest that some form of financial provision would be needed for those whose resignation, in the event of the ordination of women, would be a matter of conscience. (It is important to spell this out because it is frequently and incorrectly asserted that Parliament bounced the Church of England into the present provisions.)

Most opponents of the ordination of women had always made it clear that they could neither function alongside women priests nor relate in the normal way to those bishops who ordained them. It would, in other words, be impossible for them to live in such a church. The report came before the Synod; but was side-lined by the then House of Bishops. The bishops were extremely concerned about division in the Church, and seemed unwilling or unable to comprehend the deeply held convictions of those opposed to the legislation (in spite of the fact that a considerable number of bishops were themselves opposed to the ordination of women to the priesthood!). When in due course the bishops reported back to the Synod, they recommended only that there should be financial provisions and that both bishops and parishes should have the right to refuse the ministry of ordained women.

In July 1988, a draft Measure emerged, accompanied by a draft Financial Provisions Measure. The legislation which came before Synod contained provisions which the bishops hoped would keep the peace: power for PCCs to prevent women priests from celebrating the Eucharist or giving Absolution; power for PCCs to prevent a woman priest being appointed as incumbent or priest-in-charge; and power for diocesan bishops completely to bar women priests from their dioceses.

Without those provisions, it is inconceivable that the Measure would have been approved by the General Synod. The plain fact is that sexual discrimination for religious reasons was an integral part of that draft Measure, not just in these provisions, but pre-eminently in Clause 2, which made it clear that women could not be consecrated to the office of Bishop. Despite the many protestations of those who now seek to rescind it, sexual discrimination in matters of order was not introduced by the later Act of Synod. Memories are short. During the debate on the draft Measure in November 1989, what is more, there was an attempt to limit the safeguards to 20 years. It was decisively and comprehensively lost. The claim so often made that the safeguards were temporary is simply untrue!

During that November 1989 debate, the Archdeacon of Leicester, David Silk (later Bishop of Ballarat), moved a motion to set up dioceses into which traditionalist parishes could be gathered. The motion was lost but I recall what I said that day:

> I must tell members of Synod that one of the things that I have found difficult in the past couple of years is the number of people on the other side who say to me and to my friends, 'You don't mean it, do you?' That is a very common expression in this Synod. I have noticed in the Synod when people say, 'This would be unacceptable to me,' people around me say, 'No, no.' There is unwillingness, I suggest, on the part of some to accept

other people's thresholds and limits. (*Report of Proceedings*, November 1989, p. 1036)

The draft Financial Provisions Measure was designed to protect the rights of clergy. Because they are self-employed, priests are unable to sue for constructive dismissal or to act in many of the other ways available to those in secular employment. Parliamentarians were extremely concerned that clergy should not lose their livelihood because of substantial changes in the Church's doctrine and practice. In February 1990, when the Financial Provisions Measure was being debated, Professor MacLean prophesied that fewer than 200 traditionalists would resign under the Measure. I argued that the number would be considerably higher. It was a further illustration of the inability to apprehend the depth of opponents' unease and their difficulties with changes in the Church's governance and ministry. Colin James, the then Bishop of Winchester, claimed that there would be:

> many more refugees unless his liberal colleagues displayed more understanding of the predicament in which his fellow traditionalists found themselves . . . They were a very precious element of Anglican tradition and should be safeguarded. (*Report of Proceedings*, February 1990, p. 142)

Meanwhile, deeply disturbed because they realized that there could be no place for them in the Church of England without adequate ecclesial provision, opponents founded Cost of Conscience. Following meetings around the country of many hundreds of clergy, culminating in a gathering of over 1,000 in Church House, Westminster, they published the pamphlet *Alternative Episcopal Oversight* (1990). It argued eloquently and forcefully that it would be impossible for opponents to remain in the Church of England unless radical provisions were made. It developed, and provided a theological rationale for, two of the proposals in the 1986 McClean Report. Effectively it asked for a parallel jurisdiction. The problem was that the majority wanted to reserve to itself the right to decide what provision should meet the consciences of the substantial minority (authoritatively numbered at the time at some 3,000 bishops, priests and deacons, together with a substantial body of lay people, female and male). Neither side appeared to be listening to the other.

Eventually, on 11 November 1992, the Measure scraped through the General Synod, narrowly gaining the necessary two-thirds majority in each House. It was then referred (as are all Measures of the General Synod) to the Ecclesiastical Committee of Parliament. The General Synod always sends a representative group to appear before the committee, and I was one of those who was present and gave evidence. Though the majority of the 30 members of the committee were in favour of the ordination of women, they were extremely concerned both for the peace of the realm and the protection of those of Her Majesty's subjects who would, in conscience, be unable to accept the new order. The archbishops and others underwent searching questioning about the legislation from members of the committee, who were of the opinion that the proposed provisions were inadequate. Several private meetings took place between the leadership of the General Synod and members of the Ecclesiastical Committee. It was made plain that any legislation would need to protect the rights and interests of those opposed to the innovation. What the Church and nation faced was the risk of an upheaval parallel to the Great Ejection of 1662.

The difficulty for the Church was that opponents knew that their consciences were being pushed to breaking point, and that this was clearly seen by many both in the national press and in Parliament. The House of Bishops, however, seemed unable to grasp the magnitude of the problem. Many imagined that opponents would simply accept the new situation. It was against this background that the House met in Manchester in January 1993. It is a tribute to the two archbishops of the time that the statement issued afterwards contained the bare bones of what was to become the Act of Synod.

The Ecclesiastical Committee met again on 5 July that year. Many members of the Committee argued strongly that the provision for opponents needed to be by means of a further Measure. The Archbishop of Canterbury laid before its members the Episcopal Ministry Act of Synod. He told the Committee: 'an Act of Synod expresses such commitment and carries compelling moral authority' (*Proceedings*, p. 126). The archbishops and others resisted a further Measure because they believed it would set in stone any provisions made, and because a Measure was not deliverable within the necessary timescale. Brian McHenry, addressing the Committee, said, 'once it [the Act] is in place I think it would be very difficult indeed for those who are unhappy about this concept to dislodge it' (*Proceedings*, p. 133).

Archbishop John Habgood has recently looked back at what happened:

> What the Act did was to extend to clergy the same right to discriminate as that given to parishes. It has allowed objectors to distance themselves from the actual ordination of women as priests, and to receive pastoral care from likeminded bishops, just as lay people can distance themselves from the Measure if their parish chooses to invoke its restrictive clauses. No time limit was set on the Act, and those of us who promoted it were relying on the Gamaliel principle (Acts 5.38–39), whereby in due course it should become plain to all those open to God's guidance, when the time has come that it is no longer needed. We assumed that members of the Church of England would be open-minded enough, and generous enough, to learn from each other, and to ask themselves on the basis of each other's experience whether this new ministry is clearly being blessed by God or not. (*New Directions*, March 2004)

What were the consequences of the ordination of women? Forward in Faith had been established in 1992 and rapidly became the main mouthpiece for opponents of the Measure. The majority of traditionalists felt that, although the Act of Synod was considerably less than they needed, they should try to live and work with it. It was essential to build up confidence if extended episcopal care was to be made to work. The first two PEVs did much to lay the foundations for this new confidence, on which the subsequent PEVs and I have built. Even with the support of Forward in Faith and the work of the PEVs, however, departures from the Church of England were substantial. Though the majority of opponents believed they could work with the Act of Synod, a substantial minority could not.

In an historically unprecedented development, 4 bishops left the Church of England – Graham Leonard, Richard Rutt,

Conrad Meyer and John Klyberg. Under the Financial Provisions Measure, 441 priests resigned; although 31 returned, the net loss amounted to 410. But to these must be added many more, mostly young priests, who were ineligible for the financial provisions, as well as many retired priests. The total loss approaches 600; without the Act of Synod, it would have been nearer 2,000!

At least 33 former members of General Synod are known to have left the Church of England, including the government minister John Selwyn Gummer. Ann Widdecombe, another government minister, but not a member of Synod, also joined the Roman Catholic Church. There were other high profile departures, including the Duchess of Kent (who, it has to be said, never publicly linked her conversion with the issue of the ordination of women), but no record exists of the number of lay people who have left the Church of England. But many of the priests who have stayed report losing key members of their congregations and the total must surely run into thousands.

It is often claimed that, when the last payment has been made, the Financial Provisions Measure will have cost the Church of England £27.5 million. This cannot be true. If those 430 clergy had continued in stipendiary ministry, their stipends would have cost substantially more. The *real* loss, however, is not financial: it is in the experienced and committed ministry which they exercised. If you add to this the loss from giving by committed laity, and the demotivating effect upon many priests unable to avail themselves of the Act of Synod, the total impact is substantial.

It was hoped that the decade following the ordination of women would be a decade of expansion – the Decade of Evangelism. Although there are some bright spots, the Church is in a considerably worse state than it was in 1992. Electoral rolls have declined from 1,398,000 in 1990 to 1,200,000 in 2004. There have been similar drops in the average Sunday attendance figures. Many dioceses are facing serious financial problems.

I am not suggesting a direct causal link between this decline and the ordination of women. The issue is more complex than that, for decline is not uniform and has characterized all the mainstream Christian denominations in the West, especially in western Europe. The author Bob Jackson, in *Hope for the Church*, examines the statistics and other research and finds

some signs of growth. He reported recently that these signs can
be found particularly in parishes which had passed the Resolutions and in evangelical parishes. My own experience bears this
out, as the parishes for which I care are either holding their own
or growing substantially. These signs of hope convince me more
than ever that the Church and nation need us. But the question
remains: do our fellow Christians value us?

I know that many thought the Act of Synod would create a
ghetto, in which opposition would wither on the vine. This has
not happened, and the number of resolution parishes is still
growing. In the parishes that I care for, the average age of the
clergy is less than that in the Church at large. Opponents of the
ordination of women as priests and bishops are not a problem
that will go away. I find increased confidence and commitment
everywhere I go. On the eve of Pentecost 2000, our millennium
celebration *Christ Our Future* at the London Arena had over
1,000 priests concelebrating with the Archbishop of York and
32 other bishops (including some from overseas); 9,000 laity
attended. It was the largest millennium service in the country.
Over 2,000 clergy support our general stance within the Church
of England; in the worldwide Anglican Communion the numbers
would of course be much greater.

It is sometimes claimed that our constituency is sexist and
abusive of women. I can find very little evidence for this. There
have been many accusations, but a careful study of the published
literature will show that an overwhelming majority of examples
of alleged sexist behaviour and prejudice come from those who
support the ordination of women but betray misogynist tenden-
cies. In my personal experience, most Act of Synod parishes are
willing to treat women priests as fellow workers in the vineyard
and only regret that they are unable to accept their priesthood.

Preaching on 3 March 2004 in St Bartholomew's, Leeds, at a
service to celebrate the tenth Anniversary of the Act of Synod, the
Archbishop of York remarked:

And perhaps those who are currently seeking the rescinding
the Act of Synod might turn their minds back to ten years ago
– a reasonably short time in the history and life of the Church.
They might recall that some of the very same people are those

who were at the time ten years ago giving very clear assurances about its continuance and survival, not least at the time when the Ecclesiastical Committee of Parliament was raising precisely the same questions about its durability and thus to coin a phrase 'desirous of adding a Measure to a Measure', hence this is exactly what they foresaw might or could happen. It would not only be a tragedy if the Act of Synod were to be rescinded; it would be an act of betrayal and trigger a new crisis for our Church.

In 1991, soon after the announcement of his move from Bath and Wells to Canterbury, George Carey created an uproar by describing, in an interview with the *Reader's Digest*, 'the idea that only a male can represent Christ at the altar . . . [as] . . . a most serious heresy'. But, as is well known, he very rapidly came to understand the delicacy of the situation and was indeed quite supportive of traditionalists, doing his best to stop the Church of England tearing itself apart over the issue of women priests.

Because he recognized that the Act of Synod could no longer work if women were ordained as bishops, Dr Carey suggested, at a meeting with Forward in Faith in York in 2002, that we should set up a working party to study the question of women in the episcopate and to produce a report parallel to that of the House of Bishops' working party, which was to study the subject under the chairmanship of the Bishop of Rochester. In fact, we set up two working parties – one theological and one legal. They have worked in parallel but independently of each other for some two and a half years, and their reports are now published in this book.

We are very grateful to Cardinal Cormac Murphy O'Connor for asking Fr Aidan Nichols, OP, to be the Roman Catholic observer on the Theological Working Party, and similarly to Archbishop Gregorios for asking Bishop Kallistos Ware to be the Orthodox observer. Both have contributed substantially to the theological debate.

We are also very grateful to those who agreed to be our assessors: Dr Mary Tanner as assessor to the Theological Report, Fr Robin Ellis as assessor to the Legal Report and Mr Oswald Clark, who has been an assessor to both. Dr Brian Hanson acted as legal assessor to the Theological Group. Both working parties have taken evidence from a large number of people, including virtually all the traditional catholic bishops in the Church of England.

This report is intended to be a contribution to the formal debate upon which the Church will inevitably embark. The present nightmare for the Church of England is that the 1993 Measure has created a dual ministry, effectively putting Canon A4 on the recognition of ministers in cold storage. Manifestly, this is unsatisfactory for both sides of the debate. I believe that a formal, proper arrangement – a structural solution – for traditionalists, would give both sides what they want. The Church of England could go forward cohesively and with integrity. Its members, on whichever side, would no longer feel threatened or challenged by those with whom they disagree.

The choice facing us all is stark: are we to engage upon an endless war of attrition which harms the gospel and fails to recognize the integrity and rights of Christian conscience; or do we have the generosity and charity to give each other the space we all need?

Liz Carney: *So while the two integrities exists, is there any possibility that a woman will be consecrated bishop?*
John Habgood: *I think that I'm probably out of line here and I'm not in any case in any position to do anything about it, but I would have argued against it.*
from an interview in *File on Four*, BBC Radio 4, 7 October, 1997

✠ John Fulham

Abbreviations

ARCIC	Anglican–Roman-Catholic International Commission
ASB	*Alternative Service Book 1980*
CTS Do	Catholic Truth Society, Doctrine Series
Ecc LJ	*Ecclesiastical Law Journal*
FiF	Forward in Faith
GS	General Synod
PCC	parochial church council
PAB	Provincial Assistant Bishop
PEV	Provincial Episcopal Visitor
RSV	Revised Standard Version of the Bible

Part One

Women Bishops:
A Theological Enquiry

I

Introduction

1.1   In November 1992, the General Synod of the Church of England gave final approval to legislation enabling the ordination of women as priests. That legislation, which duly passed the following year, explicitly excluded any provision for the episcopal ordination of women. Inevitably, debate and discussion on the rightness or otherwise of allowing women to become bishops has continued – indeed, has accelerated – since the 1992 vote and the first ordinations of women priests in 1994.

1.2   The Church now awaits the report of a commission chaired by the Bishop of Rochester on the theology of women and the episcopate. Numbers of diocesan synod motions have been brought to the General Synod, requesting the immediate drafting of a further Measure to enable women to become bishops. Meanwhile, in the Church of England at large, a significant minority of bishops, priests, deacons and lay people has not received the priestly ministry of women, and, for the same reasons and more, would certainly not receive the episcopal ministry of a woman.

1.3   This report is written by a working party comprising a group of Anglican clergy (bishops and priests) and lay people[1] who seek to uphold the tradition of the Church

---

[1] A list of members of this working party, and of those who have assisted it in its work, appears as Appendix 1 below.

down the ages. With the overwhelming number of Christians throughout the world today, they affirm that the office and ministry of bishop (and priest) in the Church of God is restricted to males. In this report, we shall argue that this tradition is neither casual nor trivial; neither culturally conditioned nor merely provisional. It is an intimate and integral part of the salvation won for us in Jesus Christ, and of the life of his Body on earth, the Church.

1.4   In order to seek to understand the classical view of the ordained ministry, it is necessary to look at underlying theological issues: the Fatherhood of God and the necessary maleness of the incarnate Son. We shall consider the sacramental consonance between Our Lord in his maleness and the maleness of the bishop, whose office as teacher, shepherd of souls, president of the eucharistic banquet and guarantor of unity continues the mission of Jesus Christ. Jesus is the One sent by the Father, and who in turn sends his apostles into the world.

1.5   We shall look not only at those texts in the New Testament traditionally associated with the question of 'headship', but also, and crucially, at the rich metaphor in the Scriptures which can be termed *nuptial imagery*. We shall contend that as Christ the Bridegroom seeks out and saves the Church, his bride, so the bishop stands in a nuptial relationship with the flock entrusted to his care.

1.6   We shall argue that, if the chief pastor of the diocese – the one, indeed, whose Eucharist constitutes the diocese as a sacramental reality rather than simply as an administrative unit – were to be a woman, then not only symbolic likeness, but the reality to which that symbolism points, and in which it participates, would be ruptured.

1.7   Our discussion of the primary issues will inevitably

involve not only questions about Christian ministry (and ordained ministry in particular), but also wider issues. We shall ask how the Church is to understand God's saving purposes as revealed by his gracious creation of humankind in two complementary genders. We shall affirm our belief that it is as much part of God's good purposes to redeem us as male and female, as to create us so. We shall argue that a right understanding of what it is to be created male and female (which necessarily informs a right understanding of ministry in the Church) requires a proper celebration of the distinctiveness of the sexes, rather than a blurring of sexual difference.

1.8   Having argued these fundamental principles, we shall go on to look at some of the issues which particularly bear on the question of women bishops in the Church of England and the Anglican Communion. Ecclesiology *is* theology. The consequences of decisions about Holy Order, which touch so fundamentally on the life of the Christian community, are not second-order matters. They are of central importance to our life together in the Church, the Body of Christ on earth. We recognize that there will be many readers of this report who are agnostic about one or more of the theological arguments which we shall present, yet whose doctrine of the Church, and the lack of consensus within it for rejecting those premises, would make it impossible for them to accept the ordination of women. Thus we shall revisit the issue of authority as it relates to the Church of England's ability to make decisions on such fundamental issues as Holy Order. We shall ask what consequences follow when such decisions are contrary to the doctrine and practice of the universal Church, East and West. The two great churches (numerically and geographically) constitute overwhelmingly the greater part of Christianity today. To them the Church of England bears an historic 'family likeness'. They are the rock from which she was hewn.

1.9   We shall want to challenge the view that the Church of England possesses authority to make such changes on its own account. We shall argue that to choose to exercise authority in this way is decisively and radically to change the Church of England's self-understanding.[2] We shall look at some of the consequences of an episcopate which no longer enjoys mutual recognition throughout our Communion; and at some of the strategies which have evolved for dealing with this situation of impaired communion both here and elsewhere. We shall glance, also, at a possible future strategy for dealing with a new situation where the integrity and acceptability of the episcopate has been called into question – so-called *team episcope*. We shall highlight what we believe to be critical questions which must be asked of such an approach.

1.10   Finally, we shall look at the consequences for the Church of England in the event of a decision to proceed to the ordination of women as bishops. We shall present proposals for the future, to enable those who retain the understanding of episcopacy which the Church universal has held down the ages to remain within the family of the Anglican Communion, living an authentically catholic ecclesial life as loyal members of the Church of England.

1.11   The writing of this report has presented its authors with a unique problem. Even Pope John Paul II has made it clear that his office is to restate authoritatively and clearly the tradition of the Church: that Our Lord chose only male apostles, and that his example is bind-

---

[2] 'The Church of England . . . belongs to the true and apostolic Church of Christ' (Canon Al); see also the *Preface* to the *Declaration of Assent* (Canon C15); and note also this statement by the House of Bishops: 'The Church of England traces its origins back to the beginnings of Christianity in England and is continuous with the Church of the Apostles and Fathers.' (*The Eucharist: sacrament of unity* GS Misc 632, London, 2001, p. 14 para. 30.)

ing on the Church for all time. The Pope has left it to theologians to seek to provide a coherent *rationale* for the free, sovereign and gracious action of God in Christ. That is what this report sets out to do: to defend and explain what (in one sense) needs no further defence. We seek to defend the unvarying tradition of the Catholic Church – that Bride for whom Our Lord died, with whom he promised to remain 'to the end of the age', and whose life is guided, in all things, by the Holy Spirit. For many of us it is enough to say what Holy Church teaches, and has always taught. There is therefore almost a presumption in this report – a presumption that we may indeed *justify the ways of God to man*. The reader is urged to take the willing acknowledgement of this presumption as an apology for any deficiencies in what follows.

2

The Breadth of the Task

2.1 Introduction

2.1.1 This report arises, in the first instance, as one part of
a response to the motion passed by the General Synod
of 1995–2000, in the name of the then Archdeacon of
Tonbridge (the Venerable Judith Rose). Archdeacon
Rose's motion read:

> That this Synod ask the House of Bishops to initiate
> further theological study on the episcopate, focuss-
> ing on the issues that need to be addressed in prepara-
> tion for the debate on women in the episcopate in the
> Church of England, and to make a progress report
> on this study to Synod in the next two years.

2.1.2 The deliberations and discussions of our working
party, however, have necessarily been set in a wider
context. The question of whether women can be admitted to the episcopate, we quickly realized, is inseparable from questions which touch on the doctrines of
God and creation, of Christology and the Incarnation,
and of the nature and function, within the whole life of
the Church, of the work of both priest and bishop. It is
with these fundamental theological questions that we
begin.

2.1.3 The main premise of all our arguments needs to be
stated from the start. It is this: that we believe that we
can trust God's revelation of himself in Scripture. We
believe that the insights into the divine nature which

the narratives of Scripture disclose are neither capricious nor misleading, but point us to the truth. In this chapter we draw attention to five factors which provide the context in which our work has been undertaken.

- The free choice of Jesus Christ and the obedience of the Church to the example of the Lord.
- The ministry of the Church as a continuation of the mission of the Son.
- The sacramental and symbolic continuity between the High Priesthood of Christ and the ministerial priesthood in the Church.
- The grammar of the divine.
- Salvation history as narrative.

2.2   The free choice of Jesus Christ and the obedience of the Church to the example of the Lord

2.2.1   The free choice by Jesus Christ of twelve men to be his Apostles is the strongest and simplest reason for remaining faithful to the unbroken tradition of the Church in the matter of Holy Order. After that, all else could be said to be theological speculation.

2.2.2   The Twelve (whose number is restored by the election of Matthias after the betrayal and suicide of Judas Iscariot) constitute the New Israel – each in his own person symbolizing the renewal of the twelve tribes of the Old Covenant. At the same time they point forward to the new Temple, the eschatological people of God, and so to the heavenly banquet of the Kingdom (of which the Eucharist is the earthly foreshadowing). We shall consider later this 'forward-looking' aspect to what it means to be an apostle (and, by extension, to be a bishop and part of the apostolic college).

2.2.3   The free choice of Jesus Christ in electing only men to
         be numbered among the Twelve is the most important
         argument for Christians of the Orthodox Churches.[3]
         For the Roman Catholic Church, we note the words of
         Pope John Paul II in *Ordinatio sacerdotalis:* [4]

> The Church has always acknowledged as a perennial
> norm her Lord's way of acting in choosing the twelve
> men whom he made the foundation of his Church.

Sara Butler[5] recalls Cardinal Joseph Ratzinger's essay,
'The Limits of Church Authority', in *L'Osservatore
Romano* of 29 June 1994, in which he explains that the
Pope

> wished to emphasize the limits to the Church's author-
> ity by calling attention to the will of Christ, and that
> he leaves the task of elaborating the anthropological
> implications of this choice to the theologians.

2.2.4   As we seek now to begin doing our theology, we too
         stand under that free choice of Jesus Christ as norma-
         tive for the life of the Church.

2.3   The ministry of the Church as a continuation of the mission of the Son

2.3.1   At the heart of our understanding of the episcopate
         and the presbyterate lies that network of relation-
         ships which constitutes the great *motif* of mission in
         the Fourth Gospel. The Son sends his disciples into the

---

[3] We are grateful to Bishop Kallistos of Diokleia, the Orthodox observer
on our Working Party, for a clear expression of this principle. It should be
noted that the question of the ordination of women has yet to be discussed in
a thorough and systematic way by the Orthodox. Bishop Kallistos' *personal*
view, however, is that the matter should be regarded as an open question.

[4] John Paul II, 'Ordinatio sacerdotalis', *Acta Apostolicae Sedis* 86 (1994),
pp. 545–8.

[5] In 'The Ordination of Women: A New Obstacle to the Recognition of
Anglican Orders', in R. William Franklin (ed.), *Anglican Orders: Essays on
the Centenary of Apostolicae Curae 1896–1996*.

world to continue his work, just as the Father sent the Son. We will argue that the priest and, *par excellence,* the bishop, is set apart to do the work of Christ, even as the Son is sent by the Father.

2.3.2 It is important to emphasize at once that no neglect or denial of the mission of the whole people of God is implied here. All people, without distinction (as Galatians 3.28 points out) find their salvation in Christ. But we want to assert that it is given to the bishop (and the priest) to represent Christ as the High Priest, the Bridegroom, and the new Adam. He is the head of the redeemed human race and of the household of God. The sex of the bishop (and priest) is not irrelevant, but integral rather, to this representation.

2.4 The sacramental and symbolic continuity between the High Priesthood of Christ and the ministerial priesthood in the Church

2.4.1 The argument here, of course, requires that a sacramental and symbolic continuity exists between the High Priesthood of Jesus Christ and the work of the bishop (and priest) in continuing the work of that High Priesthood. In particular, it requires a direct connection to be made between Jesus the High Priest and the bishop as he presides over the Eucharist at which 'we, the first-fruits of his death and resurrection, are offered by Christ to the Father'.[6]

2.4.2 We will look at the way in which, in the office and work of the bishop, different strands coalesce: the bishop as chief celebrant of the Eucharist (and thus – as Ignatius and Cyprian among others saw him – 'High

---

[6] *Eucharistic Presidency: A Theological Statement by the House of Bishops of the General Synod,* 1997, p. 35.

Priest' of the mysteries of the New Covenant);[7] the bishop as teacher (unfolded particularly in the writings of St Irenaeus);[8] the bishop as the one who exercises *episcope* or oversight. All of these illustrate different but connected aspects of the bishop's role as *paterfamilias* of the household of the new people of God.

2.4.3 We recognize that not all Anglicans share our understanding of the episcopate linking it both sacramentally and symbolically with the High Priesthood of Christ. It is important to emphasize that this is the view of the members of this working party and of many in the Church of England for whom they speak. We hope that it will be recognized that it is held with seriousness and integrity. It is shared, moreover, with catholic Christians in this and other communions. It possesses a theological coherence worthy of respect.

2.5 **The grammar of the divine**

2.5.1 To affirm this symbolic connection is, of course, to raise a question about the maleness of Jesus himself, and, in turn, about the language with which we (and, crucially, with which the Scriptures) habitually speak of God.

---

[7] 'In the Eucharist, the bishop or priest "was" the high priest and therefore the Lord . . . He took into the holy of holies the bread and wine of the new bloodless sacrifice which became the body and blood of the Lord; this effected the atonement and renewal of the creation, and thus established on earth the expected Kingdom.' Margaret Barker, *The Great High Priest*, 2003, p. 58.

[8] Both the Anglican liturgical scholar Dom Gregory Dix and, more recently, the Orthodox theologian John Zizioulas agree that while the role of the bishop as *teacher* emerges more strongly as the need authoritatively to refute heresy increases, the older model is the 'mystical' one of the bishop as High Priest, the icon of the Son and/or of the Father sending the Son. Zizioulas in particular argues that the teaching office of the episcopate can never overshadow its High Priestly function, because the teaching in the bishop's sermon is always primarily to do with the sacramental mystery being proclaimed.

2.5.2   For the Christian, as for the Israelite, all our speech about the divine must be by way of analogy, metaphor and image. God is mystery. God is ultimately beyond all human knowledge and imagining. Yet we cannot allow this proper understanding of the apophatic way to prevent us from saying anything at all about God. Nor does it imply that, since no human language can do justice to the divine nature, the language that is used of God is a matter of indifference, and can never be of decisive significance in the life of the Church. To take such an approach is, brutally, to cease to believe in a God who makes himself known. It is to cease to understand Christianity as a revealed religion.

2.5.3   The witness of Scripture is that the One who is Absolute has chosen to enter into a relationship with his creation. He has thereby put himself within the arena of human knowledge and imagining. More than that, God has called into existence a community of faith. That community (like all communities) has its own patterns of language and narrative. The language which both creates and expresses that faith community cannot be lightly changed or cast aside. To do so is not merely to change the way in which the narrative of the community is related, but to change the story itself. To put it another way, to be members of the community of faith requires us to stand within the tradition by which that community has been formed. Language-patterns are not incidental to the tradition, but intimately meshed with it.

2.6   Salvation history as narrative

2.6.1   The great Christian 'story', the story of salvation history as it is unfolded in the Scriptures (which has, as its hero – to continue the literary analogy – a male victim who dies a violent and bloody death), resonates and speaks with clarity in every age and with every culture. Its symbols and archetypes are universal.

2.6.2   The power of the 'story', moreover, resides in paradox: in the confounding of expectations and in the reversal of roles.[9] At the heart of the biblical narrative is the idea of *kenosis* (the self-emptying of the Godhead at the Incarnation, and the self-offering and self-abandonment of the Son on the Cross). Just as it is impossible to give away that which you do not already possess, just as only those who have power are in a position to renounce it, so we believe the Bible story to be unimaginable without *normative* use of male language to describe (by analogy) the First Person of the Trinity, and of the Incarnation of the Second Person as a male. Without that language it would, quite simply, be a different story.

2.6.3   The matter can be put succinctly: is it remotely imaginable that the foundational 'story' of Christian tradition could revolve around a female Saviour, crucified on Calvary? Surely, whatever might be involved in such an event, it would be something quite different from the death of Jesus Christ. His sacrificial death not only fulfils the scriptural pattern (looking back to Joseph, to Isaac and, reaching back even beyond the inauguration of the covenant with Abraham, to Abel), it also resonates with human instinct and human experience in general. Both affirm the necessity of a male redeemer to meet, to absolve and to heal the consequences of (overwhelmingly male) violence and sin.

---

[9] A classic example of this motif of role reversal is found in the Johannine account of the appearance of the risen Christ first to Mary Magdalen. The impact of the story lies in its 'shock value': Mary is not herself one of the Apostles, but is *apostola Apostolorum*, the 'apostle of the Apostles'. In Jewish tradition a lone woman could not be a witness in a court of law, which required three male witnesses. The ironic point is that she who cannot witness is made to do so to those who have been called as witnesses. The whole force of this, of course, is quite lost if Mary is simply counted, in the usual feminist way, as an Apostle like all the rest.

2.7   Conclusion

2.7.1   These are large and complex themes. They can perhaps be summarized thus.

- First, that the community of faith must continue to stand within the language-patterns which have both formed it and express its foundational beliefs.
- Second, that the narratives of the faith community (as unfolded in the Scriptures) turn on a number of key symbols and archetypes which have universal resonance, and which cannot be changed or cast aside without fundamentally altering the narrative itself. (That they have universal resonance should not surprise us, for they accord with the patterns of creation which is God's own work.)
- Third, that the most fundamental of all the symbols of the Judaeo-Christian narrative is that of the redemptive sacrifice of a male. That symbol finds its fulfilment in the atoning death of Jesus Christ on the Cross. (At that point, of course, we move also from symbol to reality – the deepest reality there can be, God's own life. This is no longer 'story', but the meta-narrative in which all things are subsumed.)

2.7.2   Taking these three points together, we believe that a woman representing this heroic male figure of self-sacrifice (as a bishop or priest, we believe, necessarily does), at best jeopardizes, and at worst threatens to destroy, the foundational narrative of the faith community to which we belong.[10] We arrive, at last,

---

[10] That the Church of England has always behaved as if this were indeed the case might be suggested by the fact that in all of her ordinals, down to and including that in the *Alternative Service Book 1980*, the minister presenting a candidate for ordination to the bishop addresses him as 'Reverend Father in God', a particular title which is intended, surely, to convey far more than merely the gender of the prelate. This form of address is retained in the proposed revision of the ordinal to accompany *Common Worship* recently published in draft by the Liturgical Commission of the General Synod.

at the point at which C. S. Lewis arrived, at the end of his thoughtful, and humble, essay, 'Priestesses in the Church?'[11]

> With the Church, we are farther in: for there we are dealing with male and female not merely as facts of nature but as the live and awful shadows of realities utterly beyond our control and largely beyond our direct knowledge. Or rather, we are not dealing with them but (as we shall soon learn if we meddle) they are dealing with us.

2.7.3   The language of God in Scripture is definitive for us, we conclude, because it both forms and expresses the community of faith in which we stand. It bears more than a merely casual or transitory significance. Scriptural language – the word of God about God – invites us, with Jesus, to speak of God as Father, and to be drawn to share (by adoption) in that relationship between Father and Son which unfolds in the earthly mission of Jesus Christ. All this is merely to say that we seek to do our theology as classical Anglicans, holding that 'Holy Scripture containeth all things necessary to salvation.'[12]

---

[11] Originally published under the title 'Notes on the Way', *Time and Tide*, 29 (14 August 1948).

[12] Article VI.

3

The Fatherhood of God

3.1 Introduction

3.1.1 We turn now to the way in which God is revealed as
Father: first by analogy in the Old Testament, and then,
in the New Testament, as one not only described as
acting *like* a father (that is to say, in ways in which the
analogy of human fatherhood is merely helpful), but of
whom the term *Father* becomes a proper name. This
development is found especially in the Fourth Gospel,
but is also present in some of the writings of St Paul.

3.2 The Old Testament

3.2.1 The overwhelming evidence of the Hebrew Scriptures
is of a people who habitually use the masculine form
for the divine Name, and call on God as 'Father'. In
fact, the Old Testament is remarkably reticent in its use
of the term. This is surely because, as Thomas Smail has
so clearly explained,[13] it wants to put as much distance
as possible between the one true and living God, the
God of Israel, and the pagan notion of the god as the
generative source who has a natural relationship with
his people. The God of Abraham, Isaac and Jacob – the
God who is I AM – is the transcendent and all-holy
one. He creates the universe outside of himself and by

---

[13] In his *The Forgotten Father: Rediscovering the Heart of the Christian
Gospel*, 1987, pp. 36ff.

the pure exercise of his will. Creator and created do not
share the same nature. Every created thing reflects, in
some way or another, the essence of the Creator: this
is true in particular of mankind, the 'image of God',
whose being is made up, in part, of sexually differentiated corporeality.[14]

3.2.2   There is an austerity in the Old Testament about
the use of 'fatherhood' as a way of describing God's
relationship to his chosen people. It safeguards that
relationship as one of covenant, election and will. It is
not one of affinity in nature or generation.

3.2.3   But there is a paradox here. It is precisely by its most
careful use of the term *Father* that the Old Testament
reinforces our awareness of the term as necessary and
indispensable. While God may be spoken of, from time
to time, as behaving or acting in a motherly way, or ex-
hibiting maternal feelings towards his people, the very
rarity of these occasions renders the images arresting,
indeed startling. *Father* and *Fatherhood*, on the other
hand, remain the only *proper analogies* for God (who
is, of course, without gender).

3.2.4   What the Hebrew Scriptures so desperately want to
convey about God is that he is set apart from the gods.
God does not create from within himself; he does not
bear and give birth to the creation. To such another
god the terms *mother* and *motherhood* would be appropriate, expressing 'her' action of creation. From the
choices available by analogy from human experience,
only the term *Father* and the relationship suggested
by *Fatherhood* does justice to the action of the God of
Israel. It is biological fathers who take the initiative in
creating new life. They bring it to being not within, but
outside, their own bodies.

---

[14] Genesis 1.27.

3.2.5   We can explore further the notion of the 'Fatherhood' of the God of Israel. As Manfred Hauke has observed,[15] the term is suggestive not only of the transcendence of YHWH, but also of his power (authority) and benevolence. It enables God's love, compassion and mercy, of which the Old Testament so frequently speaks, to be tellingly 'counterpointed' with his omnipotence, righteousness and holiness. The masculine language used of God in the Old Testament thus inaugurates a succession of images. Indeed, they are more than simply images, for they constitute, rather than merely symbolize, a reality. These images are continued in the *kenosis* (self-emptying) of the Word at the Incarnation, in the passion and death of the Son of God, and in the sacramental re-presentation of the sacrifice of the Son on the altar at the Eucharist.

3.2.6   Members of the Working Party have variously described this pattern of the emptying out of the male – the historical reality of Calvary, prefigured by analogy in the attributes by which YHWH is characterized in the Old Testament – as 'gracious patriarchy', 'benevolent patriarchy', or (recognizing the almost irredeemably negative connotations of the word 'patriarchy', or of any phrase containing it, to the contemporary sensibility), a '*Paterology* of divine love and sacrifice'.[16]

3.2.7   Briefly: we can say that because there is a greater continuity between mother and child than between father and child, a pantheist religion (that is, one in which god and the creation are more or less a continuum) will naturally prefer maternal symbols. Judaism (and hence Christianity), which emphasizes the divine transcendence (and immanence made possible only as

---

[15] *Women in the Priesthood?* 1986, pp. 221ff.

[16] We are grateful to Fr Aidan Nichols, OP, for suggesting this term, which offers an account of the study of the nature of the First Person of the Holy Trinity, the Father, as 'Christology' and 'Pneumatology' to denote that of the Second and Third persons.

a consequence of transcendence) will represent this through paternal symbols.

3.2.8   In the Old Testament, the key terms used of the God of Israel – even though the Hebrew writings are sparing with their use of the actual word 'father' – all belong to the paternal 'family' of symbols: 'king', 'master', 'judge' and 'husband'.

3.2.9   All this may be summarized thus:

- The imagery of the Old Testament, taken as a whole, offers us a picture of God who possesses *personal paternal authority* (not 'paternalism'), but who condescends to exercise that authority graciously, mercifully and compassionately.
- The demonstration of these divine attributes (that is, grace, mercy, compassion and so on) is all the more telling because of the essential *paternity* (rather than *maternity*) through which God chooses to reveal himself.

3.3   The New Testament

3.3.1   With the Incarnation, the coming into the world of the eternal Son at the conception of Jesus Christ in the womb of Mary, the Fatherhood of God not merely gains prominence, but becomes the defining characteristic of the relationship between God and his people.

3.3.2   There never has been a time when Christians did not call God 'Father'. In the New Testament, the term is used on over 250 separate occasions. It is both normative and central.[17] Jesus commands his disciples to pray,

---

[17] We could scarcely improve on the words of O. Quick in *The Christian Sacraments*, Nisbet, 1927, p. 164: 'It is clear that Our Lord did insist upon the truth of God's Fatherhood so strongly and in such a special sense that

'Our Father'.[18] In the Garden of Gethsemane[19] and on the Cross[20] in the hour of his agony, Jesus himself prays to his Father. He speaks of the Temple as his Father's house.[21] He commands the disciples to exercise mercy even as their Father is merciful,[22] and to call no man on earth their father, as they have but one Father who is in heaven.[23]

3.3.3 The most sustained invocation by Jesus of his *Father* is found in the Fourth Gospel.[24] The Johannine usage requires particular attention, for it exemplifies *par excellence* the development (already present in the synoptics) of the way in which 'Father' is deployed, from analogy into proper name. God is no longer said to be *like* a father. Jesus names him as such. We might even say that in chapter 17 of St John's Gospel the name of God (the Name hidden in the Tetragrammaton, YHWH, of Exodus 3) is revealed to be 'Father'.[25]

3.3.4 Three different but related elements establish the critical importance of the Fatherhood of God in the New Testament:

- Jesus says that God is 'like a father';
- Jesus calls God 'Father' (by virtue of his unique relationship with him);

---

this teaching may legitimately be said to form a fundamental principle of his message as well as a mark of its originality.'

[18] Matthew 6.9.

[19] Mark 14.36 and parallels. In St Mark's account, Jesus prays *Abba*, the term of familiarity and intimacy taken up by St Paul in the Letter to the Romans and the Letter to the Galatians.

[20] Luke 23.34.

[21] Luke 2.49.

[22] Luke 6.36.

[23] Matthew 23.9.

[24] John 14—17, *passim*; and note also Matthew 11.25–8 (the so-called 'Johannine bolt in the synoptic blue').

[25] It is perhaps no accident that *Father* is the first of the attributes – or names – to be ascribed to God in the Creeds, preceding 'maker' or 'creator'.

- Jesus invites us to call God 'Father', to share in that relationship which is ours not by nature but by adoption.

3.3.5   In the initiation rites of the early Church (rites which many scholars believe St Paul to be alluding to directly in the Letter to the Galatians),[26] the emergent catechumen comes up out of the waters of baptism shouting, 'Abba!', denoting precisely that he or she has been admitted into the community of those who are enabled to call upon God by his proper Name.[27]

3.3.6   There is nothing controversial here, and we emphasize these points only because they have not been sufficiently prominent. Jesus consistently and deliberately speaks of the Father; he understands himself to be the Father's Son; he urges those who listen to him to see themselves as those who must think of God as Father and pray to him as such. The New Testament, moreover, has far more to say than simply to establish that the relationship between Jesus and the one who sends him is most conveniently and helpfully cast in terms of that of a father and a son. Jesus Christ is *the* representative of the Father, the one upon whom has been bestowed 'the Name which is above every other name',[28] the one who is 'the image of the unseen God',[29] who 're-

---

[26] Galatians 4.7.

[27] An understanding of baptism continued in, for example, the initiation rites of the modern Roman Catholic Church. The celebrant addresses 'the parents, godparents and the whole assembly' as he invites them to pray the Our Father. 'These children have been reborn in baptism. They are now called children of God, for so indeed they are. In confirmation they will receive the fullness of God's Spirit. In Holy Communion they will share the banquet of Christ's sacrifice, calling God their Father in the midst of the Church. In their name, in the spirit of our common sonship, let us pray together in the words our Lord has given us: . . .' Note the following: they are able to call God Father because they are his children through baptism; the context in which they do this is as members of the eucharistic community.

[28] Philippians 2.9.

[29] Colossians 1.15.

flects the glory of God and bears the very stamp of his nature'.[30] 'I and the Father are one,' Jesus says in the Fourth Gospel, and 'He who has seen me has seen the Father.'[31] It is as *Son*, the divine Second Person of the Trinity existing as man,[32] incarnate specifically as a male, that God makes the full and final revelation of himself in Jesus Christ. And it is Jesus Christ who speaks, normatively, frequently, and with specific and deliberate emphasis, of his Father who is in heaven. The commission given by the Lord to his disciples is to go out and to baptize all the nations, 'in the name of the Father and of the Son and of the Holy Spirit'.[33]

3.4   Excursus: an objection

3.4.1   Before we leave these biblical themes of fatherhood in the Old and New Testaments, we might pause to consider the objection that any emphasis on the 'Fatherhood' of God will lead to a mistaken deifying of one sex at the expense of the other, and that such imagery needs to be either discarded altogether or 'balanced' by an equal sense of God as 'mother'.

3.4.2   Our first response, *of course*, is to say again – as every faithful Israelite would have agreed – that in his essential nature, God has no gender. Second, we must surely agree with George W. Rutler[34] that *while it may be maintained that the motherhood of God is a half-truth in that he gives character and birth and nurture to creation, it is a also a half-lie which the Fatherhood of God is not.* The God of revelation, the God of human experience, claims sexual language about himself, and

---

[30] Hebrews 1.3.
[31] John 10.30; 14.9.
[32] 'Christ is the Logos, God himself, existing as man.' Thomas G. Weinandy, OFM Cap., in *Does God Change?* St Bede's, 1985.
[33] Matthew 28.19.
[34] In *Priest and Priestess*, 2003, p. 35.

that sexual language is overwhelmingly male. To seek to evacuate such language of any meaning is to turn the God of the Bible, the God of Abraham, Isaac and Jacob, into a pale shadow of himself,[35] and to substitute for I AM the 'Supreme Being' of the Deist and neoclassical revolutionary – an Idea (and ideas, of course, are always easily manipulated by men), rather than a person.

3.4.3   The 'paternal family' of symbols points to something *personal*. If we take 'king' as our example again, then we must agree with Hauke[36] that we can imagine what it means to say that God is King in a way that we could never imagine God as President – or, indeed, as a collective or committee of government. To remove or ignore sexual imagery is necessarily to downplay and degrade all that we know (by revelation) of God as the *living* God. To insist on speaking of God as 'mother' as much as 'father', is to replace the God whom we meet in the pages of Scripture with another deity of our own invention.

3.4.4   The divine image, nevertheless, is every bit as much in women as in men (Genesis 1.27 again), and God's revelation of himself as Father in no way threatens the fact that he is Father both to women and to men alike.

3.4.5   We argue, then, that (beginning with the Old Testament), 'gracious patriarchy', 'benevolent patriarchy', or the 'divine paterology of love and sacrifice' is indeed the pattern of the Scriptures. It is the pattern which the coming of Christ and the inauguration of the New Covenant fulfil, and which the tradition of the Church takes up with alacrity. To that understanding, in both its pastoral and sacramental life, the Church is called to remain faithful.

---

[35] Rutler, ibid., p. 73: 'To dispense with the maleness of God is also to dispense with some of the most revealing metaphors of scripture.'
[36] *Women in the Priesthood?*, p. 226.

4

Incarnation and Headship

4.1   A male incarnation

4.1.1   'What is the significance of the maleness of the Incarnation?' It is a question which the Church of England has posed directly before. The authors of the 1986 Report of the Faith and Order Advisory Group, *The Priesthood of the Ordained Ministry*, published by the Board for Mission and Unity of the General Synod, wrote as follows:

> The ordained priest has a representative function, both in representing Christ to the people and the people to God. Can such a function be appropriately exercised by women as well as men? This involves considering what significance is to be placed upon the maleness of Jesus and whether it is therefore appropriate for women to represent Christ to the people. It also raises questions concerning the significance of male and female in the order of creation and whether women can represent the whole Church before God as men have traditionally done.[37]

4.1.2   We note that the 1986 report asked the question in the form in which we have asked it: 'What is the significance of the maleness of Jesus?' An alternative question ('Is it significant that the Incarnation is male?') carries,

---

[37] Chapter 11, 'The Ordination of Women to the Priesthood', p. 87.

subliminally, a different set of presuppositions. That is
the question favoured by those who want to emphasize
only the (undifferentiated) humanity of Jesus Christ,
and so to render his maleness a matter of indifference.
They want, in a well-known phrase, to suggest that the
maleness of Jesus is not '*soteriologically significant*'.
We shall return to this point later in the report, in the
particular context of the use which has been made both
of Galatians 3.28 and of the famous *dictum* of St Gregory Nazianzen, 'the unassumed is unhealed'.[38]

4.1.3   To turn the maleness of Christ into, as it were, a merely
trivial detail, is, we believe, seriously to damage the
classical doctrine of the Incarnation and of the person
of Christ. There is, quite simply, no way of existing
as a human being without also existing in either the
male or female sex.[39] Sexual differentiation is of a different order from other characteristics which separate
individuals one from another – race, colour, height,
and so on. Natural theology, scientific and cultural
observation, experience and revelation all cohere. The
creation of humankind in two complementary sexes is
fundamental to the narratives of Genesis 1 and 2, and
is prelapsarian: even in paradise Adam needs Eve and
humankind exists as male and female. There can, then,
be no incarnation which is a true incarnation, in which
the Godhead assumes human nature in a sexually undifferentiated manner – such a human nature does not
exist.[40]

---

[38] See 7.2 and 9.1–3 below.

[39] We omit from this discussion the matter of so-called *intersex* children:
an important issue in medicine and in psychology, but hardly germane to
the substantive point.

[40] As Theodore the Studite (759–826) wrote: 'For Christ would not possess a human nature at all unless it dwells in him, in his particular person, in
individual existence. If it were not so, the Incarnation would be a fictitious
fantasy. . .' Christoph Schönborn, commenting on this passage in *God's
Human Face*, Ignatius Press, 1994, p. 223, adds, 'If Christ had taken on the
general human nature only, then he could not be recognised as a man except

4.1.4   Even if imaginable, such an 'incarnation' would be
either *docetic* (merely carrying the outward appearance
of human nature, but not truly being so), or *adoptionist*
(whereby the redeemer was raised or exalted to share
the divine nature at a particular moment in his life and
mission). Neither of these would be novel Christological interpretations – but neither of them would be the
faith of the Church, rooted in the Scriptures, defined
in the great Councils, and as received by the Church
of England. Neither would enable us to find in Jesus
Christ the Saviour who is both truly God and truly
man from the first moment of his conception.[41]

4.1.5   God must take human flesh as male or female: there is
no other way. And – given all that we have said about
the *Fatherhood* of God, and about the Saviour as the
one who 'bears his image and likeness' – the only possibility is for the Redeemer to be born as a male, including both sexes (male by virtue of his own humanity;
female by virtue of the one from whom that human
nature is derived, Mary, the Theotokos and Mother of
the Lord).[42] E. L. Mascall offers a masterly analysis,
grounded in sound Christological reasoning, of the

---

on an intellectual and conceptual level. Christ, of course, has assumed also
the general human nature, but since this nature exists in fact exclusively in
the particular individual, Christ is true man only if his humanity exists as
this specific, individual manifestation.'

[41] Could God have chosen to have become incarnate in the female sex?
Presumably the answer to this interesting piece of theological speculation
is as hypothetical as the question! But we believe that the answer must be
'No.' A divine daughter might have preached a heavenly Mother: though,
for reasons which we hope are by now apparent, that would have inaugurated a quite different religion from Christianity. A divine daughter who
still spoke of her Father in heaven could not be the 'image and likeness' of
that Father. Nor, of course, would a female incarnation have any place for
the involvement of the male sex: only a human mother conceiving the Son
ensures that both male and female share in the work of salvation. All of this
is interesting: but what is important is not what might have happened, but
what *did* happen: God's revelation of himself as Father and Son.

[42] God born as a female – a woman born of a woman – would, of course,
exclude the male entirely from the mystery of the Incarnation.

complementarity of male and female in the mystery of
the Incarnation. It is a useful and forthright corrective
to any mistaken implication that the maleness of Jesus
Christ somehow implies a superiority of the male over
the female:

> It was *male human nature* the Son of God united to
> his divine person; it was a *female human person* who
> was chosen to be his Mother. On the other hand, no
> *male human person* was chosen to be the Messiah.
> (To suppose so was the error of the adoptionists),
> and no *female human nature* was assumed by a divine
> person. Thus from one point of view the Incarnation
> exalts the male above the female while from another
> point of view it exalts the female sex above the male.
> In no woman has *human nature* been raised to the
> dignity which it possesses in Jesus of Nazareth, but
> in no *male human person* has there been given the
> dignity comparable to that which Mary enjoys as the
> Mother of God . . .[43]

4.1.6   The maleness of Jesus Christ is generative of a whole
family of images, each of which is critical in our understanding of his work of redemption and salvation:

- Christ the Bridegroom,
- Christ the High Priest,
- Christ the Sacrifice for the sins of the whole world.

4.1.7   We consider these in Chapters 5 and 6. First, however, we need to examine the collection of ideas and
texts which cluster around what we can call 'Christ the
Head of the redeemed human race'. This is of particular importance for two reasons:

- Because one of the most frequently deployed arguments by the proponents of the ordination of

---

[43] 'The Ministry of Women', a letter in *Theology*, 57 (413).

women to the episcopate and priesthood is that an exclusively male priesthood is 'unrepresentative' of half the human race, and suggests that women are somehow less made in the image of God, or less fully redeemed in Christ, than men.

• Because that argument turns on assertions and interpretations which are applicable, by extension, to the incarnation of Christ himself. The logic obliges us to say that women, if they are unrepresented by a priesthood of only men, are excluded from the fruits of the incarnation, death, resurrection and ascension of a redeemer who is both divine and human, but a mere male. To put it bluntly, if only a priesthood which includes women as well as men can represent women at the altar, how can a male redeemer bring women to salvation?[44]

4.2   Christ, Adam and Headship

4.2.1   The key texts here are to be found in Romans[45] and 1 Corinthians,[46] and their use of, and reflection on, the creation narratives of Genesis 1—3. To summarize: as the Scriptures consistently portray Adam as both the created origin of the human race, male and female, and its representative, so Jesus, the new Adam, is similarly both head and representative of the new humanity redeemed in him. While the Old Testament texts nowhere use such terms as 'headship', they clearly establish a pattern in which the male can represent the whole of the human race in a manner in which the

---

[44] There are similarities with the arguments sometimes employed to diminish the role of the Blessed Virgin Mary in Christian devotion. What relevance, it is sometimes asked, can a sinless virgin mother have in the lives of ordinary Christian women? We might as well ask what relevance can a sinless and celibate virgin Saviour have for any of us?

[45] 5.12–21ff.

[46] 11.3, 12; 15.21–3.

female cannot.[47] The Incarnation, as we have seen, does not obliterate, blur, or cancel the creation of mankind in two sexes, male and female: rather, it demonstrates that we are saved human beings – but also saved men and saved women: 'Sexual distinctions are fulfilled in Christ, accentuated and affirmed, and they indeed form a significant part of salvation history.'[48]

4.2.2   The pattern of imagery which usually clusters under the title 'headship' does not imply the *dominance* of man over woman. It portrays the equal but different – that is to say, complementary – roles of the sexes in the mystery of creation. Adam is not complete without Eve; Eve is Adam's helper.

4.2.3   In the New Testament, the relationship between the sexes is, as it were, a 'type' of two foundational relationships involving God himself: that between Christ and his Church; and that between the Father and the Son.[49] The relations between the Persons of the Holy Trinity are, of course, relations of *equal* Persons, differentiated precisely by the manner in which they relate one to another: the Father *is* Father because he is Father of the Son, the Son *is* Son only inasmuch as he is Son of the Father, and so on. The Fatherhood of the First Person of the Trinity expresses his role as the source, origin or principle of the other two Persons. It does not imply his 'superiority' over them.

4.2.4   So with male and female. The Pauline texts point to the mutuality, interdependence and equality of the sexes (as Father and Son are equal and interdependent). They indicate also their distinction and difference

---

[47] See Genesis 2.18–23ff. Eve is created to be Adam's 'help meet', bone of his bone and flesh of his flesh. The word *woman* literally translates 'from man': woman, *'ischscha* (lit: 'female man' is taken out of *'isch,* 'man').

[48] G. Richmond Bridge, *Women and the Apostolic Ministry?,* 1997, p. 15.

[49] 1 Corinthians 11.3. The text, of course, actually reads 'the head of Christ is God'.

within the ordered economy of creation and redemption (as Father and Son are different and distinct within the Godhead).[50]

4.2.5   Perhaps the most important text (in the light of which all other reference to the headship of Christ over the Church, and male over female, must be read) is Paul's prayer in his letter to the Church at Ephesus, 'For this reason I bow my knees before the Father, from whom every family in heaven and on earth is named . . .'.[51] Paul kneels to the Father (*pater*) from whom the whole family (*pasa patria*) derives its name. This text is one among a cluster of similar texts, both scriptural and patristic, which will help us to understand the network of relationships which, we argue, draw together the headship of Christ, the household of the people of the New Covenant, the eucharistic table (by which the people of God is constituted), and the presidency of the bishop who presides in Christ's place over the *ekklesia* brought together in eucharistic fellowship.[52]

4.2.6   The Pauline prayer forcefully reminds us that *all* other relationships (domestic, ecclesiastical, and so on) are subject to, and patterned on, the divine Fatherhood of the One Father. Developing this idea, Gerald Bray has written usefully:

> If we look carefully at the 'hierarchy' presented by the Apostle Paul, we realise that ontologically speaking, Father and Son are equal in the Godhead, whereas male and female are equal in their common

---

[50] And see also Faith and Order Advisory Group, *The Priesthood of the Ordained Ministry*, pp. 87–8: 'Texts in 1 Corinthians and 1 Timothy speak of the subordination of women to men and man as the head of woman. What implications has this for the exercise of a priestly ministry which is to lead the community and exercise authority in the community?'

[51] Ephesians 5.15 ('Family' is a questionable rendering; see Part Three, Paper 2).

[52] See the paper attached to this report as Paper 2, 'The Gender and Number of Bishops', by Fr John Hunwicke.

humanity. It is between the divine and the human
that the great gulf of inequality is fixed, and so whatever the hierarchy of headship is supposed to stand
for, it cannot be that . . . Men and women are linked
to God the Father and the Son because as human
beings they are created in the image and likeness
of God. Headship therefore refers to a pattern of
relationships within a divine order which transcends
the distinction between created and uncreated
being. The Son [is] subordinate to the Father . . .
because that is his place in a divine order in which
the individuality of each of the persons is affirmed
and protected. Father and Son need each other to
be themselves, and this mutuality is worked out in
the submissiveness of the Son just as much as it is in
the 'authority' of the Father who raises him from the
dead and thereby validates his sacrifice. Similarly,
male and female need each other in order to be themselves, and their interrelationship is also expressed in
terms of submission and sacrifice. The whole pattern
of our salvation is worked out in this complex structure of 'order', which the Church is called to proclaim and reflect in its public worship.[53]

4.2.7   Bray's analysis helpfully reminds us of the complementarity of the Persons of the Holy Trinity, and the
complementarity of the sexes which, however dimly,
reflects that aspect of the divine life. It also (in the final
sentence quoted above) reminds us that – again, however dimly – the Church, and especially the Church at
worship, the life of the Church as eucharistic community, does participate in the divine reality.[54] It should

---

[53] G. Bray, 'Bishops, Presbyters and Women', 2002, in *The Theologian –
the internet journal for integrated theology*, www.theologian.org.uk

[54] We might summarize the argument thus: The Scriptures portray the un-
folding mystery of a kenotic or benevolent patriarchy, which has its primary
focus in the passion of the Lord. The Pauline Epistles (episodically, since
they are occasional and not systematic works) apply that mystery to the
social and liturgical life of the Church, and to the relations of the sexes.

show forth, in its rites, signs and sacramental symbols, something of that divine reality and that divine ordering of creation.

4.2.8   The place of men and women in the life of the Body, their visible complementarity and mutuality, may in fact be of the same order as the requirement to use bread and wine for the Eucharist,[55] or (pure, clean) water for the administration of the sacrament of Holy Baptism. Like them, it is not a matter of indifference, which can be adapted at whim, according to local cultural conditions. It is of the essence of what is not just being symbolized, but actually conveyed. Bluntly, the question might be this: would the force of the visual sign and symbol of a female bishop (exercising the ministry which we shall examine in more detail in a later part of this report) be such as to undermine, threaten or (to use a less aggressive image) cause simply and quietly to wither away those fundamental theological truths we have been discussing: the Fatherhood of God and the divine Sonship of Jesus Christ?

4.2.9   Gerald Bray goes on to comment more specifically on the ministerial roles of women and men in the Church, insisting that 'neither [the woman's] ability to do the job, nor her fundamental equality with men is at stake'. Such an inference is no more valid, he argues, than is the conclusion that the Son is in some way inferior to the Father because the Second Person of the Trinity became incarnate and offered himself sacrificially for the salvation of sinful men. Relationship, mutuality is all – whether between the Persons of the Trinity in the Godhead, or the male sex and the female sex in created humanity.

---

[55] 'The bread, whether leavened or unleavened, shall be of the best and purest wheat flour that conveniently may be gotten, and the wine the fermented juice of the grape, good and wholesome.' (Canon B17) 'The essential signs of the Eucharistic sacrament are wheat bread and grape wine', *Catechism of the Catholic Church*, #1412, p. 318. The Catechism in the Book of Common Prayer states that the 'outward part or sign of the Lord's Supper [is] Bread and Wine'.

5

Bridegroom and Bride

5.1   Christ the Bridegroom

5.1.1   The centrality and importance of this relationship and mutuality in the whole consideration of God, Christ, male and female leads naturally on to one of the most significant of all the biblical symbols bearing on our theme: that of Bridegroom and Bride.[56] It is in the language and the visual representation of this particular symbolism (which of necessity demands a complementarity and not an interchangeability of the two 'parties' or 'partners' concerned) that we find unfolded for us a profound mystery of creation and redemption, which overflows into the life of the Church and her ministry.

5.1.2   The origins of the symbol lie in the Old Testament. The salvation offered by God to men and women and the union with him to which they are called – in short, the Covenant – took, from the Old Testament prophets onwards, the privileged form of a nuptial mystery. The Chosen People is seen by God as an ardently loved spouse. Both the Jewish and the Christian traditions have unfolded the depth of this intimacy by reading and rereading the Song of Songs: the divine Bridegroom will remain faithful even when the Bride betrays his love, when Israel is unfaithful to God (Hosea 1—3; Jeremiah 2).[57]

---

[56] See Part Three, Paper 1, 'The Bishop as Bridegroom of his Church: A Roman Catholic Contribution', by Fr Aidan Nichols, OP.

[57] *Inter Insigniores* ('Declaration on the Question of Admission of

5.1.3 The book of the prophet Isaiah also uses the analogy of husband and wife to represent the manner in which God speaks to his Chosen People.[58] It is in chapter 54 that the Lord, speaking through the prophet, says to his people Israel, 'For your Maker is your husband.'[59] Baruch, prophet of restoration and return from exile, closes the prophecy which bears his name with a vision of Jerusalem looking to the East, watching for the day, and the ingathering of the nations. In so doing, she is casting off her garments of mourning and widowhood, and adorning herself with jewels, with a diadem fit for a bride. She is expecting the return of her husband. In the well known passage in chapter 61, Trito-Isaiah speaks of being 'clothed with the garments of salvation [and] covered with the robe of righteousness, as a bridegroom decks himself with a garland, and as a bride adorns herself with her jewels'.[60]

5.1.4 These, of course, are a few examples out of many. The love of God in the Old Testament is the love of a husband (who is eternally faithful) for a wife (who may well be faithless). Readers will call others to mind. It is a divine love, but a love which can properly be described in the language of a man's love for a woman; the bridegroom's love for the bride.

5.1.5 Just as the analogy of the Fatherhood of God is used fitfully in the Old Testament, but with massively increased frequency (and significance) in the New, so too is the portrayal of the relationship between God and

---

Women to the Ministerial Priesthood', Sacred Congregation for the Doctrine of the Faith, October 1976), Section 5: 'The ministerial priesthood in the light of the mystery of Christ'.

[58] This passage is discussed in another key text from the contemporary Roman Catholic Church, the Apostolic Letter of Pope John Paul II *Mulieris Dignitatem*, or, 'On the Dignity and Vocation of Women', 1988, ch. 7.

[59] And see also Psalm 45.

[60] Isaiah 61.10–11.

humanity as that of a nuptial mystery given renewed and greatly augmented force with the coming of Christ and the establishment of the New Covenant. Jesus is the Bridegroom who comes to consummate the divine love for the new people of God. Through his work of salvation, enacted in his Incarnation, passion, death, resurrection and ascension, and through his obedience to the mission entrusted to him by his Father, he spends himself for her.

5.1.6   It is difficult to overemphasize the importance of nuptial imagery in the New Testament. In the Synoptic Gospels, parables woven around the theme of the wedding banquet abound. There are stories (such as that of the wise and foolish virgins)[61] which point towards the need to be prepared for the coming of the Bridegroom, the One who is sent to marry the Bride. There are those (such as the parable of the wedding garment)[62] which portray the kingdom of heaven itself as a marriage feast. Either way, the key image is the same: in the advent of Jesus Christ to the world, there is a fulfilment of all that has been promised and foreshadowed in those many Old Testament images of Israel as the bride of God.[63]

5.1.7   In the Fourth Gospel, the first miracle performed by Our Lord – the turning of the water into wine – takes place at a wedding feast. St John's symbolic narrative leaves us in little doubt that it is Jesus himself who is the true Bridegroom. John the Baptist's words[64] make

---

[61] Matthew 25.1–13 and parallels.

[62] Matthew 22.1–14.

[63] For the people of the New Covenant, there continues to be a foreshadowing of the coming kingdom of God in the marriage feast of the eucharistic table. This eschatological dimension to the celebration of the Lord's Supper, and the Bishop's role in that celebration as the President (or *paterfamilias*) of the eucharistic household, and the bridegroom of his flock (or, normatively, his diocese) is central to the argument we are developing.

[64] John 3.29ff.

explicit what the episode at Cana in Galilee implies. The Forerunner says of the One who will come after him, 'he who has the bride is the bridegroom; the friend of the bridegroom, who stands and hears him, rejoices greatly at the bridegroom's voice'. The climax of the Revelation of St John the Divine turns on the nuptial imagery of the heavenly marriage feast. The New Jerusalem is the Bride; the Lamb her Husband.[65]

5.2   The Bridegroom and the nuptial mystery

5.2.1   It is in the letters of St Paul that the mystery of Christ the Bridegroom is more fully developed. In the Second Letter to the Corinthians, the Apostle speaks of his 'divine jealousy' for the Church in that place. 'I betrothed you to Christ to present you as a pure bride to her one husband,' he says.[66] It is in the Letter to the Ephesians, in the well-known passage in chapter 5,[67] that the fullest expression of the love of Christ for his people according to the analogy of the nuptial mystery is to be found. Here is the explicit linkage of the kenotic headship which Christ exercises over the Church with that exercised by man over woman. The quotation from Genesis which St Paul places at the heart of his argument (teaching that 'a man shall leave his father and mother and be joined to his wife, and the two shall become one flesh') shows that, for the Apostle, the mysteries of creation, redemption and the life of the Christian household are so closely interwoven as to be inseparable.

5.2.2   For Paul the fundamental patterns of relationship between the sexes within the redeemed Body of Christ are based on a distinction which is there from the first

---

[65] Revelation 19.7–10; 21.1–4, 9, 17.
[66] 2 Corinthians 11.2.
[67] Ephesians 5.21–33.

moment of the creation. As we have seen when considering the Incarnation of the Word, those patterns are not abolished by the coming of Christ. They are restored, healed and deepened. In being so healed and deepened, they are also radically redeemed. They are enabled to disclose something of the very nature of God himself.[68]

5.2.3   The submission of wives to husbands, enjoined upon Christians in Ephesians 5, is itself an outworking of that ultimate headship of Jesus Christ over the Church, which devolves upon him as the offspring of the divine Father. At a more basic level, we can say, emphatically, that redemption does not mean the smoothing away of difference. The Redeemer himself comes as Bridegroom in order to win back the Bride, in order to give himself in sacrificial love for her, even as she is called to submit herself to him.[69] As Gerhard Müller has put it, in a passage well worth quoting at some length:

> When the husband – imitating that loving devotion that leads to self-emptying and obeying the divine command to be an image of the *kenosis* of the son of God – empties himself, too, of all self-love, desire to dominate, self-sufficiency, and airs of superiority, then he is the reflected glory and the image of God according to the standard of Christ, who in his obedience to the Father is in God's image. The husband is

---

[68] As C. S. Lewis wrote (in *Undeceptions*) London, 1971: 'One of the ends for which sex was created was to symbolize to us the hidden things of God . . . We have no authority to take the living and sensitive figures which God has painted on the canvas of our nature and shift them about as if they were mere geometric figures.'

[69] And *hypotasso*, submit, means precisely that. It is used 40 times in the New Testament, and every time means 'to place oneself under the authority of another'. While St Paul certainly *modifies*, in a subtle and profound way, the call to submission by telling the Christians at Ephesus to be subject *to one another*, that modification does not alter the substantive meaning of the word itself.

designated head of his wife, not for the sake of theologically legitimising a relation of dominance, but in order to align the husband's conduct with the mind of Christ, who by virtue of his mission (as Head of the Church) loved the Church and gave himself up for her, so as to become 'one flesh' (= a loving union) with her . . .

. . . Both spouses, personally and in their marital union, are representatives (as a unity of head and body, original glory and reflected glory): they are an image and likeness of the love of God being poured out on men in Christ . . .

. . . In the mystery of sacramental marriage is revealed the most profound significance of the fact that man is made in the image and likeness of God; as husband and wife, man symbolizes God's dominion, as the source of created being in the uncreated Love of God . . . Christ is the Lord of the *basileia* [kingdom] of God . . . the *Kyrios* by virtue of his *kenosis* and his obedience to the revelation of the glory of God the Father, a glory that is reflected in the salvation of mankind (cf. Philippians 2.6–11).

Woman (a wife) is described as 'the glory of man' (1 Corinthians 11.7) and symbolically represents, in her natural relation to man (her husband), the bridal response of faith and love made by the Church, which Christ by his devotion has made into his Body.[70]

5.2.4 Among the many helpful points made by Müller, it is especially important to note his insistence that the pattern of authority and submission which St Paul unfolds in this letter is by no means intended to justify (still less to sanctify) abusive or unjust structures of human behaviour. This is of crucial importance to the question with which this report is principally concerned: that of the admissibility (or inadmissibility) of women to Holy Orders, and specifically to the episcopate. The

---

[70] Gerhard Müller, *Priesthood and Diaconate*, 2000, pp. 102–3.

argument from *justice*[71] is one often advanced to further the case for the ordination of women – where justice (to put it simply) is equivalent to the interchangeability of the sexes. Ephesians 5 (and other similar texts) points us to a better way: the profound complementarity of the sexes, their necessary difference in the scheme of salvation. Difference implies absolutely no domination of the one by the other in a cruel, oppressive or unjust way.

5.3   The Church, the Bride and the whole people of God

5.3.1   Another key aspect to the great analogy of the 'Bride' in the Letter to the Ephesians is that it helps us to understand that *the whole human race, male as well as female*, is to be included in the Church which is the Bride. Each person is called to accept Christ the redeemer's offer of love and to respond to that initiative in his or her own life. It is central to our argument that the restriction of ordination as bishops (and priests) to men alone does not exclude women from full equality before God. The inclusiveness of the Church, the Bride of Christ, embraces both women and men through faith and baptism. (Here we touch again on a right understanding of Galatians 3.28.)

5.3.2   This insight is critical to the theology of priesthood in the writings of Hans Urs von Balthasar.[72] Balthasar's sense of the Marian, Johannine and Petrine characters of the Church and her ministry is a helpful one, and worth exploring briefly. To sum up the first and third of these categories or charisms (which are the most pertinent to our discussion), we can say that it is given

---

[71] See 9.3 below.

[72] For a good summary of his thinking in this field, see Paul McPartlan, 'The Marian Church: Hans Urs von Balthasar and the Ordination of Women', in William McLoughlin and Jill Pinnock (eds), *Mary is for Everyone: Essays on Mary and Ecumenism*, 1997.

to the whole Church to carry forward the Marian gift of active receptivity to the will and Word of God. The Church, in her Marian role, numbers among her members both male and female. To Peter, and to the Petrine office which continues *his* work, is given the responsibility, variously, of shepherding, encouraging and building up the flock entrusted to him, and also of carrying forward Christ's work as Judge – that office which Christ in turn received from his Father.

5.3.3   A critical distinction between the Marian and Petrine charisms is that, whereas the Church (which encompasses both women and men) is Mary, the successors of Peter can only *represent* him who is the Chief Shepherd, Judge, and Bridegroom. And that they can do so only in a way which never allows them to claim any of the divine dignity for themselves. This is why, for Balthasar, there can be no suggestion that to restrict priestly ordination to men is to assign an inferior or second-class status to women. It is the primary calling of *all* Christians, of all the baptized, to be Mary. They are to make her (gloriously feminine) open response to God their own.

5.3.4   As Brendan Leahy has put it:

Echoing Bouyer, von Balthasar sees the man-priest, therefore, as being simultaneously both more and less than himself in that as sexual being he only represents what he is not (the Lord) and transmits what he does not really possess (the Lord's real presence and sacraments). Woman, on the other hand, reposes in herself and is entirely her own being, that is, the total reality of a created being before God as partner, receiving, bearing, maturing and nurturing his Word in the Spirit.[73]

---

[73] *The Marian Profile in the Ecclesiology of Hans Urs von Balthasar*, 2000, p. 180.

5.3.5 Or, as John O'Donnell has it:

> The ordained members of the community, those who receive the office of representing Christ in the community, represent Christ in his masculine function. But the ordained are first and foremost baptised Christians. As the baptised they are feminine, they are receptive of Christ's grace, they must imitate Marian openness to the word. Hence Peter has a subordinate role in regard to Mary. As regards authority, Mary stands under Peter. But as regards the essence of the Church, Peter must be inserted within the Marian Church. His institutional authority has no sense apart from the Church of love. In this sense, Balthasar would argue that in no way does woman have less in the Church. For woman represents the essence of what it means to be Church.[74]

5.3.6 Both Leahy and O'Donnell help to make the vital point (developing Balthasar himself) that ordination is in no sense about conferring power or superiority upon the person ordained. The history of the Church is studded with the examples of many women – St Hilda of Whitby and St Catherine of Siena, to name but two – who have exercised enormous authority in both the ecclesiastical and secular spheres. None of them, of course, were priests. The highest calling is to follow the way of receptivity, the Marian calling. We are to live in a way which is above all defined by the Johannine gift of love.

5.3.7 Following (as we believe) von Balthasar and others, we want to resist the notion that the episcopate is susceptible to secular definitions of 'equal opportunities' and 'justice'.[75] 'Justice' lies in the equal standing of men

---

[74] In *Hans Urs von Balthasar*, quoted in McLoughlin and Pinnock, *Mary is for Everyone*, p. 51.

[75] We would strongly resist, for example, the gloss placed upon the appointment of Canon June Osborne as Dean of Salisbury Cathedral in *The Times* of 13 December 2003. In its Leader column of that day, the assertion

and women before the Father as those redeemed in Christ. But the priesthood and the episcopate belong to the world of sacramental signs. The *symbol* of Christ the Bridegroom, the Son who is *homoousios* with the Father, must be male. The male is called to *represent* what he cannot *be* (Shepherd, Teacher, Judge). Jesus is those things. Yet the Church can no more do without such representation than the Lord can do without Peter.

5.3.8   We shall return to this very important point when we come to consider the bishop as Bridegroom of his flock, and, in particular, our understanding of the bishop at the Eucharist as the sacramental sign of the Father sending his Son to his people, to gather them to himself as the Bridegroom seeks out and marries the Bride.

5.4   The Bridegroom in the tradition

5.4.1   The scriptural image of Christ the Bridegroom (and its converse, the Church as Bride) is one that is central to the thinking of the early Fathers. For Origen, Christ in his self-giving love is seen as Bridegroom of both Church and individual soul. For St Cyril of Alexandria, the incarnate Word is also the Bridegroom, wooing fallen humanity. St Ambrose weaves together creation of humanity and the redemptive work of Christ to suggest a series of parallels between Adam and Eve, the Bride and the Bridegroom, and Christ and the Church.

---

is made that Canon Osborne will 'prove' by her conduct in office that the opponents of the ordination of women are motivated by 'pure prejudice', as it is clear that she will perform the administrative, managerial and financial duties of the role of Dean as well as, if not better than, any man. Such a merely functional view of Holy Orders would be anathema to Balthasar (and, indeed, to all those who stand in the great tradition of the undivided Church). *The Times* further compared Canon Osborne's appointment to the admission of girl choristers at the Cathedral, a comparison which scarcely requires further comment.

That the significance of the image persists beyond the patristic age and into Anglican tradition can be seen in this quotation from Bishop John Jewel (1522–71), that great defender of the claims of the Church of England. He writes:

> And that this Church is the kingdom, the body, and the spouse of Christ; and that Christ alone is the prince of this kingdom; that Christ alone is the head of this body; and that Christ alone is the bridegroom of this spouse.[76]

5.4.2   In the nineteenth century, the image is central to one of the best-known hymns:

> *From heaven he came and sought her*
> *To be his holy Bride*
> *With his own life he bought her*
> *And for her life he died.*[77]

More pertinently, perhaps, the particular image of the Church as Bride has been newly chosen for inclusion in the draft *Common Worship* ordinal.[78] The Archbishop addresses the candidate for the episcopate thus:

---

[76] *Apologia Ecclesiae Anglicanae* II. And see the Form of Solemnization of Matrimony in the Book of Common Prayer; (from the Preface) 'Matrimony [is] an honourable estate, instituted of God in the time of man's innocency, signifying unto us the mystical union that is betwixt Christ and his Church'; (from the Prayers) 'O God, who has consecrated the state of Matrimony to such an excellent mystery, that in it is signified and represented the spiritual marriage and unity betwixt Christ and his Church: Look mercifully upon these thy servants, that both this man may love his wife, according to thy Word, (as Christ did love his spouse the Church, who gave himself for it, loving and cherishing it even as his own flesh).'

[77] S. J. Stone, 'The Church's One Foundation'. Commenting on this verse, Eric Routley adds, 'The metaphor of marriage is pressed to the uttermost. Christ's relation with the Church is one of utter self-giving. In the world of time Christ so trusts the Church and so commits himself to the Church, that his continuing ministry is incomplete without it. The Church is founded in the self-giving and self-surrender of Christ.' (E. Routley, *Hymns and the Faith*, John Murray, London, 1955, p. 243)

[78] GS 1535. At the time of writing, it remains to be seen whether this image survives the Revision Committee.

N, remember always with thanksgiving that God has entrusted to your care Christ's own flock, his beloved bride, his household, bought by the shedding of his blood on the cross.

Such a choice of words, and of this image in particular, in a revision of the ordination rites, surely suggests a deep consciousness among Anglicans of the intimate connexion between the nuptial mystery of Christ and his Church and the relationship between the bishop and the local church to which, by virtue of his office, he is espoused.

5.5   Excursus: an objection

5.5.1   To the foregoing arguments an objection is frequently raised by those who support the ordination of women as bishops and priests:

If both men and women can participate in the Church, the Bride, by baptism, why cannot they equally so participate in the Bridegroom, by ordination?

Leaving to one side, for the moment, Galatians 3.28,[79] we believe that this question can be addressed as follows.

5.5.2   The Church does not require any further sacramental symbolism in order to be what it is: all who are baptized *are* the Church by virtue of their baptism. But in order to represent the High Priesthood of Christ, further sacramental symbolism *is* required – namely, the ordained minister, who visibly carries in his human person the likeness of the Son. While it is true that the priest represents the whole Church at the celebration

---

[79] See 7.2. below.

of the Eucharist (acting *in persona ecclesiae*), he does so only because first he represents Christ himself, and acts *in persona Christi*: more specifically, *in persona Christi capitis*, in the person of Christ who is the head of the Church.

5.5.3   As St Thomas Aquinas has it, the priest 'enacts the image of Christ, in whose person and by whose power he pronounces the words of consecration'.[80] Thomas understands the need for the priest to be male in terms of the congruity of sacramental signs. There is a 'natural resemblance' which must exist between the matter of the sacrament and the thing signified. It is because the priest has to be the sign and image of Christ that only men can be ordained to the priesthood. The priest must be conformed, in his humanity, to Christ the Head. As Theodore the Studite puts it, centuries before Aquinas, the priest is *mimema Christou*: he takes the part of Christ. Or again, to use another key image, the priest is the *icon* of Christ, confronting us at the altar with the reality and particularity of the Incarnation.

5.5.4   The iconographic relationship between the celebrant of the Eucharist and Christ does not require, as has sometimes been suggested, that the priest 'matches' the person of Jesus in every particular physical detail. That is not the way that icons 'work'. But it does require that fundamental congruity of which Theodore and Thomas speak, of which maleness is surely an essential part.

5.5.5   The importance of sacramental symbolism, and the iconographic relationship between the priest and Christ must not (it should be stressed once again) be taken as suggestive of a superiority of the male over the female, nor as a negative comment on the wider ministry of women in the Church.

---

[80] *Summa Theologiae* III. 83. I. ad 3.

5.5.6   The Working Party has given considerable attention to the urgent need to articulate and to act upon a theology for 'catholic women'.[81] In order both to guard against the clericalism of which Balthasar is rightly so suspicious, and in order truly to become 'Mary', her vocation, the Church needs to ask deeply and searchingly, what are those vocations to which women are being called by God in the life of his Church and Bride. While acknowledging that there is always more work to be done, we want, here and now, to rejoice in and to celebrate the fact that women are foremost in all the activities which constitute the domestic, civil and ecclesial Christian communities. It is a primary task of the apostolic ministry to support, encourage and enable those ministries. Furthermore, the most fruitful expressions of women's ministry in the life of the Church of England, notably women in the religious life, the Order of Deaconesses and women as catechists, evangelists, spiritual directors and parish workers, were formed by the Catholic tradition. The dangers to be avoided at all costs are that of clericalism (an over-emphasis on the ordained ministry) and the erosion of *difference* between ministries.

---

[81] To use a shorthand which has been employed by (no doubt among others) the present Bishop of Ebbsfleet.

6

Priesthood and Sacrifice

6.1 The Old Covenant

6.1.1 From Christ the Bridegroom we turn to Christ our great High Priest, the sacrifice for our sins. We should not, of course, draw too sharp a distinction between these two aspects of Christ's work of redemption, nor in any way present them as alternatives. It is the same self-giving love which Christ demonstrates as Bridegroom of the Church which he consummates in the sacrifice of himself as priest-victim on the Cross. In the Book of Revelation nuptial and sacrificial images coincide. The Church is portrayed as the wife of the Lamb.[82]

6.1.2 We have already alluded[83] to the 'metanarrative' of Holy Scripture, which has as its focus the sacrificial death of Jesus Christ, and to the way in which that redemptive self-offering of the Son of God completes and fulfils the pattern established in a sequence of examples of the death – or near-death – of key (male) figures in the Old Testament: Abel, Isaac, Joseph, and so on.[84]

---

[82] E.g. Revelation 19.9.

[83] See 2.6 above.

[84] We might characterize the role played by these three foundational characters in the great story of the Hebrew Scriptures as, respectively, the first victim of violence (whose death requires expiation); the one who demonstrates that God is not only the author of sacrifice but will himself provide the victim; and the one betrayed by his brethren, who is ransomed, and who redeems those who have betrayed him. In each case, the mystery of the Cross is foreshadowed.

6.1.3   More generally (though this report cannot do justice to so wide a topic) we may say that the entire Jewish priest-hood and sacrificial system was summed up once and for all in Jesus' death on the Cross. The Jewish priest-hood was, of course, a priesthood exercised by men, and by men only. This was not (as is all too frequently alleged) as a result of social or cultural conditioning. It was, rather, in deliberate contradistinction to the pre-vailing culture of the ancient Near East, characterized as it was by the widespread occurrence of priestesses serving the shrines of pagan deities (male and female) and cults.

6.1.4   There were priestesses in Mesopotamia, in Egypt, and in the Canaanite environment (cultures whose socio-logical structures, in other respects, exercised a not inconsiderable influence upon Israel); but among the chosen people of God – none at all. Why is this? We believe that the answer is in part to do with the under-standing of sacrifice as it developed in the Hebrew reli-gion.

6.1.5   The 'theology' of sacrifice in the Old Testament is complex and many-layered. What is made emphati-cally clear in the texts is a rejection of the deification of sexual intercourse, as in the fertility cults of Canaan. Those cults had temple prostitution at their heart. For the Israelites sexuality was not a divine activity, but a relationship between created beings. At the heart of Israelite religion is an awareness of the awful other-ness of God. That religion is about *covenant* with him; about the offering of thanks and praise (especially, of course, thanksgiving for deliverance from slavery in Egypt in the Passover rites); about expiation for sin (deriving from the account of Aaron and the 'scape-goat' in Leviticus,[85] and culminating in the Temple

---

[85] Leviticus 16.21–2.

ritual of the annual Day of Atonement). All this is an expression of the utter and complete dependence of man upon God for everything, even life itself.

6.1.6   In all of these overlapping and complementary under-standings of sacrifice in the Old Testament, it must be remembered (distinguishing the Israelite view once again from that of all other cults) that, as Ian Bradley comments, sacrifice for the Jews was always about the 'provision and gift of God'.[86]

6.1.7   Do these comments take us any further in understand-ing why the Jewish priesthood should have been re-stricted to males? There is, of course, the brute fact that only males would be physically able to slay the larger animals. That this might appear to be 'merely' a practi-cal or pragmatic consideration should not lead us to belittle its significance. We can offer two important answers to the question, each picking up on key themes which we have already discussed.

- First, only a male priesthood would do justice to the Hebrew consciousness of one transcendent God, wholly other than his creation.
- Second, only a male priesthood could represent the whole of the community before God, in a way in which the female could not. (We might note, in passing, that not any or every Israelite male could become a priest, of course, but only those 'elected' by God himself to that office by virtue of their member-ship of the tribe of Levi and their Aaronic descent.)

6.1.8   There is, of course, much more to be said about the exercise of priesthood in Old Testament Judaism. For our purposes, the key points are these:

- First, that for Jesus Christ to be the one who fulfils

---

[86] *The Power of Sacrifice*, 1995, p. 90.

both sacrifice and priesthood as unfolded in the
narrative of the Hebrew Scriptures and in the worship of the people of the first covenant, his maleness
is not insignificant, but of central importance.

- Second, that the priesthood of the New Covenant
(in a particular way the effective representation and
continuation of the ministry of Christ), though in one
sense something radically new, had its roots in the
distant past. It did not, in Manfred Hauke's phrase,
'descend from the heavens like a UFO from outer
space'.[87] Rather, it was prepared for – anticipated
and foreshadowed – over many centuries in the history of the Jewish people, the first to answer God's
call (as one of the collects for Good Friday now has
it). That history was not negated or cancelled out
by the coming of Christ, but rather completed and
fulfilled by it.

6.2.   The New Covenant in the blood of Christ

6.2.1   Arthur Middleton has written:

> There is an essential continuity between the Old
> Covenant and the New, which is organic rather than
> merely historic. There are quite literally, vital con-
> cepts such as Atonement, sacrifice, and redemption,
> whose only explanation is in terms of that continuity.
> Jesus claimed an identity with that same Covenant
> represented by Moses and Elijah, a living participa-
> tion in a continuity of life which was to find its fulfil-
> ment in him, the New Covenant. The selection by
> Jesus of men for his priestly work can therefore be
> no accident of cultural determinism. . . . [The essence
> of the Judaic-Christian tradition is sacrificial and]
> sacrifice is a specifically male prerogative whose deep

---

[87] *Women in the Priesthood?* p. 207.

roots reach back into primitive times. Abraham, not
Sarah, is asked by God to prepare Isaac for sacrifice.
Christ is the priest of the eternal covenant that is
sealed by his sacrificial death. His priesthood does
not derive from comparison with human priests, but
derives from a priesthood that is eternally his as the
one mediator between God and men. The authentic
type of the one eternal priest, as the Epistle to the
Hebrews points out, is to be found in the mysteri-
ous figure of Melchizedek, King of Salem and priest
of the most High. This King-Priest whom no name
can fully describe, and who is without beginning
or end, appears on the stage of history but is not of
history, because he transcends the limitations of the
human predicament. Hence the psalmist sees him as
a type of Messiah, a 'priest for ever after the order of
Melchizedek'.[88]

6.2.2   The whole Jewish priesthood and sacrificial system was
consummated once for all in Jesus' death on the Cross.
We who are under the New Covenant now look back
on the ordinances of the Old and see that they were a
kind of prefiguration – a *type* of the person, priesthood
and sacrifice of Christ. The whole of the Old Testament was a preparation for the moment of his death
on the Cross, and for the morning of his resurrection.
We live about as long *after* the crucifixion as Abraham
lived before it; and we look on the ordinances of the
New Covenant – the sacraments, the sacred ministry,
the Church itself – as a kind of 'post-figuration' of the
person, priesthood and sacrifice of Christ. They are a
continuation in time of the Incarnation. Just as that
unity was safeguarded in anticipation of the Cross by
an all-male Jewish priesthood (and an all-masculine
sacral language), so it is observed in retrospect by the

[88] 'The mystery of Christ and women priests', pp. 9–10, 20–1, in 'The
Office and Role of a Bishop in the Understanding of the Ancient Fathers and
the Anglican Divines' – a paper delivered to the Working Party.

priests[89] of the New Covenant being male (and by the masculine sacral language made normative in the 'Our Father').

6.2.3   In making the case for the continuity of the priesthood of the Old Covenant and the ordained priesthood as exercised in the Christian Church, we do not mean, of course, to suggest that there is no decisive, radical and irrevocable change in the nature and significance of the priestly ministry of the latter as distinct from the former. To the contrary: the passion and death of Jesus Christ brings to an end, once and for all, the necessity of the sacrifices of the Jewish cult. This is the point made, *par excellence,* by the Letter to the Hebrews. It is Christ's own one, full, perfect and sufficient sacrifice of himself which will now be made present in the life of the Church, under the forms of bread and wine in the Eucharist.

6.2.4   Yet the tradition attests that the Eucharist is no mere reminder of the Cross. It is not simply a prompt to pious mental recollection, but a *sacrifice*: the unbloody sacrifice of the people of God, the people of the New and Everlasting Covenant. At the earliest period of the history of the Church, St Justin, St Irenaeus and the author of the *Didache*, among others, refer to the Eucharist as a sacrifice – '*the* sacrifice', or even 'the pure sacrifice' of Christians. St Cyprian – in words which bear especially on our present investigation into the issues which surround the ordination of women as bishops – writes this:

> If our Lord and God Christ Jesus is himself the high priest of God the Father, and offered himself as a sacrifice to the Father, commanding this to be done

---

[89] The word 'priest' in Christian usage is used first, of course, to denote the *bishop*.

as a memorial of himself – then certainly the priest[90] truly performs his office in the place of Christ, imitating that which Christ did, and offering in the Church to God the Father a real and complete sacrifice.[91]

6.2.5 The classical Anglican understanding of the Sacrament has always made room for a doctrine of eucharistic sacrifice. It is especially a characteristic of the writings of the late-sixteenth- and seventeenth-century Divines.[92] Examples are too numerous to be quoted here, but attention must especially be drawn to the writings of Lancelot Andrewes (1555–1626), Bishop of Chichester, Ely and finally Winchester, who constantly used sacrificial language of the Holy Eucharist and promoted such an understanding of the rites through his own liturgical and ceremonial practice.

6.2.6 Jeremy Taylor (1613–67), writing in his *The Great Exemplar, The History of the Life and Death of Holy Jesus*[93] says this:

As it [the Eucharist] is a Commemoration and Representation of Christ's death, so it is a Commemorative Sacrifice ... There [in Heaven] He [Christ] sits, a High Priest continually, and offers still the same one perfect Sacrifice; that is, still represents it as having been once finished and still consummate, in order to perpetual and never failing events. And this also his ministers do on earth. They offer up the same Sacrifice to God, the Sacrifice of the Cross by prayers, and a commemorating rite and representment, according

---

[90] Cyprian's word here is *sacerdos*, literally translated as 'priest', but almost certainly designating (as has already been noted) what we would understand by a *bishop*.

[91] Cyprian, *Epistles* 63.14.

[92] See especially K. Stevenson, *Covenant of Grace Renewed*, Darton, Longman & Todd, 1994.

[93] Part III, section xv; quoted in P. E. More and F. L. Cross (eds), *Anglicanism*, SPCK, 1935, p. 495.

to His holy Institution . . . As Christ is a Priest in Heaven for ever and yet does not sacrifice Himself afresh nor yet without a Sacrifice could He be a Priest, but by a daily ministration and intercession represents His sacrifice to God and offers Himself as sacrificed, so He does upon earth by the ministry of His servants. He is offered to God; that is, He is by prayers and the Sacrament represented or offered up to God as sacrificed, which in effect is a celebration of His Death, and the applying it to the present and future necessities of the Church as we are capable by a ministry like to His in Heaven.

6.2.7   We can notice also the work of John Bramhall (1594–1663), Archbishop of Armagh, who wrote in his *Replication* of 1654:[94]

We acknowledge an Eucharistical sacrifice of praise and thanksgiving; a commemorative Sacrifice or a memorial of the Sacrifice of the Cross; a representative sacrifice, or a representation of the Passion of Christ before the eyes of His heavenly Father; an impetrative Sacrifice, or an impetration of the fruit and benefit of His Passion by way of real prayer; and lastly an applicative Sacrifice, or an application of His Merits unto our souls.

6.2.8   In their reply of 1897 *Sæpius Officio* to the Bull of Pope Leo XIII *Apostolicæ Curæ*, which had condemned Anglican Orders, the then Archbishops of Canterbury and York defended the position of the Church of England on eucharistic sacrifice:

Further we truly teach the doctrine of Eucharistic sacrifice . . . We continue a perpetual memory of the precious death of Christ . . . For first we offer the sacrifice of praise and thanksgiving; then next we

---

[94] Quoted in More and Cross, *Anglicanism*, p. 496.

plead and represent before the Father the sacrifice of the cross, and by it we confidently entreat remission of sins and all other benefits of the Lord's passion for all the whole Church; and lastly we offer the sacrifice of ourselves to the Creator of all things which we have already signified by the oblations of His creatures. This whole action, in which the people has necessarily to take its part with the Priest, we are accustomed to call the Eucharistic sacrifice.[95]

6.2.9   The sacrifices of the Old Covenant (the one perfect and complete sacrifice of Calvary) and the sacrifice of the memorial meal of the New Covenant are held together in that nuanced and profound manner which is truly expressive of the mystery of the Eucharist as the Church has received it. We find agreement between Anglicans and Roman Catholics on a common understanding of eucharistic sacrifice in the 1979 *Elucidation* of the statements on eucharistic doctrine in the ARCIC I *Final Report*:

it is possible to say that at the same time there is only one unrepeatable sacrifice in the historical sense, but that the eucharist is a sacrifice in the sacramental, provided that it is clear that this is not a repetition of the historical sacrifice.[96]

while of the ordained priesthood, the 1979 *Elucidation* (in this case of the Statements on Ministry and Ordination) says:

the ordained ministry is called priestly principally because it has a particular sacramental relationship with Christ as High Priest. At the Eucharist, Christ's people do what he commanded in memory of himself, and Christ unites them sacramentally with himself in his self-offering. But in this action it is only the ordained minister who presides at the eucharist,

[95] *Sæpius Officio*, Church Literature Association, 1977, pp. 13–14.
[96] Section 5.

in which, in the name of Christ and on behalf of his Church, he recites the narrative of the institution of the Last Supper, and invokes the Holy Spirit upon the gifts.[97]

6.2.10   We repeat the question which we asked in a slightly different context earlier in this report: is the subtle and profound network of relationships which exists between the sacrifices of the Old Covenant, the Sacrifice of Calvary, the celebration of the Eucharist, and the person of the ordained president at the Eucharist, damaged or jeopardized where the continuity of natural symbolism guaranteed by a male priest is no longer present?[98]

6.2.11   It could be argued that the Church of England has already given its view on this question, by permitting the ordination of women to the priesthood. We are convinced both that there is every justification in revisiting the theological issues at stake in the debate over the priesthood of women (many of which, we suggest, were given scant attention at the time) and that with the particular emphasis in the ministry of the bishop resting on his role as normative chief celebrant of the Eucharist, these questions will inevitably surface again.

6.3   Conclusion

Seeking to summarize the different emphases in the person and work of Jesus Christ which we have discussed in Chapters 4–6 (Christ as Head of redeemed

---

[97] Section 2.
[98] Margaret Barker, in *The Great High Priest* (chs. 4ff.), provides fascinating material for reflection in connection with this question, when she suggests that the original understanding of the Eucharist might have derived not chiefly from the Passover, but rather from the ritual of the Day of Atonement.

humanity; Christ as Bridegroom; Christ as High Priest; Christ as Sacrifice), and their significance for the gender of bishops and priests we can do no better than quote from an unpublished contribution to the deliberations of the Working Party. Our ecumenical observer representing the Roman Catholic Church, Fr Aidan Nichols, OP, has written thus, in an unpublished paper submitted to the Working Party:

> In the Atonement, Jesus acts as the great High Priest, representing all humanity to the Father and the Father to it. His male identity in the first case, his bearing of a male-gendered divine name in the second, are among the necessary conditions of the atoning act. By that act, the incarnate Son not only reveals the new state of divine–human relations his vicarious death brings about. He also renders that new state of affairs potentially fruitful for all individual human persons. This he does through becoming the Bridegroom of the Church, whose existence and flourishing as the effective inauguration of the Kingdom of God is the final cause of his sacrifice. By his Spirit, he generates children, both male and female, for the heavenly Father, in the sacramental mysteries, notably baptism and the Eucharist. He does so, these liturgical acts attest, through the 'mother', holy Church, in whose 'womb', or communion, it is that new sons and daughters are born.
>
> Via the apostolate, the ministerial priest (bishop for the particular church, presbyter for the local church) represents Christ as the High Priest of human salvation, Head of redeemed humanity, Bridegroom of the Church. This representation takes place in the sacramental order: that is, the order of dominically instituted effective signs. Entry on this office must meet the conditions set by the symbolism appropriate to the sacrament in question . . . it seems abundantly clear that the male gender must not be the least of these conditions.

7

Ministry in the Early Church

7.1   The Apostolic College in the New Testament

7.1.1   We deliberately placed the calling of the Twelve (and
the significance for the subsequent unbroken practice
of the Church of the *maleness* of the Twelve) at the
very beginning of this report.[99]

> From the beginning it was . . . evident that there was a
> 'pre-eminence' given to those called 'Apostles' in the
> Gospel record. Jesus chose Twelve, representing the
> New Israel, and commissioned them to preach the
> good news of the Kingdom. After the resurrection,
> their commission was renewed, and they emerged as
> the nucleus of the new messianic community.[100]

7.1.2   The Twelve are called – called, we do well to remember, with no discernible qualification for that call
beyond the decision of Jesus Christ, freely made, to call
them. They were to share in the Lord's mission in a
particular and distinctive way. They were sent out (*apo-
stellein*) to do the work of the Son: to preach and to
heal in his name, with his authority (*exousia*), and to
accomplish his saving work in word and sign.[101] It is to
the Twelve exclusively that Jesus addresses much of his
teaching. They (or a smaller group from among them)
are present at the most significant moments in his ministry. They are representatives of the twelve tribes of

---

[99] See 2.2 above.
[100] Faith and Order Advisory Group, *The Priesthood of the Ordained
Ministry*, p. 18.
[101] Mark 3.13–19; 6.6–13ff.

the people of the first covenant, and thereby together a sign of the new age of the Kingdom. Thus they also together constitute the foundation stones of the new Temple, that is, of the eschatological people of God. Because they share in Jesus' mission and actually represent him, those who hear their words hear the words of Christ.[102] To them is given the instruction to carry out, in word and symbolic action, the eucharistic memorial of the New Covenant.

7.1.3   Alongside the foundational Twelve, others in the New Testament are called 'apostles'. Matthias, of course, who was elected to fill the vacancy created by the falling away of Judas Iscariot; Barnabas and Silas; and, most famously of all, Paul. It was imperative for Paul's own claims and understanding of the call he had received from God that his apostolate should be seen to stand on the same footing as that of the Twelve. Those to whom the title 'apostle' is given in the texts are easily distinguished from the many helpers and enablers who supported and set forward the apostolic ministry.

7.1.4   There is no need here to attempt to give a full account, still less a synthesis, of the mosaic of different ministries to which the New Testament bears witness. We can agree again with the Faith and Order Advisory Group that 'there is no uniform pattern of church order to be found within the pages of the New Testament'.[103]

7.1.5   Nevertheless, we can recognize with confidence what is happening in the emergent Christian communities. We can discern the tradition – the passing on – of the apostolic ministry of oversight, teaching and the celebration of the mysteries of the New Covenant. This is effected either by the appointment of what have been termed 'apostolic delegates' (for example, Timothy),

---

[102] Luke 10.16; 1 Thessalonians 21.3.
[103] *The Priesthood of the Ordained Ministry*, p. 20.

or (to summarize brutally) of local elders or leaders, who assume the oversight of scattered Christian communities and churches. The most frequent – though of course by no means the only – terms for these 'leaders' are *presbyteroi* and *episkopoi*: terms which, we freely acknowledge, cannot always and absolutely be differentiated in the New Testament. Their specific functions cannot in each instance be described with precision. Nevertheless, we can suggest with at least a presumption of truth (a presumption greatly strengthened by the non-scriptural but primitive sources to which we shall presently turn) that the New Testament points us towards the emergence of a ministry with at least two orders (bishops and deacons[104] or bishop-presbyters and deacons). This may possibly be raised to three, if we accept that already in the New Testament there are those presbyters who exercise *episcope* in a manner which is distinct from all the rest.

7.1.6   By the time of the Pastoral Epistles, an ordained ministry with full authority has developed, and with these we see, in some places, the first beginnings of monoepiscopacy. We naturally stress the witness of the Scriptures that the ministry of *presbyteroi* and *episkopoi* is male. There is no evidence of, or endorsement for, the exercise of oversight or liturgical leadership by women: the opposite is the case.[105]

7.1.7   It is not the intention of this report to offer a detailed exegesis of each of the important Pauline texts.[106] We want instead to emphasize the general conclusions which can be drawn from the New Testament material. Teaching, oversight and liturgical presidency

---

[104] Philippians 1.1.

[105] See e.g. 1 Corinthians 14.33–6 (possibly a specific prohibition by St Paul of female presidency at the Eucharist); 1 Timothy 3; Titus 1.5ff.; etc.

[106] A very thorough, and balanced, job in this regard is done by the *Report of the Study Concerning the Ordination of Women* undertaken by the Anglican Mission in America, 2003.

are associated one with another (each being a related aspect of headship over the household of the new People of God). The emergent ministry is entrusted to men, whose headship images the Headship of Jesus Christ (the new Adam) over the whole human race.[107] 'Headship' does not imply the superiority of men over women, but rather the complementarity of the sexes in the life of the household of God, as in creation itself. Ephesians 5 (and related texts) leave us in no doubt that it is St Paul's firm intention as much to emphasize the mutuality of relationships between the sexes, and the love which the husband owes to his wife, as it is to point out the necessary maleness of representative ministry and oversight.

7.2   Galatians 3.28 – the abolition of difference?[108]

7.2.1   *Diversity, difference* and *complementarity* are terms which have been employed frequently in advancing the key arguments of this report. There is, however, one biblical text which is often used to suggest that, in Christ, these concepts are so radically redefined as to be virtually abolished; and that a consequence of this redefinition or abolition is that all orders of ministry must be open equally to both women and men. That text, of course, is to be found in the Letter of St Paul to the Galatians 3.27–9:

---

[107] Professor Frances Young, in a paper delivered to the Methodist Sacramental Fellowship Public Meeting at the Methodist Conference in Leeds in 1994 (published as *Presbyteral Ministry in the Catholic Tradition, or, Why Shouldn't Women Be Priests?*) argues forcibly that there is no New Testament (or any other) precedent for women exercising an episcopal or presbyteral ministry. She advances the case for the ordination of women as *presbyters* on other grounds, but admits frankly that this would be a change in the practice of the Church, and not a return to its origins.

[108] For a longer treatment of the issues raised by this passage, see 'Fatherhood, Headship and Tradition' by Fr Geoffrey Kirk, Part Three, Paper 3.

> For as many of you as were baptised into Christ have put on Christ. There is neither Jew nor Greek, there is neither slave nor free, there is neither male nor female; for you are all one in Christ Jesus. And if you are Christ's, then you are Abraham's offspring, heirs according to promise.

7.2.2   To suggest that St Paul intends, by this text, to sweep away all distinction between men and women is, we believe, fundamentally to misread and misunderstand him. There is nothing in Galatians – and nothing, therefore, in this passage – about ordination, or about ministry of a particular kind. Paul is teaching that salvation in Christ is open to all through baptism: it is in this sense that men and women are equal, as Jews and Greeks, and slaves and freemen, are equal also. Salvation comes – for all – through entry into the Church by baptism, and through participation in the life of the mystical body of Christ. Such a proclamation is very far from arguing that all orders of ministry within the Church must be open to male and female alike. It is, precisely, new life in Christ by baptism which is re-demptive; not admission into the orders of deacon or presbyter or overseer. Paul would not suggest – and we must not suggest – that ordination is somehow a neces-sary part of salvation, and therefore must be open to women as well as men, in order that women too may be saved.

7.2.3   If we reflect for a moment on the entirety of Paul's writ-ings, then it becomes evident that Galatians 3 could not mean what some have taken it to have meant – the eradication of any distinction between male and female. Paul's thinking must be taken as a whole. His understanding of the relationship between the sexes is patterned upon difference and complementarity, as we have seen. Man is head of the woman as Christ is Head of the Church; husband and wife relate to one another as the Bridegroom (Christ) relates to his Bride (the Church). Christology, ecclesiology and anthropology are deeply interwoven. To find in Galatians 3 a radical agenda for the elimination of difference between the sexes would be to lift it out of context, and to cut the threads of the whole Pauline understanding of God, Christ and humankind.

7.2.4   For Paul, we are saved not *from* sexual difference, but *in* it. Sexual difference is preserved and redeemed in the New Covenant, not abolished or taken away.[109] So it is with the other two elements in the Apostle's threefold saying in Galatians 3.28. Paul continues to believe that Jews and gentiles are different (he could scarcely have written the Letter to the Romans had he not so believed). He continues to believe that there will exist slaves as well as freemen. The point to be grasped about Galatians 3.28 is that it is neither a prescription for the organization of a Christian society, nor a programme for the authorized ministry of the Church.

7.3   A female apostle?

7.3.1   There is another specific reference in the writings of St Paul, however, which must be given a little more detailed attention, for it is – mistakenly, in our view – also frequently cited as a proof text by those who argue in favour of the ordination of women as bishops. This is, of course, the reference to Junias or Junia, in the Letter to the Romans (16.7). The name appears in a lengthy list of those to whom the Apostle wishes to

---

[109] Various forms of dualistic Gnosticism taught the contrary. See *New Testament Apocrypha* (Edgar Hennecke, 1965), vol. ii, pp. 169–9 and 289–9, especially: '. . . I will make her male, that she too may become a living spirit, resembling you males. For every woman who makes herself male will enter the Kingdom of Heaven.' It is not surprising that, in such circles, eucharistic presidency by women is not unknown. The oddity is that, even in these groups, the practice appears to have been uncommon.

send greeting. The controversy it has sparked may be indicated simply by juxtaposing the translations of the relevant verses in the Revised Standard, and then the New Revised Standard, Versions of the Bible. The RSV first:

> Greet Andronicus and Junias . . . they are men of note among the apostles.

and now the NRSV:

> Greet Andronicus and Junia . . . they are prominent among the apostles.

A male *known to the apostles* has become a *famous female apostle*!

7.3.2   How did this happen, and which translation is to be preferred? There are two issues to be addressed.

- First, there is the question of whether the person mentioned in the text is male or female. Of this we cannot be sure: *Iounian* could be the accusative of the masculine noun or it could be that of the feminine *Iounia*.
- Second, and more importantly, there is the question of how we understand what it is St Paul is intending to convey.

7.3.3   If the person in question (male or female!) *was* an apostle, then that term is being used very oddly. The context suggests that St Paul, feeling justifiably uncertain about the quality of the reception he is likely to receive from the Christian groups in Rome, is attempting to put together a list of Roman Christians who might be prepared to vouch for him. To hide a couple of 'prominent' apostles in the middle of such a list is curious. And if they *were* 'prominent apostles' it seems equally remarkable that the Roman Christians need to be informed about them.

7.3.4   The sense of the phrase *episemoi en tois apostolois* is
         crucial. Does it mean 'notable members of the group of
         apostles' or '[not apostles themselves but] well-known
         among [i.e. *to*] the apostles'? An answer can only be
         found, if at all, in a survey of ancient Greek usage.
         M. H. Burer and O. B. Wallace[110] examined the phrase
         episemos en . . . in the whole of extant Greek literature
         and concluded that the latter translation is the correct
         one: that is, the Apostles (probably the leaders of the
         Jerusalem community whose views would weigh heav-
         ily with those Jewish Christians in Rome who might
         be uneasy about St Paul) both knew and respected
         Andronicus and Junia(s).

7.3.5   We are left with the conclusion that those who claim
         Junia as the first woman apostle stand on shaky
         ground. The disputed interpretation of one verse in one
         letter of St Paul can hardly call into question the clear
         witness of the Pauline corpus taken in its entirety.

7.4   **The testimony of the Fathers in the Apostolic Age**

7.4.1   *Let the Bishop preside in the place of God.*[111] It is in
         the writings of the Apostolic Fathers that a coherent
         picture of the office and work of the bishop in the early
         Church is built up. In the letters of St Ignatius of Anti-
         och the bishop is seen as the one who guarantees the
         unity of the Church, and does so primarily in his office
         as the one celebrant of the one Eucharist.[112] The bishop
         is the representative, and the image, of the divine
         Father: he is *typon tou patros*, a 'type of the Father'.[113]
         St Ignatius urges the Christians in Smyrna to 'follow

---

[110] *New Testament Studies* 47 (1) (January 2001).

[111] Ignatius of Antioch, *To the Magnesians*, 6.

[112] See especially John D. Zizioulas, *Eucharist, Bishop, Church: The Unity of the Church in the Divine Eucharist and the Bishop during the First Three Centuries*, 2001.

[113] *To the Trallians*, 3

your bishop . . . as obediently as Jesus Christ followed the Father'.[114]

7.4.2   The Church is where the bishop is:

> The sole Eucharist you should consider valid is one that is celebrated by the bishop himself, or some person authorized by him. Where the bishop is to be seen, there let all his people be; just as wherever Jesus Christ is present, we have the catholic Church.[115]

The bishop both personifies the whole of his flock, and unites that flock with one another and with Christ in the Eucharist: union with the bishop is equivalent to union with God. As another well-known passage from St Ignatius has it:

> Make certain, therefore, that you all observe one common Eucharist; for there is but one Body of Our Lord Jesus Christ, and but one cup of union with His Blood, and one single altar of sacrifice – even as also there is but one bishop, with his clergy and my own fellow-servants the deacons. This will ensure that all your doings are in accord with the will of God.[116]

7.4.3   In a fascinating passage, John Zizioulas links the account of the Eucharist in the writings of St Ignatius with the worship of heaven as portrayed in the Revelation of St John the Divine. In so doing he draws together the work of the bishop as eucharistic celebrant, his iconic function as the type of the Father, and the unity of the Church in Christ:

> The task of the Bishop was from the beginning principally liturgical consisting in the offering of

---

[114] *To the Smyrnaeans*, 8
[115] Ibid.
[116] *To the Philadelphians*, 4.

the Divine Eucharist. This is attested in very early texts. If we combine the information Ignatius gives us about the Bishop with the image of the Eucharistic assembly that the author of the Apocalypse has in mind, we see that the Bishop is described as 'presiding in the place of God,' precisely because in the Eucharistic assembly he occupied that place, which the Apocalypse describes as 'the throne of God and of the Lamb,' in the heavenly assembly, the image of which the Apocalypse takes from the celebration of the Divine Eucharist in the Church. The very title of 'Bishop' (*episkopos*) is used by Ignatius most probably because . . . the *episkopos par excellence* is God, Whose place in the Eucharistic assembly was now occupied by the Bishop who presided over it. Everything in the vision of the Apocalypse revolves around the altar which is before the throne of God. Before it stands the multitude of the saved, and around the throne in a circle the twenty-four presbyters. The metaphor is plainly taken from the Eucharistic assembly at which the Bishop sat on his throne before the altar with the presbyters in a circle around him. This was from the beginning the place the Bishop occupied as the one who offered the Divine Eucharist, and for this reason the Church saw him as the image and type of God or of Christ. . . . In the Divine Eucharist, the Church was manifested in space and time as the body of Christ, and also as a canonical unity. In this way the unity of the Divine Eucharist became the font of the Church's unity in the body of Christ, and also of her unity '*in the Bishop*'.[117]

7.4.4   Gregory Dix and Zizioulas are agreed concerning the priority of the nature of episcopacy attested in the letters of St Ignatius. By referring briefly to other patristic sources, we can build up a picture of the

---

[117] *Eucharist, Bishop, Church*, pp. 66–7.

several different aspects which become important in the Church's developing understanding of the work of the bishop. St Clement of Rome, writing to the Christians in Corinth, asserts that the key to understanding the authority of the Apostles is that it rests on the authority of Christ himself:

> the apostles received the Gospel for us from the Lord Jesus Christ; Jesus Christ was God's ambassador. Thus Christ is sent from God, and the apostles from Christ.[118]

7.4.5   The ordination rites of Hippolytus (*c*. AD 215)[119] turn on the image of the bishop not as Father, but rather as *alter Christus*, another Christ. The prayer for the consecration of a bishop asks that the candidate for office might have bestowed upon him by God that same 'princely Spirit' by which Jesus himself had exercised his own offices of Good Shepherd of God's 'holy flock', and High Priest, 'propitiating' God by the offering of the Church's eucharistic sacrifice.

7.4.6   For St Irenaeus, it is the teaching office of the bishop which comes into the foreground. The bishop is apostolic witness and guardian of the tradition – not so much *alter Christus* as *alter apostolus,* the representative of the Apostles. Irenaeus' attitude both to the bishop's teaching authority and to the apostolic succession is summed up in this well-known observation:

> We should obey those presbyters in the Church who have their succession from the apostles, and who, together with succession in the episcopate, have received the assured charisma of the truth.[120]

---

[118] *1 Clement*, 42.
[119] Some scholars date these to the fourth century.
[120] *Against the Heresies*, 4.40.2.

Kallistos Ware has commented:

> Outward continuity in apostolic succession serves as the sign and guarantee of inward continuity in apostolic faith . . . its purpose is to preserve the continuity of doctrinal teaching, the fullness of Catholic faith and life.[121]

Thus the apostolic succession as a visible expression of the bishop's ministry is the servant of his calling, as the representative of his Church, to guard and hand on the *paradosis*.

7.4.7   The writings of St Cyprian (middle of the third century) contribute the important insight that it is only in fellowship with their bishop that the local congregation can be assured of participation in the universal Church of God:

> Hence you should know that the bishop is in the Church, and the Church in the bishop, and that if anyone is not with the bishop, he is not in the Church.[122]

For Cyprian, it is because the episcopate is united that the whole Church is one. That oneness is made visible by the communion which exists among the bishops, and which results in their common action throughout the world. In each community the bishop is at once the symbol, the guardian and the instrument of this unity. The episcopate, which belongs to each bishop, belongs to him as one of a great brotherhood linked by manifold ties into a corporate unity:

> The episcopate is one; the individual members each

---

[121] 'Patterns of Episcopacy in the Early Church and Today: An Orthodox View', in Peter Moore (ed.), *Bishops: But What Kind? Reflections on Episcopacy*, 1982.
[122] Cyprian, *Letters*, 66.7.

have a part, and the parts make up a solid whole.[123]

The existence of a local church implies a bishop as the ministerial sign of its organic life; conversely, a bishop has the absolute duty to embody for the local community the faith and practice of the whole Church, and to teach and instruct them in it. It is the responsibility of the people to sever themselves from the ministry of a bishop who has fallen into heresy.

7.5   Conclusions

7.5.1   What conclusions can we draw from the theology of the episcopate as it is found in the testimony of Ignatius, Irenaeus and Cyprian? We have identified a number of crucial strands which we now draw together.

- The bishop is 'high priest' and the principal liturgical minister of the Church.[124]
- He is the focus of unity, for the community at whose eucharistic offering he is the celebrant, and through which the very unity of that community is expressed.
- He is the instrument of unity between churches.
- He is the successor to the Apostles, continuing that mission which Christ himself instituted in commissioning the Twelve.
- He is a type, or *eikon*, both of the Father and of the Son as sent by the Father.
- He is the guardian of the tradition, and the teacher of the faith.

7.5.2   While the spread of the faith both numerically and geographically increasingly brings about the delegation

---

[123] Cyprian, *De Catholicae Ecclesiae Unitate*.
[124] Later, St Gregory Nazianzen will speak of the (presbyter or) bishop as a liturgist, one called to celebrate 'those mystic and elevating rites which are our greatest and most precious privilege'.

of a number of episcopal functions to the presbyterate (most notably in terms of liturgical celebrations),
the evidence of the early centuries points conclusively
to the distinctive and foundational role of the bishop
within the ministry of the Church. Bishops are not
merely presbyters with added 'voltage' as St John
Chrysostom was to suggest in his reply to St Jerome in
the fourth century. Chrysostom wrote, ' "bishops" are
superior to "presbyters" only in the power of ordination and in this respect alone have they advantage over
presbyters'. On the contrary, in the pre-Nicene age, we
can say that 'the bishop is the fundamental continuing
apostolic ministry in the Church'.[125]

7.5.3   The question of the nature of the relationship between
the bishop and the presbyter is of course highly pertinent to the present debate. For now, it can be stated
in general terms that, as the Church developed in the
early centuries, the presbyterate, though it retained a
distinctive character, became ever more dependent on
the episcopate. Presbyters belong to the apostolic succession only through their ordination by the bishops
who embody that succession. Their ministry is a share
in the ministry of the bishop.

---

[125] Aidan Nichols, OP, *Holy Order*, 1990, p. 47. The presbyterate, like
the episcopate, is of apostolic foundation and is attested in Scripture, but the
two are distinct in origin, and presbyters are neither merely nor originally
'mini-bishops', just as bishops are neither merely nor originally 'super-
presbyters'. In chapter 6 he sets out the teaching of the Second Vatican
Council in the light of the recovery of this patristic understanding.

8

The Episcopate and the Church of England

8.1   Is there an 'Anglican' doctrine of episcopacy?

8.1.1   When members of the General Synod were given the opportunity in July 2002 to put questions to the Bishop of Rochester's working party following the presentation to the Synod of their progress report,[126] Fr Simon Killwick asked whether there would be contained in the final report 'a clear statement . . . which would tell us what bishops are, what they are for, why they are necessary'.[127]

8.1.2   We make the same point by asking: has the Church of England sought always to hold to, and to hand on, that patristic understanding of the office and work of the bishop which can be characterized, in summary, as focus and instrument of unity, chief pastor and liturgical minister of the Church? Has it included with this, by virtue of the requirement that all presbyters be episcopally ordained, the understanding that bishops are the fount of all sacramental ministry? Does it hold that bishops are to be both teachers and guardians of the faith?

8.1.3   To these questions, we answer with a resounding 'Yes'.

---

[126] GS 1457.
[127] *Report of Proceedings: General Synod, July 2002*, p. 203.

We can look directly to the Canons of the Church of England, which still refer to the diocesan bishop as the 'Father in God' to all in his diocese, and as chief pastor and principal minister of that diocese.[128] The continuing use of the term 'Reverend Father in God' in the Anglican ordination rites has already been noted.[129] The proposed Declaration to be made at the ordination of a bishop in the draft *Common Worship* rites says this:

> Bishops are called to serve and care for the flock of Christ . . . As principal ministers of word and sacrament and stewards of the mysteries of God, they are to preside at the Eucharist and lead the offering of prayer and praise.

Bishops are to be the 'chief pastors', sharing oversight with their priests.

8.1.4   This text, of course, is but the latest expression of a consistent Anglican tradition. One of the most notable features of the English Reformation was, famously, the care that was taken to retain the historic threefold Order of bishops, priests and deacons. The Ordinal annexed to the *Book of Common Prayer* speaks only of the making of bishops, priests and deacons 'in the Church of God', a phrase which persists into modern times. It was (and here we summarize the well-known story) the intention of the reformers not to innovate, but to restore the English Church to the primitive Catholicism from which it had deviated. This (reformed) Catholic Church in England was to share the unbroken and uninterrupted ministry of the Catholic Church, ex-

---

[128] Canon C18. It is interesting to note that in the Pope's recent teaching document on the episcopate, *Pastores Gregis*, a renewed encouragement is given to the faithful to kiss the bishop's hand, in token of his spiritual fatherhood.

[129] See n. 10, above.

isting (as the preface to the Ordinal has it) in threefold form since the time of the Apostles. Continuity with the undivided Catholic Church of the age of the Fathers was not only assumed in the Prayer Book and Ordinal,[130] and by the retention of the Catholic Creeds and Sacraments, but also in the Canons of 1604. Canon 30 clearly states that the purpose of reformation was not to divide, or separate from the unity of the Church, save only 'in those particular points wherein they were fallen both from themselves in their ancient integrity and from the Apostolic Churches, which were their first founders'.

8.1.5　The history of the Church of England from the time of the Reformation onwards is studded with examples of the determination of Anglican divines to retain the historic episcopate. From the time of Elizabeth I, to take but two examples, there is the care taken over the consecration of Matthew Parker as Archbishop of Canterbury,[131] and the issuing (with royal authority) of the Prayer Book in Latin (for use at Oxford, Cambridge and Eton) in which we find 'priest' represented by *sacerdos*.[132]

8.1.6　Richard Hooker (1554–1600), in the *Laws of Ecclesiastical Polity*, sets out to show that to 'be a bishop now' (that is, in the England of Elizabeth I) is the same as it was in ancient times,[133] and to defend the episcopate as

---

[130] And, indeed, in the retention of the names and titles of the historic sees.

[131] See, most conveniently, E. Denny and T. A. Lacey, *De Hierarchia Anglicana*, 1895, p. 210.

[132] This is the word used by Bishop Eric Kemp in his translation of the Preface to the 1968 proposed Anglican–Methodist Ordinal into Latin to convey (to ecumenical partners among others) what the Church of England intended by its use of the word 'priest'. This Ordinal was the basis of the Ordinal in the Methodist Service Book of 1975 and of the Series 3 Ordinal of 1977, authorized in 1978 and incorporated into the *ASB* of 1980.

[133] Vol. ii, bk vii, ch. 2 i.

fundamental to the life of the Church. The 'first institution of bishops was from heaven, was even of God', and bishops could not only 'beget children to God in baptism' but also could 'create fathers to the people of God' in ordination. Space does not permit us to rehearse the whole struggle against (bishop-denying) Puritanism which convulsed the English religious landscape in the seventeenth century. Historians of the English Civil War, whatever their overall judgement of the record of Charles 1, will almost all agree that, had he consented to the abolition of episcopacy and embraced Presbyterianism, he would certainly not have lost his head, nor in all likelihood his kingdom.

8.1.7   John Cosin (1594–1672), preaching at the consecration of Francis White as Bishop of Carlisle in 1626, said that an essential part of the work of the bishop is to preserve unity, for which purpose the Spirit of unity is given ('Receive the Holy Ghost') during the prayer of consecration. He continues:

> Bishops are sent by [God] to mediate and pray for the people, to be ministers of reconciliation, as St Paul speaks, *and in a manner to be sacrificers too, representers at the altar here, and appliers of the Sacrifice made once for all*; without which last act the first will do no good. (emphasis ours)[134]

For Jeremy Taylor (1613–67), the episcopal office is the surest guarantee of the solidarity and unity of the Church, and is divinely instituted, founded in the apostolical tradition, and an essential mark of Catholic practice. William Sancroft (1617–93) (Archbishop of Canterbury 1678–91) maintains in his sermon preached at Westminster Abbey on 2 December 1660, at the first consecration of new bishops since the Restoration, that bishops are at once the representatives of Christ

---

[134] John Cosin, *Works*, Library of Anglo-Catholic Theology, 1843, vol. i, p. 87.

to their flocks, and of their Church before God. In the eighteenth century, men such as William Wake (1657–1737) (Archbishop of Canterbury 1716–37), John Potter (1674–1747) (Archbishop of Canterbury 1737–47) and Samuel Horsley (1733–1805) (Bishop of St David's 1788–94) all wrote and preached about the spiritual authority of the episcopate as it derives from the first Apostles and in turn from Christ himself, and about the continuation of the episcopal office – ancient, catholic and reformed – in the Church of England.

8.1.8 As we come closer to modern times, we recall that the *proximate* cause of the launch of what was to become the Oxford or Tractarian Movement in John Keble's Assize Sermon of 1833 was the intended reform by the Whig government of the Irish bishoprics. The theological and ecclesiological issue at stake for Keble was the sacred nature of the episcopate, being not an office of state to be interfered with by the secular power, but rather of divine origin and nature.

8.2 The nature of the episcopate and the ordination of women as bishops

8.2.1 We now turn directly to the theological consequences of ordaining women as bishops in the tradition to which the early Fathers bear witness and to which the Church of England has adhered (as much after the upheavals of the sixteenth century as before them).

8.2.2 It is frequently argued that to ordain women as bishops is not to *change* the episcopate, but rather simply to *enlarge its scope*, so that it includes women as well as men. We hold otherwise. The office and work of women bishops will not be – cannot be – continuous with that of the historic episcopate. On the contrary it is a wilful departure from the tradition, with the expressed aim of amending the faults and eliminating the prejudices of those who initiated and formed it.

8.2.3   Earlier in this report we gave much attention to the example of Jesus Christ in choosing twelve men to be his Apostles, and to what we can broadly term the argument of *sacramental symbolism*. We argued that the male gender is a necessary condition of the particular manner in which the bishop (and the priest) represent God to the people, continuing the Lord's work as Bridegroom of his Church. Those arguments, we believe, are powerful – indeed decisive. They are consequent upon core doctrines: the revelation of God as Father, the Incarnation of God in a male human person, the authority of Scripture, the creation of humankind by God in two complementary sexes, male and female.

8.2.4   That we hold these opinions in solidarity with the greater part of Christendom, both Eastern and Western, makes us poignantly aware of other significant problems, which are to do with the bishop as the instrument of unity, and with the continuity of the historic episcopate within the Church of England.

8.2.5   These problems can be clarified in terms employed by the Cameron Report,[135] chapter 4 of which begins with an analysis of the function of the episcopate in three 'planes' of the Church's life: the unity of the local community; unity between communities; and what we might call the 'vertical' plane of unity – the unity of the Church from generation to succeeding generation, expressed in the handing on of the tradition in continuity with the Apostles.

8.2.6   The authors of the report acknowledge a debt to the 'Lima Statement', *Baptism, Eucharist and Ministry*,[136] and it is worth quoting here the extract from that important WCC text which underpins the 'three

---

[135] The Report of the Archbishops' Group on the Episcopate, 1990, GS 944.
[136] Published by the World Council of Churches, 1982.

planes' theology of the episcopate in *Episcopal Ministry:*

> Bishops preach the Word, preside at the Sacraments, and administer discipline in such a way as to be representative-pastoral ministers of oversight, continuity and unity in the Church. They have pastoral oversight of an area to which they are called. They serve the apostolicity and unity of the Church's teaching, worship and sacramental life. They have responsibility for leadership in the Church's mission. They relate the Christian community in their area to the wider Church, and the universal Church to their community. They, in communion with the presbyters and deacons and the whole community, are responsible for the orderly transfer of ministerial authority in the Church.[137]

8.2.7 Keeping in mind the principles of both the Cameron Report and the WCC statement, we can proceed to look more closely at the reasons why we believe women bishops would be unable to fulfil the essence of episcopal ministry as the tradition understands it.

8.3 Unity and communion

8.3.1 Following a decision to proceed with the lawful consecration of women to the episcopate, it is plain (and agreed by all) that there would be a minority of bishops, priests, deacons and lay people in the Church of England who would not accept those so consecrated as true bishops. What the size of that minority might be is difficult to gauge with accuracy (nor is it strictly relevant to the argument). It is, however, reasonable to assume that it would include all those bishops who do not presently ordain women to the priesthood, together with clergy and people of those parishes which

---

[137] *Baptism, Eucharist, Ministry,* M29, in Meyer and Vischer, *Growth in Agreement,* pp. 489–90.

have petitioned for Extended Episcopal Care under the Episcopal Ministry Act of Synod 1993 and those, ordained and lay, who have not hitherto been able or willing to avail themselves of that provision.

8.3.2 This constituency would hold to its position in good conscience, and in accord with the provisions of the 1993 Measure which permitted the ordination of women to the priesthood in the Church of England. That Measure presumed that not everyone would accept the priestly ministry of women; that such a stance was wholly compatible with the doctrine of the Church of England and that it ought to command respect in the Church. The law recognized that it was necessary to ensure that those unable in conscience to accept the priestly ministry of women could distance themselves from it through the mechanism of the Schedules with which it concluded.

8.3.3 By the 1993 Measure, the Church of England proceeded to ordain priests whose ministry, it freely acknowledged, would not be acceptable to all. Their ministry was agreed to be provisional or conditional, inasmuch as it was not obligatory for all members of the Church of England to accept their priestly ministry (although of course those who did so accept it accounted them true priests). Impairment of communion at the presbyteral level was, and remains, the consequence of that deliberate decision.

8.3.4 With the ordination of women as bishops (and the inability to accept their episcopal ministry by those who presently cannot accept the ministry of women priests), full communion would no longer exist between the bishops of the Church of England. Communion would not simply be impaired, but fractured – broken. There would exist bishops who would not be recognized as such by other bishops. The unity of the Church would be disrupted in the very ministry which exists to effect and express it. In what sense, it might be asked, would there continue to be one Church of England in such a case, when episcopal Orders were no longer mutually recognized and interchangeable?[138]

8.3.5 Along with the breakdown of communion between bishops (and the consequent collapse of the bishop's historic role as the instrument of unity between dioceses and provinces), the ordination of women to the episcopate would also ensure that the bishop could no longer guarantee the sacramental unity of the local Church. (This is acknowledged to be at the heart of episcopal ministry by the House of Bishops of the Church of England in their Occasional Paper *Bishops in Communion*.)[139] We would have moved far away from that intimate connection we have found from St Ignatius onwards between the bishop, his Eucharist, the Church and her unity.

8.3.6 But there is more. If the sacramental ministry of a woman bishop is not accepted by all, then not only her celebrations of the Eucharist, but also the ordinations of priests and deacons carried out by her, are in doubt. The Church of England would soon find itself faced with a situation in which not only were the Orders of women bishops (and priests) not everywhere recognized and mutually interchangeable, but where those of men ordained by women bishops were also called into question. A whole class of male priests would come into existence whose sacramental ministry was held to be at best doubtful by many faithful Anglicans.

---

[138] We are grateful to Fr David Houlding for his paper on behalf of the Catholic Group in General Synod, delivered to the Bishop of Rochester's Commission on Women in the Episcopate in June 2003 – Appendix 3.

[139] 'In episcopally ordered churches, bishops, as chief pastors, have a particular concern for the unity and *koinonia* of the Church.' *Bishops in Communion: Collegiality in the Service of the Koinonia of the Church*, GS Misc. 580, 2000.

8.3.7   In the matter of the sacraments, of course, it ought to
          be the *least* doubtful course which is to be pursued.[140]
          Sacraments (so the Church of England has always
          taught and teaches still) exist to be trustworthy and
          authoritative channels of God's grace. The sacramen-
          tal mysteries are seals of the reliability of a faithful God
          – and the ordained ministry which guarantees them
          has the Lord's seal upon it.[141] Yet the Church of Eng-
          land, should it decide to proceed with the ordination of
          women as bishops, would be bringing about precisely
          the opposite state of affairs.

8.3.8   Further issues of critical importance cluster around
          the role of the diocesan bishop as the 'ordinary' of the
          diocese. At present (as the Episcopal Ministry Act of
          Synod 1993 makes clear) *all* clergy continue to recog-
          nize the diocesan bishop as the ordinary by whom (or
          on whose behalf) they are instituted or licensed, and to
          whom they owe canonical obedience. Were women to
          be ordained to the episcopate, all this would change.
          While it is true that the actions of those bishops who
          have ordained women to the priesthood have result-
          ed in an impairment of communion with those who
          cannot accept such ordinations, the ministry of those
          bishops in ordaining men, and in administering confir-
          mation, is beyond challenge. No-one doubts that it is
          indeed the Holy Eucharist at which they preside. The
          new situation would be radically different.

8.4   The doctrine of reception

8.4.1   There are those who are eager to make the ordina-
          tion of women as priests and bishops binding upon all

---

[140] Bishop Kenneth Kirk to the Church Assembly in 1947: 'Where
sacraments are concerned the Church is always obliged to take the least
doubtful course.'

[141] Notice the language of absolute certainty used in the BCP in which,
for example, absolution after auricular confession is recommended 'to the
quieting of . . . conscience and avoiding of all scruple and doubtfulness'.

Anglicans and to move to the consecration of women bishops by a one-clause measure, with no provision for opponents. We believe that the terms of the 1993 Measure make such an approach impossible. Revision of that Measure moreover would require not only Synodical but also Parliamentary assent.

8.4.2   There are, however, far more serious theological questions at issue than simply the question of the repeal or otherwise of one piece of legislation. The whole context of the decision-making process leading up to the vote of November 1992 was that the Church of England was embarking on an experiment. No-one was to be compelled to accept the sacramental ministry of women priests.[142] They were to be ordained on the understanding that the question of whether their priesthood would ultimately be received by the Church as a whole was genuinely an open one.[143] The Church of England acted: but only in such a manner as to admit the possibility that the action might subsequently prove to have been mistaken.[144]

8.4.3   *Reception,* it is now widely agreed, has become something of a fraught term. For some, it never implied anything more than a period of time allowed for those who did not accept an innovation to 'get used to it'.

---

[142] 'Ordination of Women to the Priesthood: Pastoral Arrangements'. Report by the House of Bishops. (*Bonds of Peace*) p. 6: 'Those who for a variety of reasons cannot conscientiously accept that women may be ordained as priests will continue to hold a legitimate and recognised position within the Church of England.'

[143] Episcopal Ministry Act of Synod 1993 s 3 (a) (i) 'The General Synod regards it as desirable that all concerned should endeavour to ensure that discernment in the wider Church of the rightness or otherwise of the Church of England's decision to ordain women to the priesthood should be as open a process as possible.'

[144] '. . . we have always said and always believed that any step of this nature may be of the Holy Spirit but may not be of the Holy Spirit. Time will tell.' Archbishop George Carey, in reply to a question at the Sacred Synod held at the Emmanuel Centre, Westminster, Thursday 28 October 1999.

In this weak sense, some proponents of the ordination of women hold that, a decade or so after the first such ordinations, the period of 'reception' is, or ought to be, over. Such an understanding of the term we hold to be wholly misguided. 'Reception', properly understood, involves the acceptance (or non-acceptance) of a development in part of the Church, by the whole Church. The Report of the Primates' Working Party (the Grindrod Report) is quoted extensively in the Cameron Report and includes just such a use of the term, in a very helpful explanation of how the ordination of a woman as bishop in one province of the Anglican Communion would be fed into the life of the whole Communion:

- The development should be offered to the Anglican Communion in an open process of reception.
- The development could not be expressed as the mind of the Church until it had been accepted by the whole Communion. Even then there would necessarily be a tentativeness about it until it had been accepted by the universal Church.
- Consideration of the ordination of women to the presbyterate and episcopate within the Communion would need to continue with provinces listening to one another's thoughts and experience, aiding one another in theological reflection and exercising mutual sensitivity and care.
- Debate in the wider fellowship of the churches ought to be encouraged, particularly within existing bilateral and multilateral dialogues.[145]

8.4.4 The Primates recognize that there is always something provisional, or tentative, about a development until such time as it has been accepted by all. We add that what remains the subject of open-ended dialogue between provinces must necessarily be tolerated and respected within them. In the Church of England the

---

[145] *Episcopal Ministry*, p. 242, para. 554.

ordination of women to the priesthood is still very far from having been accepted by all. We argue that it cannot be right to proceed with a second development (the ordination of women as bishops) while the first, upon which it is consequent, is still in doubt. To do so would be to bring to an abrupt and premature end any sense of the ordination of women as a development which may or may not be received by the whole Church.

8.4.5   Reception in the 'universal Church' was accorded a critical role by the Primates: so critical that even after its unanimous acceptance within the Anglican Communion, a development would remain 'tentative'. We note that there are no signs of approaching 'reception' in that wider arena to which they appeal. The teaching of the Roman Catholic Church is crystal clear. In his Apostolic Letter of 22 May 1994, *Ordinatio Sacerdotalis*, Pope John Paul II concluded his teaching with words which have often been repeated:

> Wherefore, in order that all doubt may be removed regarding a matter of great importance, a matter which pertains to the Church's divine constitution of itself, in virtue of my ministry of confirming the brethren (cf. Luke 22.32) I declare that the Church has no authority[146] whatsoever to confer priestly ordination on women, and that this judgement is to be definitively held by all the Church's faithful.

8.4.6   It is not simply that the Catholic Church does not wish to ordain women as priests, the Pope is saying, or that the time is not right so to do. Rather, the Pope is saying that it lies beyond the competence of the Church to initiate such a development. The teaching of the Pope (and of the whole Roman Magisterium, as exemplified in the Declaration *Inter Insigniores* of 1976) makes

---

[146] *'facultatem'*. This word would naturally suggest 'ability' and not merely 'authority' to do something.

it clear that the ordination of women as bishops and priests *cannot* be 'received' by the Roman Catholic Church.[147] Yet even prominent Anglicans who have ignored the declared position of the papacy and support the ordination of women as priests, have understood the importance of the reception of doctrine by the whole Catholic Church. Michael Nazir-Ali writes that a development in a particular ecclesial tradition 'eventually . . . would have to be received as authentic not only by the particular tradition in which it first arises but by the Universal Church as well'.[148] Stephen Sykes is confident of the future ordination of the women in the wider Catholic Church, to which the ordination of women in the Anglican Communion is said to have been an act of 'eschatological obedience'.[149]

8.4.7 It is perhaps as well to recall that in the more exotic by-ways of the early Christian centuries women presbyters did exist. In Montanism, a 'feminist reading' of Scripture, combined with a deft use of Galatians 3.28, and a disinclination to see soteriological significance in the maleness of Christ, was held to justify the presbyteral and eucharistic ministry of women.[150] Sometimes, particularly among Roman Catholic supporters of the ordination of women, it is suggested that the Church's consistent practice of a male ministry is not normative for us, 'because the question of ordaining women has not been raised before in the same way as it is being raised now'. It has been; but the *una Catholica* was not impressed.[151]

---

[147] Indeed, the concept of infallibility (in terms of *Lumen Gentium*, 25) has been invoked to cover the teaching embodied in *Ordinatio Sacerdotalis* (see *New Directions*, November 2002).

[148] Nazir-Ali, 'Episcopacy and Communion: Church, Culture and Change', in *Communion and Episcopacy: Essays to Mark the Centenary of the Chicago–Lambeth Quadrilateral*, 1988.

[149] In 'Foundations of an Anglican Ecclesiology', reprinted in *Unashamed Anglicanism*, 1995.

[150] Epiphanius, *Adversus Haereses*, 49.2 (PG 41. 881).

[151] What if, purely for the sake of argument, we were to concede the dubious claim that there *were* priestly women in the 'early Catholic Church',

8.5   Ecumenism

8.5.1   The restriction of the priesthood and episcopate to males only is, of course, the consistent teaching and practice not only of the Roman Catholic Church of the Latin West, but of the great churches of the East, Orthodox and Oriental, as well.

8.5.2   Why should the Church of England take any notice of the position held by other churches? We can answer that question on a number of levels.

- There is the fundamental imperative for unity of the whole Church represented by Our Lord's High Priestly prayer, 'that they may all be one'.
- There is the Church of England's claim to share the Orders of the historic, undivided Church (as already discussed at some length in this report).
- The Church of England has always maintained that a precondition for full visible unity is the mutual recognition and interchangeability of Orders.
- More particularly, there is the story of the steady progress made in recent times towards a common understanding of ministry and sacraments with the Roman Catholic Church – our largest ecumenical partner, and, to coin a well-known phrase, 'the rock from which we were hewn'.

---

and that the phenomenon subsequently died out? We are uncertain that the conclusions usually drawn from this are compelling. Was there not, according to this reading of history, thus a 'period of reception', as a result of which the common mind of the universal Church, Latin, Greek and Syrian, rejected the experiment? It is all very well to account for this by alleging an increasingly hierarchical and patriarchal mindset, which, accordingly we are told, vitiates this non-reception, but the logic of this approach deserves examination. Suppose our present 'period of reception' were *also* to lead to the rejection of this experiment. Are there not likely to be those once again who will dispute the validity of *that* verdict, on the grounds, once again, of the patriarchal discrimination inherent (as they would see it) in those who have reached such a judgement? When is a 'period of reception' finally settled – and how often does the Church have to jump through the same hoops whenever an ancient heresy or discarded innovation is revived?

8.5.3 Whatever the ups and downs of the ecumenical conversation[152] as represented by the ARCIC process, astonishing progress has been made. A new stage in the ecumenical journey between the communions of Canterbury and Rome with the setting up of the International Anglican–Roman Catholic Commission for Unity and Mission (IARCCUM) is yet in its infancy.[153] For the Church of England to innovate and to experiment by proceeding with the ordination of women to the episcopate in the face of the clearly stated position of the Roman Catholic Church, and the consistent practice of the historic churches of the East, would surely be for it deliberately to place itself outside the universal episcopate. It would be, in the matter of our relations with the Roman Catholic Church in particular, to ignore much of the agreement reached on the exercise of the Petrine primacy expressed in the most recent ARCIC Statement, *The Gift of Authority*. There we read that 'the Bishop of Rome offers a specific ministry concerning the discernment of truth'.[154]

8.5.4 In this latest ARCIC statement on authority in the Church we also find two particularly helpful comments (or rather, one comment and one question). They need to be taken with the utmost seriousness as the Church of England considers how it should proceed in the matter of the ordination of women as bishops. The comment is this:

The duty of maintaining the Church in truth is one

---

[152] Professor Henry Chadwick in his essay 'Unfinished Business', in C. Hill and E. Yarnold (eds), *Anglicans and Roman Catholics: The Search for Unity*, 1994, accepts that there was some disappointment among the members of ARCIC at the Vatican's official response to the ARCIC 1 *Final Report*, but concludes that 'the Vatican verdict deserves to be wholly supported in its evident conviction that good ecumenism is more than polite co-existence in a state of permanent eucharistic separation'.

[153] Recently imperilled by the episcopal ordination of a practising homosexual man as Bishop of New Hampshire.

[154] *The Gift of Authority*, 1999, p. 28, para. 47.

of the essential functions of the Episcopal college. It has the power to exercise this ministry because it is bound in succession to the Apostles, who were the body authorised and sent by Christ to preach the Gospels to all nations. The authenticity of the teaching of individual bishops is evident when this teaching is in solidarity with that of the whole Episcopal college. The exercise of this teaching authority requires that what it teaches be faithful to Holy Scripture and consistent with Apostolic Tradition.[155]

And the question – posed to Anglicans – follows from it. The report raises the need for the Anglican Communion to develop 'structures of authority among its provinces' and then asks:

When major new questions arise which, in fidelity to Scripture and Tradition, require a united response, will these structures assist Anglicans to participate in the *sensus fidelium* of all Christians?

It is surely to the wisdom of the Patriarch of the West that the Church of England must look for guidance if it is to remain within that *sensus fidelium* in the exercise of episcopacy.[156]

8.6   Excursus: some suggested procedures

8.6.1   All the suggestions which have surfaced thus far about how the episcopal ministry of women might somehow be exercised in a manner acceptable to those who cannot in conscience recognize it, are highly problematic.

---

[155] Ibid., p. 32, para. 44.
[156] Canon Edward Norman's Ecclesiastical Law Society Lecture, *Authority in the Anglican Communion*, though too long to quote usefully in this report, is a masterly analysis of the breakdown of the instruments of authority in classical Anglicanism, and the consequent doctrinal and ecclesiological incoherence which have resulted; see 5 *Ecc LJ* 172.

8.6.2   A separation between the juridical and sacramental
         functions of the bishop drives a wedge between the
         work of the bishop as one who has oversight and the
         one who is the chief liturgical minister and normative
         celebrant of the Eucharist. These, as we have seen, are
         intimately bound together in the tradition.

8.6.3   The model of *team episcope,* in which male bishops (in-
         cluding those opposed to the ordination of women) and
         female bishops would exist side by side, perhaps as suf-
         fragans of a male diocesan, is even more problematic.
         How can the episcopate accommodate two 'classes'
         of bishop, one of which can only aspire to suffragan/
         assistant status? What sort of Catholic understand-
         ing of the episcopate remains in such an arrangement,
         when the members of such a 'team' cannot recognize
         one another's sacramental acts? Comparisons might
         be drawn with the existence at the present time of
         clergy teams in which male opponents of the ordina-
         tion of women minister alongside women priests. The
         difference surely lies in the particular associations of
         the episcopate with the expression of the unity of the
         Church. An episcopal team constituted specifically to
         embody *disunity* would be an absurdity. To generalize
         the concept of *episcope* by downplaying the individual
         Father in God is to contradict the entire development
         which led to the emergence of the historic episcopate in
         the first place. That the bishop rightly shares his over-
         sight with a range of others, lay and ordained, in the
         exercise of his *episcope* cannot obscure the fact that the
         Bridegroom does not come as a committee, but as the
         one incarnate Son of God.[157]

---

[157] See further Paper 2 included in Part Three of this report, 'The Gender
and Number of Bishops' by Fr John Hunwicke.

9

Some Commonplace Arguments

9.1   Introduction

This report has sought to be positive in its approach – that is, to seek to explain more deeply the theological reasons which underpin the constant tradition of the Church in ordaining only males as bishops and priests. There remain, nevertheless, familiar arguments used by those in favour of the ordination of women as priests and bishops. We have looked already at two issues raised by particular biblical texts, those to do with sexual difference (Galatians 3.28),[158] and the possible existence of a female apostle (Romans 16.7).[159] But there are others – in the realms of Christology, soteriology and anthropology – whose common currency in the debate demands attention.

9.2   Soteriology and Christology

9.2.1   *What is not assumed, is not healed.* So runs the famous dictum of St Gregory of Nazianzen, with which, in particular, he refutes an Apollinarian Christology with its truncated understanding of the full humanity of Jesus Christ.[160] From this dictum, proponents of the

---

[158] See 7.2 above.
[159] See 7.3 above.
[160] Briefly: the Apollinarian heresy sells short the full humanity of Christ

ordination of women have derived an argument for a priesthood which must include men and women. Since all humanity is saved in Christ, and the priest represents Christ, therefore the priesthood must include all humanity in both sexes.

9.2.2   The argument is flawed, however, both because it confuses ordination to the ministerial priesthood with salvation in Christ by baptism (a point we explored in connection with the Galatians text), and also because it fails to understand that *all* of humanity – male and female – is saved precisely through Christ's taking of human nature upon himself, even though the Incarnation is (inevitably, as we have argued) in one sex, and that sex the male. To recruit Gregory in favour of the ordination of women using this text is to fail to do justice to the reality of the Incarnation. Jesus Christ is fully human. He is not some not-quite-human composite made up of divine and human elements, a third 'quiddity' somewhere between the fully human and the fully divine. That was the error of the Nestorians, an error which St Cyril and the Alexandrians fought to correct. Put bluntly, the misuse of Gregory leads to the conclusion that to be male (or indeed to be female) is not to be fully human, only sub-human. Full humanity subsists only in some mythical being in which male and female somehow coexist.

9.2.3   This view is simply not consistent with the Christian understanding of the human person, or indeed the person of Jesus Christ. It is a docetic ('spiritualized') view of human nature. It implies that, if only the confines of the body could be shaken off or put aside, a purer humanity, untroubled by having to exist as male or female, would emerge as a result.

---

by allowing that, at the Incarnation, Christ assumed a human body and a human soul, but that the human spirit was replaced by the divine Logos; thus while perfect in Godhead, Jesus lacked perfect manhood.

9.2.4   The argument that in order to 'do justice' to the full humanity of Christ the priesthood must be both male and female is sometimes stiffened by another: that because the priest represents the whole people of God there must be both male and female priests. This second argument is open to precisely the same objections as in the former. *Maleness* cannot damage, or limit, *humanness*. If that were so, the Incarnation would not be real. The whole of humanity can be equally represented by a male *or* a female. This report sets out the reasons why the Church teaches that bishops and priests are necessarily male. But *maleness* cannot make priests or bishops any less fully representative of the whole human race.[161]

9.2.5   Another argument for the ordination of women is based on the premise that the risen Christ has no gender, and therefore the need for symbolic or iconographic consonance between the priest/bishop and Christ does not apply. Here again there is a basic misunderstanding of the Incarnation, of the resurrection and of the ascension. It may be true, in the fullness of God's Kingdom, where they neither marry nor are given in marriage, that sexual relations between women and men will be no more. But Jesus Christ is raised from the dead in the fullness of his humanity (see Article IV). Were that not so, his resurrection would not be ours also. At his ascension, our human nature would not be raised to the Godhead. Christ's risen body, his glorious body, still bears the wounds of the Cross. There is continuity between the earthly body and the resurrection body.

---

[161] In his presidential sermon preached to the Affirming Catholicism group on General Synod at St Margaret's, Westminster, on 11 November 2002 (the 10th Anniversary of the vote in General Synod to permit the ordination of women to the priesthood), the Bishop of Salisbury said, 'A priesthood of only one sex [is] an inherently defective icon of the priesthood of Christ.' But this is again to undermine the universal salvific significance of the Incarnation, for it implies that a (male) Redeemer must in turn be a defective icon of the Father.

Christ does not leave behind his maleness at his resurrection or ascension.

9.3   'Justice'

9.3.1   It is evident to any observer of the present debate that
the advocates of innovation derive at least part of their
argument from issues of *justice*. This is the most compelling argument for some. It is contrary to Gospel
principles of fairness, it is said, that women should be
excluded, on the grounds of their sex alone, from any
order of Christian ministry; any more than they can be
excluded from any position of employment, or office,
in the secular world.

9.3.2   We do not accept that the question of the ordination
of women is a 'justice' issue. The Church, the Body of
Christ, is called to reflect the diversity of gifts, graces
and ministries which God gives to his people. It is patterned not on sameness and the erosion of difference,
but on the celebration of God's providence in creating
humanity male and female, honouring the mutuality
and complementarity of the created order. We believe
that the Church has a particular calling to embody a
different model from that of secular society, where the
distinct gifts and callings of women and men, both in
domestic and civic life, struggle to find articulation in
the face of the dictates of the 'progressive', secularist
(and largely atheist) agenda by which, increasingly,
contemporary society is governed.

9.3.3   As long as ordination as a bishop or priest is seen as
a matter of rights and entitlements, the exclusion of
women from these ministries will seem, to the secular
mind, unfair and backward-looking. But when Holy
Order is properly understood as conferring no superiority, but rather as instituted to be at the service of
the whole body of the faithful, such anxieties ought

to evaporate. The God and Father of Our Lord Jesus Christ is indeed a God of justice; but nowhere in Scripture or in the tradition can we understand that justice to be equivalent with 'equal rights' in the sense in which that phrase has been understood for the last 175 years or so. Whatever the issues raised by the question of the possible admission of women to the presbyterate and episcopate, we would go so far as to say that, theologically, the matter cannot be one of *justice* as the world understands it.

10

Conclusion

10.1   It has been our intention, in this report, to seek to elu-
cidate why the mind of the Church has consistently
favoured the ordination only of males as bishops and
priests. We believe that the question of the gender of
the ordained ministry touches upon profound theological questions: the doctrines of God, of the creation and
of the nature of humankind, of the Incarnation and of
the person of Jesus Christ. It has serious implications
for our understanding of the Church; of communion,
authority, reception, and of the place of the Church of
England within the one, holy, catholic and apostolic
Church of Christ.

10.2   In considering, specifically, the question of the ordination of women to the *episcopate,* we have seen how the
classical understanding of the office and work of the
bishop as focus of unity, high priest, fount of Order and
of the other sacraments of the Church, chief celebrant
at the Eucharist, and chief pastor in his diocese ensures
that the various considerations which come into play
in the matter of the ordination of women as presbyters
are sharpened, and even more clearly defined, when it
comes to a consideration of the possibility of women
bishops.

10.3   We have recalled the unvarying practice of by far the
greater part of the Church Catholic down the ages,
founded on the example of Our Lord himself, that only

males are admitted as priests and bishops, and we have considered what it might mean for the Church of England further to depart from that consistent practice. That the Church of England has always understood the episcopate to be a foundational sign of its unity with the whole Church past and present, there can be no doubt. As the House of Bishops' report *Eucharistic Presidency* makes clear:

> The historical succession of ordained ministry serves this continuity [the continuity of Christ's own teaching and mission], and in the Anglican Communion, as in many others, this continuity finds particular expression in Episcopal succession. In line with much contemporary ecumenical understanding we believe that the historic episcopate is a sign of, and serves, the apostolicity of the whole Church, continuing a call to fidelity and unity, a summons to witness to, and a commission to realise more fully, 'the permanent characteristics of the Church of the apostles'.[162]

We recall the point made in paragraph 1.8 above. To alter one of the foundational 'signs . . . of the apostolicity of the whole Church' without the consent of the whole Church is to do grave damage to the ecclesial identity and self-understanding of the Church of England.

10.4 Can an episcopate which no longer conforms to one of the identifying marks of the historic order of bishops – its maleness – continue to be a sign of continuity, of apostolicity, of fidelity and unity? That, we believe, is the crucial question which now confronts the Church of England.

10.5 We offer two final reflections. The first concerns the particular circumstances in which the Church of England finds itself. Memories are short. In 1992/4, the

---

[162] *Eucharistic Presidency*, Church House Publishing, 1997, p. 33.

Church of England proceeded with the ordination of women to the priesthood. It went ahead in a context of open reception, and with assurances made in good faith to those who were not persuaded that the innovation was faithful to the will of God. Those promises were made within the family of the Christian community, made within the Body of Christ. They are not trivial things. They cannot easily be dispensed with when political expediency or opportunity allow. It would be a grave scandal were those promises to be abandoned, diminished or distorted only a decade after they were made. By no criteria hitherto articulated within the Anglican Communion, still less according to the tenets of the universal Church, can the period of reception as to the rightness of the ordination of women be held to be complete. How can the Church proceed to ordain women as bishops, and still hold true to the assurances of 1992–4, and honour the process of reception?

10.6 Second: we must all – proponents of innovation and adherents to the tradition alike – grapple with the question: can the Church change? How do we discern what is true and what is false development within the Body of Christ? For the Church of England, change – departure from the tradition – can only be entertained after serious thought and with maximum consensus, as the report *Eucharistic Presidency* makes clear:

> [We recognize that] the faith of the Church is received and drawn out for each age through traditions which have been tested, cherished, handed on and inhabited through the centuries. It would be foolish to set aside lightly the long, sustained, and many-sided tradition which has resisted lay presidency. Careful and generous attention must be paid to the reasons why the restriction of Eucharistic presidency to priests/presbyters emerged so quickly and became the unbroken practice of the Church for centuries.[163]

---

[163] *Eucharistic Presidency*, p. 5.

Could we not rewrite this paragraph, substituting 'women in the episcopate' for 'lay presidency', and altering the last sentence to describe the restriction of the priesthood and episcopate to males?

10.7   That doyen of the doctrine of development, John Henry Newman, numbered among his hallmarks of authentic development in the doctrine or practice of the Church the following:

- it would have its roots clearly in primitive belief and practice, and be suggested in ecclesial life before it actually comes to pass;
- it would build upon, and not contradict, what had gone before;
- it would be conducive to the promotion of unity within the life of the Church.

10.8   Anglican polity is not to be judged or measured by the words of one man alone – even the words one of the Anglican Church's most brilliant sons. But Newman's methodology does bring the question into the sharpest possible focus. Against the background of the settled mind of the great Latin Church of the West, of the unvarying practice of the Christian East, of division between provinces and within provinces in the Anglican Communion, and of a far from settled outcome in the Provinces of Canterbury and York themselves, whence would the Church of England derive her authority for entering upon further change? With what possible confidence could she identify it as an authentic development? How could the Church of England genuinely make room for those who dissent from the ministry of women bishops? The legislation allowing women to be ordained as priests was complex and controversial. For the reasons we have set out, it will be even more challenging to legislate sensibly and coherently for dissent from the ministry of women in the episcopate.

Part Two

Women Bishops:
The Way Forward for the Church

Women Bishops:
The Way Forward for
the Church

1   **Introduction**

1.1   In March 2002 the Council of Forward in Faith asked Canon Beaumont Brandie, one of its members, to convene a group of lawyers to consider what legal provision might be possible for those members of the Church of England unable to accept the ordination of women to the priesthood and episcopate in the event that the Church of England should decide to ordain women bishops.

1.2   Accordingly a group of lawyers, both ordained and lay, who practise in or have knowledge and experience of ecclesiastical law, was convened to form a working party to discuss these matters. The membership of the Legal Working Party is given at Appendix 1 to this report. This Working Party has met on eleven occasions and its members have communicated between meetings by email.

1.3   This report has the unanimous support of the members of the Legal Working Party.

2   **Background**

2.1   In October 1999 the National Assembly of Forward in Faith approved the document entitled 'The Case for a

Free Province of the Church of England'.[164] This document argued the case for establishing a new province of
the Church of England for those who are in conscience
unable to accept the ordination of women to the priesthood and the episcopate.

2.2   In an interview for the *Church Times*[165] before his confirmation of election as Archbishop of Canterbury, Dr
Rowan Williams made it clear that he believed that the
time was right to give serious consideration to the consequences of the consecration of women bishops. He is
quoted as saying:

> I would find no personal difficulty in consecrating
> a woman as a bishop, but if we go down this road
> there are large questions about what happens to the
> substantial minority for whom this would be the last
> straw – people for whom the Act of Synod would no
> longer be an adequate resort.
>
> And maybe we ought to be thinking well in
> advance about what the possibilities are. Do we
> need a Third Province solution? That has got to be
> thought through from early on in the discussion, and
> not just in haste afterwards.
>
> We have to face the reality that a lot of people
> who still identify themselves as Anglicans will not
> want to be in the kind of structural relationship they
> are now in with the rest of the Communion.

2.3   Almost a year later in an article in *New Directions*,[166]
the Archbishop reaffirmed this commitment to a structural solution:

> It is because of all this that I think it worth work-
> ing at structures in Anglicanism that don't either

---

[164] See http://www.forwardinfaith.com/about/uk_free_province.html.
[165] *Church Times*, 29 November 2002.
[166] 'The Structures of Unity', *New Directions*, September 2003.

commit us to a meaningless structural uniformity or leave us in mutual isolation. If you're not going to be a Roman Catholic, with clear universal visible tests for unity, you're going to be involved in some degree of structural complexity – and I'm assuming that as Anglicans we have enough theological reservations about the RC model of visible unity to make it worth our while exploring how 'structural complexity' can witness to the supernatural character of the Church.

2.4   In its deliberations the Working Party has not limited itself to consideration of the possibility of the formation of a new province. It has also considered whether there are other possibilities which could provide an ecclesial and structured solution for both those in favour of women bishops and priests and those who cannot accept them.

3   The present situation

3.1   The Priests (Ordination of Women) Measure 1993 allows parishes to pass certain resolutions which prevent a woman from presiding at Holy Communion or pronouncing the Absolution in the parish (Resolution A), or from becoming incumbent, priest in charge or team vicar for the benefice (Resolution B).[167] When the Ecclesiastical Committee of Parliament considered whether the Measure was expedient, especially in relation to the constitutional rights of all Her Majesty's subjects,[168] it became apparent that this provision for those who could not accept women priests was not sufficient. It was out of this difficulty that the Episcopal Ministry Act of Synod 1993 was born.

---

[167] S 3 and Sch. 1.
[168] As it was required to do under the Church of England Assembly (Powers) Act 1919, s 3(3).

3.2 Members of the Ecclesiastical Committee expressed the view that any further provision should also be by Measure. However, assurances were given to Parliament that an Act of Synod would suffice. In the light of the present calls for the Act of Synod to be rescinded, the concerns of the Ecclesiastical Committee seem justified.

3.3 The Act of Synod provides:

Whereas :

(1) The Church of England through its synodical processes has given final approval to a Measure to make provision by Canon for enabling women to be ordained to the priesthood.

(2) The bishop of each diocese continues as the ordinary of his diocese;

(3) The General Synod regards it as desirable that

(a) all concerned should endeavour to ensure that

(i) discernment in the wider Church of the rightness or otherwise of the Church of England's decision to ordain women to the priesthood should be as open a process as possible;

(ii) the highest possible degree of communion should be maintained within each diocese; and

(iii) the integrity of differing beliefs and positions concerning the ordination of women to the priesthood should be mutually recognised and respected;

(b) the practical pastoral arrangements contained in this Act of Synod should have effect in each diocese.

3.4 The Act of Synod makes it clear that the Church of England is in a period of reception with regard to the decision to admit women to the priesthood. The period of reception will only be concluded when the wider Church has reached a common mind on the matter.

Even within the Church of England, the introduction of the priestly ordination of women is subject to the Gamaliel principle,[169] whereby in due course it will become clear whether women priests are an innovation of man or God. Until such time the discernment must be as open as possible.

3.5   The practical arrangements contained in the Act are the provision of extended episcopal care by means of diocesan arrangements,[170] regional arrangements[171] or provincial arrangements.[172] It is the latter which involved the creation of the provincial episcopal visitors (often known as 'flying bishops'). Because the diocesan bishop remains the ordinary of his diocese, bishops operating under the Act can only do so at the request of the diocesan bishop.[173] Thus, it is argued, the territorial integrity of each diocese is maintained.[174]

3.6   However, the Church of England is not as territorial as is often supposed. Although most of England is part of a diocese which is subject to the ordinary jurisdiction of the diocesan bishop, this is far from universal.

3.7   Even within his diocese, the bishop, though the ordinary, cannot direct his chancellor. Though appointed by the bishop and adjudicating matters in the bishop's court, the chancellor of the diocese is independent of the bishop.[175]

---

[169] See Acts 5.38–9.   [170] Episcopal Ministry Act of Synod 1993, s 3.
[171] Ibid., s 4.   [172] Ibid., s 5.
[173] Ibid., s 4(2) (regional arrangements), s 5(3) (provincial arrangements).
[174] It has been argued that this territorial model of episcopacy that we have inherited from the Middle Ages is being challenged by modern developments. These include the desire to provide indigenous bishops in Australia, New Zealand and elsewhere, the desire of non-episcopal churches to receive episcopacy into their systems and the demand for 'enculturalization' being felt in the Roman Catholic communion. See Allen Brent, *Cultural Episcopacy and Ecumenism*, Brill, 1992.
[175] See *Tyler v United Kingdom* (Application 21283/93), 5 April 1994 E Com HR (unreported).

3.8   A diocese does not have to be a geographically contiguous area. For example, until 1985 the Diocese of Canterbury included the Archdeaconry of Croydon. This detached 'enclave' in the Diocese of Southwark was transferred to Southwark by a scheme made under the Dioceses Measure 1978 and confirmed by Order in Council.

3.9   Chaplains in the armed forces receive their licences to officiate from the Archbishop of Canterbury. Although often working at establishments situated within a diocese, chaplains are not subject to the jurisdiction of their local bishop. They have their own separate hierarchy which includes an archdeacon for each of three services and the Archbishop of Canterbury's Episcopal Representative to Her Majesty's Forces. Each of the forces has an elected Archdeaconry Synod and the Forces Synodical Council carries out many of the functions of a diocesan synod. Under present regulations the three service archdeacons represent the forces as *ex officio* members of General Synod.

3.10   There are peculiar jurisdictions where the ordinary jurisdiction of the diocesan bishop does not apply.[176] Among some of the better known are the royal peculiars of Westminster Abbey[177] and St George's Chapel, Windsor,[178] which are subject only to the visitorial jurisdiction of the Crown. Many ancient universities and colleges claim to be peculiars in that the governing body is the ordinary rather than the diocesan bishop. In some cases the bishop of another diocese is the visitor of the college.[179]

---

[176] See the article 'What is a Peculiar?' by Paul Barber, 3 *Ecc LJ* 299.
[177] The Collegiate Church of St Peter in Westminster.
[178] The Queen's Free Chapel of St George Within Her Castle of Windsor.
[179] E.g. the Bishop of Winchester is visitor to New College, Oxford.

3.11   Cathedrals are not subject to the ordinary jurisdiction of the diocesan bishop, but the dean and chapter is usually the ordinary. The bishop's consistory court has no jurisdiction over the cathedral. It is only in his visitorial capacity that the diocesan bishop has any jurisdiction over the cathedral.[180]

3.12   The Church of England extends beyond the boundaries of England. The Diocese in Europe covers Europe (except Great Britain and Ireland) and small parts of Asia and Africa. The Bishop of Gibraltar in Europe does not have the same territorial jurisdiction as his brother English diocesan bishops. There is in Europe a parallel Anglican structure of the Convocation of American Churches in Europe (part of the Protestant Episcopal Church in the United States of America). In addition the Lusitanian Church and the Spanish Reformed Episcopal Church are extra provincial dioceses under the metropolitical jurisdiction of the Archbishop of Canterbury. In parts of Europe there are, therefore, three Anglican jurisdictions operating in the same place, two of those jurisdictions being subject to the Archbishop of Canterbury.[181]

3.13   Examples of parallel jurisdictions elsewhere within the Anglican Communion can be found in New Zealand,[182] Australia[183] and South Africa.[184]

---

[180] Cathedrals Measure 1999, s 6(3); also s 3(2) and s 4.

[181] For details of how they cooperate see the *Church of England Year Book 2004*, p. 386.

[182] The Bishopric of Aotearoa, serving the Maoris, covers the same geographical area as the eight English-speaking dioceses on the two islands of New Zealand: ibid., p. 401.

[183] The Diocese of North Queensland has two assistant bishops. One is the Torres Strait Islander Bishop and the other the National Aboriginal Bishop. Both serve their cultural communities beyond the diocesan boundary.

[184] The Ethiopian Episcopal Church, formerly the Order of Ethiopia, is an autonomous church in full communion with the Church of the Province of South Africa: ibid., p. 385.

3.14   It would seem that geographical territorial jurisdiction is not, therefore, an essential element of Anglicanism or of the Church of England. Thus the view expressed by John Habgood, former Archbishop of York and one of those who devised the Act of Synod, that 'The creation of a separate province would destroy the territorial basis of the Church of England'[185] would seem to be based on a false premise.

3.15   The Act of Synod is applied differently from diocese to diocese. In some dioceses[186] a diocesan arrangement operates whereby a suffragan or assistant bishop of the diocese looks after those who are opposed.[187] In others[188] a regional arrangement exists where a bishop from a neighbouring diocese looks after those who are opposed. However, for the majority of parishes which have petitioned under the Act of Synod provincial arrangements operate so that it is a provincial episcopal visitor who provides episcopal care. This has led to the perception that these parishes are already in a *de facto* diocese or province.

3.16   Whatever the public perceptions may be, no parish receiving extended episcopal care is outside the jurisdiction of the diocesan bishop. After he has received a petition from the parish, it is the diocesan bishop who requests an appropriate bishop to provide extended episcopal care.[189] Similarly, the provincial episcopal visitors are suffragan bishops of the archbishop's diocese and subject to his jurisdiction.[190]

---

[185] John Habgood 'Thoughts on GRAS', *New Directions*, March 2004, p. 5.
[186] E.g. Blackburn, London.
[187] 'Those who are opposed' is the terminology used in the Episcopal Ministry Act of Synod, 1993, ss 2, 12(1).
[188] E.g. Carlisle, Rochester, Southwark.
[189] Episcopal Ministry Act of Synod 1993, ss 4(2), 5(3).
[190] Ibid., s 5(1), (2).

3.17   The arrangements under the Act of Synod work because those who have jurisdiction (the diocesan bishops and the archbishops) are always male bishops. They can be accepted as bishops by those who come under their jurisdiction, whatever disagreements or differences of opinion they may have with them.

3.18   Nevertheless, the attempt to separate the juridical from the pastoral and sacramental functions of the bishop has led to difficulties and anomalies even where all concerned are trying to make the arrangements work. For example, the authorizing of persons to distribute the holy sacrament of the Lord's Supper in a parish is, in law, a matter for the diocesan bishop[191] although it might seem to be a more appropriate matter for the bishop who is exercising extended (sacramental) care for the parish under the Act of Synod. Similarly, questions of selection for training for ordination and the decision whether or not to ordain are matters for the diocesan bishop, even though some other bishop may be exercising extended care for the relevant parish. The latter bishop may ultimately ordain a candidate, but he can only do so under the authority of the diocesan bishop.

3.19   Once there is the possibility of a woman bishop being a diocesan bishop or archbishop then the current provisions under the Act of Synod would not suffice. Those who could not accept women bishops would have to submit to the jurisdiction of a woman bishop, the validity of whose orders as a bishop of the One Holy Catholic and Apostolic Church they doubted. It would follow that all her episcopal actions would be doubted. Such a situation would be unacceptable.

3.20   There would be a further difficulty as soon as a woman was consecrated bishop, whether diocesan or suffragan. Any priest (male or female) ordained

---

[191] Canon B12 para. 3.

by her would not be accepted as such by those who doubted the woman bishop's orders. It would follow that as soon as she ordained a male priest uncertainty would be introduced into the whole priesthood of the Church of England. When attending a church with a male priest presiding, worshippers who doubted the orders of women bishops would need to enquire who ordained the priest. This would also be unacceptable.

3.21   The period of discernment over the rightness or otherwise of the decision by the Church of England to ordain women to the priesthood will not come to a close if the Church of England decides to ordain women bishops. The Church of England will still await the decision of the wider Church and within the Church of England itself there will still be a substantial minority who cannot and will not accept women priests or bishops. This minority would require some form of provision.

4   Incorporating women into the episcopate of the Church of England

4.1   We have considered various ways in which the Church of England might seek to incorporate women into the episcopate. For each way we have considered what practical and legal difficulties might arise for those opposed to the introduction of women bishops and what form of provision would be necessary for them.

A one-clause measure

4.2   The simplest method by which women could become bishops in the Church of England would be by means of a one-clause Measure amending section 1 of the Priests (Ordination of Women) Measure 1993 so as to remove the prohibition on women being ordained as bishops. It should be noted that this would require a two-thirds majority in each of the three Houses of the General Synod.[192]

---

[192] Priests (Ordination of Women) Measure 1993, s 11.

4.3   If this were the method adopted those opposed might, at first sight, seem to have a degree of protection since the provisions preventing a woman from presiding at Holy Communion or pronouncing the Absolution in a parish which had passed Resolution A would remain.[193] It is arguable that it would be possible to prevent (by injunction or otherwise) a woman bishop from performing these priestly acts, by relying on those provisions.

4.4   However, under the Canons of the Church of England a diocesan bishop is the principal minister within his diocese and has the right to celebrate the rites of ordination and confirmation and of conducting, ordering, controlling and authorizing all services in churches.[194] This conflict between statute law and the canons would be a highly unsatisfactory situation and would make it impossible for a woman diocesan bishop properly to fulfil all her functions. Statute law (the 1993 Measure) must prevail over the Canons.[195]

4.5   Those priests, deacons and lay workers who could not accept a woman bishop would be unable to take the oath of canonical obedience to her as required at each ordination, licensing and institution[196] or accept her authority as ordinary.[197] Similarly, churchwardens who could not accept a woman bishop would be unable to make the declaration on admission to office.[198]

4.6   Given that the Ecclesiastical Committee of Parliament is under a duty to consider the rights of all Her

---

[193] Ibid., s 3 and Sch. 1.
[194] Canon C18, para. 4.
[195] Submission of the Clergy Act 1533, s 3. Synodical Government Measure 1969, s 1(3).
[196] Canon C14.
[197] Canon C18, para. 2.
[198] Canon E1, para. 2.

Majesty's subjects[199] and the fact that financial provisions accompanied the legislation to allow women
priests,[200] we think it unlikely that Parliament would
agree to such a one-clause Measure without accompanying financial provisions for those clergy and lay
workers forced to resign.

Women suffragan bishops, but not diocesan bishops

4.7 It has been suggested that the difficulties outlined
above[201] concerning the functions and jurisdiction
of diocesan bishops throughout the diocese could
be avoided if women were permitted to be suffragan
bishops, but not diocesans. Since there would be no
ecclesiological basis for such a 'glass ceiling' beyond
which women could not rise, such a restriction would
be sexist and thus, we believe, offensive both to those
who could not accept women bishops as well as to
those who could. In any event, such a provision would
still create problems. No deacons or priests (male or
female) ordained by a woman suffragan would be
accepted as such by those who could not accept the
woman bishop. We do not, therefore, think that such
a solution would be adequate provision for those who
could not accept women bishops.

Women diocesan bishops, but not archbishops

4.8 The suggestion that women could be bishops at all
levels except archbishop is also unsatisfactory since it
does not remove the difficulties outlined above concerning women diocesans[202] (except for those in the
Dioceses of Canterbury and York).

Episcopal teams

4.9 An alternative suggestion is that there could be some
sort of team episcopate in each diocese in which there

---

[199] Church of England Assembly (Powers) Act 1919, s 3(3).
[200] See Ordination of Women (Financial Provisions) Measure 1993.
[201] See paras 4.4 and 4.5 above.
[202] Ibid.

would always be a male member of the episcopal team. This would be a departure from traditional Anglican ecclesiology where the diocesan bishop has always been seen as the chief pastor and the focus of unity for the whole diocese.[203] Thus a suffragan bishop only has such episcopal power or authority as is given him by the bishop of the diocese.[204] Were the diocesan bishop to be a woman then the problems outlined above would arise.[205]

4.10 The fact that a priest or parish may be able to relate to a male member of the episcopal team in some way would not remove the problem that it is the diocesan bishop who is principal minister and ordinary within the diocese.[206]

Extended episcopal care

4.11 Another suggestion is that those who cannot accept women bishops should be protected by some form of extended episcopal care. The basis for such provision would, presumably, be the reasoning which led to the passing of the Episcopal Ministry Act of Synod 1993. The Act of Synod operates from the starting point that the bishop of each diocese continues as the ordinary of the diocese.[207] It is thus the diocesan bishop who makes appropriate arrangements for episcopal duties to be carried in accordance with the Act of Synod.[208]

4.12 This can work at the present time, albeit with some difficulties, when the diocesan bishop must be male. But once there is the possibility of a woman diocesan further difficulties arise. The woman diocesan would have jurisdiction as the ordinary of the diocese. It would be impossible for those opposed to take the oath

---

[203] See Canon C18.
[204] Canon C20, para. 2.
[205] See paras 4.4 and 4.5 above.
[206] Canon C18, especially para. 4.
[207] Episcopal Ministry Act of Synod 1993, preamble para (2).
[208] Ibid., s 8 (1).

of canonical obedience to her or to accept her authority, jurisdiction or action in the many matters which
the canons specifically state are to be decided by the
diocesan bishop.[209]

4.13   It would thus not seem possible for any form of
extended episcopal care, where the jurisdiction of the
diocesan remains, to be sufficient provision for those
opposed to women bishops.

4.14   This is the view expressed by the Archbishop of York,
Dr David Hope, in a sermon preached to mark the
tenth anniversary of the Act of Synod. He said:

> But then given the fact that the ordination of women
> to the Episcopate is now on the agenda – *the* ques-
> tion which ought in any case to have been addressed
> in the very first instance – the question needs to be
> asked whether that Act [of Synod] can continue to
> bear the weight of this further development having
> in mind its main premise of 'extended' Episcopal
> care. Plainly it could not. Any such arrangements in

---

[209] See Canon C18, para. 4. Other matters include approval of forms
of worship (Canon B2, paras 2A and 3), form of service where alternative
forms are authorized (Canon B3, para. 4), approval of local Holy Days
(Canon B6, para. 5), dispensation from requirement to read Morning and
Evening Prayer or celebrate Holy Communion in parish churches (Canon
B14A; Canon C24, para. 2), guidance on admission to Holy Communion
(Canon B15A, para. 3), notorious offenders not to be admitted to Holy
Communion (Canon B16), preaching in parish churches (Canon B18),
baptism of such as are of riper years (Canon B24, para. 2), confirmation
(Canon B27, para. 1), granting of common licences for Holy Matrimony
(Canon B34, para. 3), of the burial of the dead (Canon B38, para. 6), of
Holy Communion elsewhere than in consecrated buildings (Canon B40),
of divine service in private chapels (Canon B41, para. 2), of relations with
other churches (Canons B43, B44), ordination (Canons C3, C4A, C5, C6),
ministers exercising their ministry (Canon C8), collation and presentation
(Canon C9), churchwardens (Canon E1), readers (Canon E6), lay workers
(Canons E7, E8), alms (Canon F10), plays, concerts, etc. in churches
(Canon F16), appointment of judge of the consistory court (Canon G2),
appointment of registrar (Canon G4).

respect of ordination of women to the Episcopate must surely be at least 'alternative' rather than merely 'extended', and that these same arrangements be in respect of 'oversight' rather than 'care' – arrangements ranging from a further development along the broad lines of the Act of Synod to an altogether more distanced third Province.[210]

4.15 An alternative oversight, where those opposed would be under another jurisdiction, entirely separate from that of the diocesan bishop, would seem to be the only satisfactory way of providing for those opposed.

Peculiar jurisdictions

4.16 There are existing peculiar jurisdictions which are not subject to the jurisdictions of the diocesan bishop[211] and we have considered whether the creation of a new peculiar jurisdiction would provide a way forward for those who could not accept women priests or bishops.

4.17 It has to be noted at the outset that the creation of a new peculiar jurisdiction would be against the trend of the last 175 years of abolishing such jurisdictions.[212]

4.18 It would, however, be possible to create a peculiar jurisdiction by Measure. The existing provincial episcopal visitors could, for example, be given a peculiar jurisdiction in respect of all parishes under their care so that those parishes would come under their oversight and jurisdiction rather than under the oversight and jurisdiction of the diocesan bishop. The provincial episcopal visitors would, in effect, have the powers of diocesan bishops. As such they would need powers to do everything which a diocesan bishop could do, so that nothing in the parishes for which they had over-

---

[210] Sermon preached at St Bartholomew's Armley, Leeds on 3 March 2004. See *New Directions*, April 2004, p. 5.

[211] See above, para. 3.10.

[212] Most peculiar jurisdictions were abolished by Orders in Council made between 1836 and 1852 under the Ecclesiastical Commissioners Acts 1836 and 1850.

sight was subject to the jurisdiction of the diocesan bishop. Faculties, for example, could not be issued by the diocesan consistory court since that is the bishop's court.

4.19   To proceed along such a route would be to create a peculiar jurisdiction which was, in effect, one or more dioceses. The difficulty with such a proposal comes when we consider the metropolitical jurisdiction of the archbishop. There are many matters which by statute law or the canons are to be referred to the archbishop.[213] If the archbishop were a woman then those within the peculiar jurisdiction could not submit to her metropolitical jurisdiction. The provincial episcopal visitors could not take the oath of canonical obedience to her as required by the canons[214] or accept consecration at her hands.

4.20   Creating an extra-provincial (or 'royal') peculiar would be a way of solving this problem of metropolitical jurisdiction. The extra-provincial peculiar could only be visited by the Crown, to the exclusion of any diocesan bishop or metropolitan.[215]

4.21   Paul Barber argues in an article in the *Ecclesiastical Law Journal*,[216] that extra-provincial peculiars are 'like

---

[213] See Canon C17 as to archbishops generally. Other matters include: presentation to benefices remaining vacant for nine months (Patronage (Benefices) Measure 1986 s 16); admission of offenders to Holy Communion (Canon B16, para. 2); appeal against revocation of minister's licence (Canon C12, para. 5), reader's licence (Canon E6, para. 3), lay worker's licence (Canon E8, para. 5); approval of forms of service (Canon B4, para. 2; Canon B5A); summoning convocations (Canon H2); permission to those ordained abroad to minister (Canon C8, para. 5); residence of priests in their benefices (Canon C25 para. 3); occupation of ministers (Canon C28, para. 3).

[214] Canon C14, para. 1.

[215] Other than the Archbishop of Canterbury's *Legatine* powers which are exercisable over extra-provincial peculiars in the same way as they are exercisable over the Province of York (see below, para. 5.25).

[216] Paul Barber, 'What is a Peculiar?' 3 *Ecc LJ* 299, at p. 302.

mini-provinces in their own right with the ordinary being in an equivalent position to the archbishop in his province'.

4.22   If the ordinary of the peculiar were also to have the jurisdiction of the metropolitan then important rights of appeal would be lost. For example, there could be no effective appeal against the revocation of a minister's licence,[217] since the person who revoked the licence, the provincial episcopal visitor, would also hold the metropolitical jurisdiction of appeal. In such a situation the aggrieved minister could only petition the Crown for redress.

4.23   We do not think that priests and people would happily submit to the ultimate jurisdiction of the Crown, rather than an ecclesiological person or body. To do so would seem to be a return to something similar to the nineteenth-century regime of Her Majesty's Privy Council being the final arbiter over church matters.

4.24   We doubt whether the Crown would agree to the creation of such a royal peculiar bearing in mind all the matters which might fall to the Crown's visitorial jurisdiction in the absence of anyone else with jurisdiction. Would the Crown, for example, wish to become involved in appeals against the revocation of licences of ministers, readers and lay workers?

4.25   It would be possible to give to some archbishop or presiding bishop outside England the metropolitical jurisdiction for the peculiar. This would be similar to the way in which the Archbishop of Canterbury exercises metropolitical jurisdiction over the extra provincial diocese of Bermuda. However, it is difficult to see who outside England would be an acceptable metropolitan to those in England. Furthermore, since

---

[217] Under Canon C12, para. 5.

he would be a bishop of an autonomous church there would be nothing to prevent that church accepting women bishops in the future, which could mean the metropolitical jurisdiction being exercised by a woman bishop. This would be unacceptable.

4.26   There is precedent in the Anglican Communion for metropolitical jurisdiction to be exercised by a body, rather than one archbishop. The Episcopal Church of Cuba is under a Metropolitan Council in matters of faith and order. The Council's members include the Primate of Canada, the Archbishop of the West Indies and the Presiding Bishop of the Episcopal Church of the United States of America or a bishop appointed by him.[218] We do not consider that such a Metropolitan Council would be acceptable in the Church of England.

4.27   For the above reasons we consider that the creation of a peculiar jurisdiction would not provide a satisfactory way of providing alternative episcopal oversight for those who cannot accept women priests and bishops.

5   **An additional province for the Church of England**

5.1   We have, therefore, concluded that the only way of achieving satisfactory alternative oversight is to create a new province (in addition to Canterbury and York) in which it would not be possible for women bishops and priests to officiate.

5.2   The creation of a new province to cater for differing views on women's ministry has precedent within the Anglican Communion. The Holy Catholic Church in Hong Kong was inaugurated as an autonomous province of the Anglican Communion in 1988 in order to

---

[218] See *Church of England Year Book 2004*, p. 386.

separate it from dioceses in South East Asia with which it had been associated under the custodianship of the Council of Churches of East Asia.[219]

5.3   We believe that it would be possible to create an additional province of the Church of England by Measure. The Church of England Assembly (Powers) Act 1919 provides that a measure may relate to any matter concerning the Church of England.[220] The additional province would, in legal terms, simply be the creation of new administrative arrangements for parts of the Church of England. Unlike the formation of the Church in Wales in 1920,[221] when a separate church was created out of parts of the Church of England, the new province would remain part of the Church of England.

5.4   Accordingly the working party has drafted a measure to create an additional province within the Church of England. This Draft Measure, together with an explanatory memorandum, follows paragraph 6.2 of this report.

5.5   The new province would not have women bishops, women priests or male priests ordained by a woman bishop officiating in it.[222] We believe that within the Provinces of Canterbury and York the suspension of Canon A4 brought about by the 1993 Measure ought to end so that all bishops, priests and deacons (male and female) should be accounted to be truly bishops, priests and deacons within those provinces and that they should be able to officiate throughout those provinces. In our view it would not be appropriate, therefore, to allow parishes or cathedrals in the provinces of Canterbury and York to pass Resolutions A or B and

---

[219] Ibid., p. 346.
[220] S 3(6).
[221] Under the Welsh Church Act 1914.
[222] Clause 9.

so the Draft Measure revokes those provisions of the 1993 Measure.[223]

5.6   Certain bishops would be within the new province by virtue of the sees they occupy (unless they choose to remain within the Province of Canterbury or the Province of York).[224] Any other bishop would be able to make a declaration that he wished to serve in the new province.[225]

5.7   We have considered whether bishops of the new province should be entitled to sit in the House of Lords. It seems likely that, even if the Lords Spiritual remain after the next stage of House of Lords reform, their number will be reduced, placing an even greater duty on those who remain. It could be that the rota for duty bishops would involve six weeks' service in a year. For those bishops in the new province this would probably be an impossible commitment. Furthermore, bishops of the new province would not be able to speak in the Lords on policy decided by the House of Bishops of Canterbury and York since they would not be members of that House of Bishops. If the bishops serving in the additional province were not to be eligible for membership of the House of Lords by virtue of their office then we would submit that the Prime Minister would not need to have a significant role in their appointment. For these reasons we propose that the bishops of the additional province should not be members of the House of Lords[226] (though there would presumably be no objection to a bishop of the new province being appointed to a life peerage).

---

[223] Clause 17.
[224] Clause 2(1), (2).
[225] Clause 2(3).
[226] Clause 1(8).

5.8   The Draft Measure provides that the canons of the new province would make provision for the appointment of future bishops. Discussions with the Prime Minister would be necessary to see how the Queen, as Supreme Governor, would retain a role in the appointment. Since we propose that bishops of the new province would not have seats in the House of Lords[227] it may be that the procedure now used for the appointment of suffragan bishops could be utilized. This involves the submission of two names by the Church to the Prime Minister, whose advice, invariably to select the first-named, the sovereign follows.[228]

5.9   Those parishes which were receiving extended epis-copal care under the Episcopal Ministry Act of Synod 1993 would be deemed to be parishes within the new province (unless they chose, by resolution of the paro-chial church council ('PCC'), to remain in the Province of Canterbury or the Province of York).[229] Other par-ishes could join the new province by resolution of the PCC at any time.[230]

5.10   We consider that the PCC is the only appropriate body to decide these matters since this is the central forum for decision-making and discussion in relation to parish affairs. It is thus the PCC which can pass Resolutions A and B under the 1993 Measure or petition the diocesan bishop under the 1993 Act of Synod. The suggestion that some other body (e.g. the annual parochial church meeting or those enrolled on the church electoral roll) should have the power to decide these matters would involve a constitutional change in the government of the Church of England. While an expression of opinion

---

[227] See above, para. 5.7.
[228] See *Senior Church Appointments: A Review of the Methods of Ap-pointment of Area and Suffragan Bishops, Deans, Provosts, Archdeacons and Residentiary Canons* (GS1019, 1992), App. II, paras 2–20.
[229] Clause 3(1).
[230] Clause 3(2).

by any parochial church meeting must be considered by the PCC,[231] the meeting cannot direct or bind the PCC. Similarly enrolment on the church electoral roll has, hitherto, not given any right to be consulted on or to decide anything, but simply to attend certain meetings and elect certain people.[232]

5.11 Parishes could move back from the new province to the Province of Canterbury or the Province of York, except that they could not do so within five years of joining the new province.[233] We believe that this five-year period will ensure a degree of stability, but without preventing a parish from participating in discernment as to the rightness or otherwise of the Church of England's decision to ordain women priests and bishops.

5.12 The possibility of moving from one diocese to another or from one province to another is not a new concept in the Church of England. Examples can be found at the level of parish,[234] deanery,[235] archdeaconry[236] and diocese.[237]

5.13 The present parochial structure of the Church of England would be maintained in the new province. Parishioners would continue to have the right to worship and to be baptized, married or buried in or from their parish church.[238] Where a parishioner did not wish to

---

[231] Parochial Church Councils (Powers) Measure 1956, s 2(3).

[232] See Church Representation Rules (Synodical Government Measure 1969, Sch 3, as amended).

[233] Clause 3(3).

[234] The parish of Edmundbyers with Muggleswick was transferred from the Diocese of Durham to the Diocese of Newcastle in 1990.

[235] The Rural Deanery of Himley was transferred from the Diocese of Lichfield to the Diocese of Worcester in 1994.

[236] The Archdeaconry of Croydon was transferred from the Diocese of Canterbury to the Diocese of Southwark in 1984.

[237] The Diocese of Southwell was transferred from the Province of Canterbury to the Province of York in 1935.

[238] Clause 7(1).

worship in his parish church then, as now, he could choose to worship elsewhere and be enrolled on the church electoral roll of that parish.[239]

5.14 This would be nothing more than an extension of the present situation where there is a juxtaposition of parishes with different theological traditions and worship styles, and people choose where to worship.

5.15 The forms of service contained in the Book of Common Prayer would continue to be available for use in the new province.[240]

5.16 Priests and deacons who were serving in parishes of the new province would be deemed to be priests of that province unless they declared in writing that they wished to stay in the Province of Canterbury or the Province of York, in which case they would have to resign their office.[241] Any other priest or deacon could make a declaration that he wished to serve in the new province, but he would have to resign from any office he held within the Province of Canterbury or York before being beneficed, licensed to serve or given permission to officiate in the new province.[242]

5.17 There would be difficulties in the new province being represented on General Synod. Measures and Canons which concern doctrinal formulae or the services or ceremonies of the Church of England or the administration of its sacraments or sacred rites must be referred to the House of Bishops and may only be presented for the approval of Synod in the form approved by the House.[243] This would no longer be a satisfactory guarantee of orthodoxy once the House of Bishops

---

[239] Church Representation Rules r 1(2).
[240] Clause 5(2).
[241] Clause 4(1).
[242] Clause 4(2).
[243] Synodical Government Measure 1969, s 2(1), Sch. 2, Art. 7(1).

included women bishops, the validity of whose orders were doubted by those in the new province.

5.18   Similarly, the Archbishops of Canterbury and York are joint presidents of the Synod and have important functions concerning the interpretation of the constitution of the Synod.[244] Those in the new province would be unable to submit to this jurisdiction if either of the archbishops were a woman.

5.19   There would be a difficulty in the Synod trying to legislate for the new province in matters where there were fundamental disagreements. There would be a danger that those representing the new province could become a minority in constant conflict with the majority.

5.20   It has been suggested that lack of representation on General Synod would mean that a new province would not be part of the Church of England. However, representation on the General Synod is not an essential test of membership of the Church of England. The Church of England existed for over three hundred years without a Church Assembly or General Synod.

5.21   We therefore conclude that the new province should not be part of the General Synod, but should have its own Provincial Synod.[245]

5.22   When the new province comes into being the existing ecclesiastical law of the Church of England would apply.[246] However, the Provincial Synod would have the power to alter and amend the existing law[247] and to pass Measures under the Church of England Assembly (Powers) Act 1919.[248]

---

[244] Ibid., Sch. 2, Art. 4(1), 12(2).
[245] Clause 6.
[246] Clause 5(1).
[247] Clause 6(3).
[248] Clause 6(3), (4).

5.23   We envisage that the Provincial Synod would often
        wish to adopt Measures passed by the General Synod,
        with any necessary modifications. This would be simi-
        lar to the way that existing measures of the General
        Synod can be adopted with modifications for the Dio-
        cese in Europe,[249] the Isle of Man[250] and the Channel
        Islands.[251]

5.24   The Draft Measure provides that the bishops of the
        new province should choose one of their number to be
        the presiding bishop.[252] He would have, within the new
        province, all the powers and jurisdiction which the law
        places on the archbishops within their respective prov-
        inces.[253]

5.25   The Archbishop of Canterbury's *legatine* powers to
        grant licences and dispensations for marriages would
        continue to be exercisable by him throughout all Eng-
        land (including the new province).[254]

5.26   The new province would be in communion with the See
        of Canterbury,[255] but neither the Archbishop of Canter-
        bury nor the Archbishop of York would have jurisdic-
        tion over the province (other than the *legatine* powers
        of the Archbishop of Canterbury).[256] This contrasts
        with current practice in the Provinces of Canterbury
        and York where, during a vacancy in an archiepiscopal
        see, the archbishop of the other province has jurisdic-
        tion in certain matters; also in appeal cases, where the

---

[249] Diocese in Europe Measure 1980.

[250] See K. F. W. Gumbley, 'Church Legislation in the Isle of Man', 3 *Ecc LJ* 240.

[251] Channel Islands (Church Legislation) Measure 1931, Synodical Government (Channel Islands) Order 1970, SI 1970/1117.

[252] Clause 2(5).

[253] Clause 18(1).

[254] Ecclesiastical Licences Act 1533, s 3; Canon C17, para. 7.

[255] Clause 1.

[256] See above, para. 5.25.

archbishop is acting as bishop of the diocese concerned, jurisdiction passes to the other archbishop.[257]

5.27 The new province would be in a similar position to the Church in Wales as regards its relationship with the See of Canterbury. This would mean that the presiding bishop of the new province should, like the Archbishop of Wales, attend meetings of Anglican primates (something which the Archbishop of York has never done).

5.28 Initially the presiding bishop would have all the functions and duties of a diocesan bishop throughout the whole province.[258] However, it would be possible for the Provincial Synod to make provision by Measure or Canon for these functions and duties to be delegated or divided among the bishops in whatever method seemed most convenient. We envisage that such provision would be necessary, but consider that decisions about such matters would best be left until it is known how many parishes and clergy are going to be part of the province.

5.29 One or more archdeacons would need to be appointed (for the purposes of faculty jurisdiction and other matters where they have a specific duty), but there is nothing to prevent them being in episcopal orders or being beneficed clergy. Again these matters would be best left until the number and geographical spread of parishes of the new province is known.

5.30 The new province would need its own financial structures and so the Measure provides for the creation of

---

[257] E.g. presentation to benefices remaining vacant for nine months (Patronage (Benefices) Measure 1986, ss 16, 39(1)); admission of offenders to Holy Communion (Canon B16, para. 2); appeal against revocation of minister's licence (Canon C12, para. 5), reader's licence (Canon E6, para. 3), lay worker's licence (Canon E8, para. 5).

[258] Clause 18(1). Examples of some of these are given at n. 209 above.

a board of finance for the province[259] and for the possibility of funds being transferred by the Church Commissioners.[260] Parish assets held by diocesan boards of finance would be transferred to the provincial board of finance.[261]

5.31 Pension arrangements for clergy and lay workers would continue to operate under the present legislation.[262]

5.32 The new province would have responsibilities for some Church of England schools and so provision is made for a Board of Education.[263] In the case of schools which serve parishes of both the new province and either Canterbury or York, then local arrangements would have to be made to ensure fair representation and proper governance of the schools. This would be similar to present arrangements in ecumenical schools. With care and sensitivity to the views of all concerned this should be possible.

5.33 Hospitals and other institutions seeking to appoint a Church of England chaplain would be free to employ clergy of the new province and those of Canterbury and York, since all would be clergy of the Church of England.

5.34 In the case of hospitals it is assumed that health trusts would continue to seek to respect the patients' religious and cultural beliefs at all times. As such, we assume that trusts would ensure that a priest of the new province was made available when requested. This would be an extension of the present practice whereby hospitals ensure that a male priest is available when requested.[264]

---

[259] Clause 12(1).   [260] Clause 11.   [261] Clause 12(2).
[262] Clause 10.   [263] Clause 14.
[264] As they are required to do under the document *Pastoral Implications*, issued as an annex to the House of Bishops Code of Practice on Women Priests issued in January 1994.

5.35   The Draft Measure provides the basic legal framework for the new province. Much preparatory work
would need to be done between the Measure receiving
the Royal Assent and the new province being established.[265] In particular preparations would be necessary for the first meeting of the Provincial Synod in
view of its duty to consider Canons relating to membership, elections and procedures of the Synod[266] and the
method of appointment of future bishops.[267]

6   Conclusion

6.1   An additional province in the Church of England
would allow the Provinces of Canterbury and York to
ordain women to the episcopate while providing adequate safeguards for those who in conscience cannot
accept women priests and bishops. Both those who
support women priests and bishops and those who
oppose them would be able to remain in the Church
of England. The creation of the province would enable
the period of discernment as to the rightness or otherwise of the decision to ordain women to continue for
as long as is necessary. We believe that the creation of
a new province provides the only acceptable way forward for the Church of England if it decides to ordain
women bishops.

6.2   In the event that the Church of England resolves to
ordain women to the episcopate, we offer the following Draft Measure (and the Explanatory Memorandum which follows it) to the Church as the means by
which it will be enabled to move forward in faith.

---

[265] Clause 1 provides that the Archbishops of Canterbury and York shall,
in consultation with the bishops of the new province, appoint the day on
which the new province shall be established.

[266] Clause 6(2).

[267] Clause 2(6).

Draft of a Measure to be Passed by the General Synod of the Church of England

To make provision for the establishment of an additional Province for bishops, clergy and laity who are unable to accept the ordination of women to the presbyterate and to the episcopate and for connected purposes

Establishment of the Province

1 On such day (hereinafter referred to as 'the appointed day') as the Archbishops of Canterbury and York shall jointly appoint and with the concurrence of the bishops referred to in section 2(1) hereof the Province of [such title as shall be decided] (hereinafter referred to as 'the Province') shall be established being a province in communion with the See of Canterbury.

Bishops of the Province

2(1) The Bishops of Beverley, Ebbsfleet and Richborough shall be the first bishops of the Province provided that any of the said bishops may declare in writing before the appointed day that he wishes to remain in the Province of Canterbury or the Province of York as the case may be.

2(2) The Bishop of Fulham and any other bishops who on the appointed day have care of parishes where arrangements for episcopal duties are in place in accordance with the Episcopal Ministry Act of Synod 1993 shall be bishops of the Province, provided that any such bishop may declare in writing before the appointed day that he wishes to remain in the Province of Canterbury or the Province of York as the case may be.

2(3) Any other bishop residing in the Province of Canterbury or the Province of York may declare in writing in the form set out in Part III of Schedule 1 to this Measure that he wishes to serve as a bishop in the Province and, on being accepted for service in the Province, any see held by him shall thereupon be vacated and, if he was in receipt of a Writ of Summons from the House of Lords, he shall cease to be a Lord of Parliament.

2(4) The Episcopal Endowments and Stipends Measure 1943 shall continue to apply to those bishops referred to in subsections (1) and (2) above who are serving in the Province.

2(5) The bishops referred to in subsections (1) and (2) above together with any other bishop who on the appointed day has made the declaration set out in Part III of Schedule 1 to this Measure shall choose one of their number to be the presiding bishop.

2(6) The Canons of the Province shall provide for the method of appointment of future bishops of the Province.

2(7) No bishop other than those referred to in subsections (1) and (2) above may officiate in the Province unless he holds a licence or permission to officiate issued by the presiding bishop. The presiding bishop shall be responsible for assigning the care of parishes to bishops serving in the Province. Bishops with responsibility for parishes are hereinafter referred to in this Measure as 'the relevant bishop of the Province'.

2(8) No bishop of the Province shall as such be summoned to or be qualified to sit and vote as a Lord of Parliament.

Parishes and institutions

3(1) All parishes where arrangements for episcopal duties are in place prior to the appointed day in accordance with the Episcopal Ministry Act of Synod 1993 shall be parishes in the Province provided that the parochial church council of the parish may before the appointed day resolve to rescind the resolutions under the Priests (Ordination of Women) Measure 1993 and the said Episcopal Ministry Act of Synod 1993 whereupon the parish will remain in the Province of Canterbury or the Province of York as the case may be on the appointed day.

3(2) Subject to the following provisions of this section, any parochial church council of a parish in the Province of Canterbury or the Province of York may on or after the appointed day pass the resolution set out in Part I of Schedule 1 to this Measure and such resolution shall continue in force until rescinded.

3(3) Subject to the following provisions of this section, a parochial church council of a parish which is a constituent part of the Province by virtue of subsection (1) above or which has passed the resolution under subsection (2) above may pass the resolution set out in Part II of the said Schedule and thereafter the parish shall (subject to subsection (10) hereof) revert to the relevant diocese in the Province of Canterbury or the Province of York as the case may be. Provided always that no motion in the form set out in Part II of the said Schedule may be considered by a parochial church council within five years of the appointed day or of the passing of the resolution set out in Part I of the said Schedule whichever is the later.

3(4) A motion for a resolution in the form set out in Part I of the said Schedule shall not be considered by a parochial church council if the incumbent or priest in charge of the benefice concerned, or any team vicar or assistant curate for that benefice, is a woman ordained to the office of priest.

3(5) A resolution shall not be passed by a parochial church council under subsection (2) or (3) above unless –
(a) the secretary of the council has given to the members of the council at least four weeks' notice of the time and place of the meeting at which the motion proposing the resolution is to be considered; and

(b) the meeting is attended by at least one half of the members of the council entitled to attend.

3(6) Where a resolution under subsection (2) above is in force, the parish shall (together with the parishes referred to in subsection (1) above) be deemed to be a constituent part of the Province and not a parish in the Province of Canterbury or the Province of York as the case may be.

3(7) Subsections (1) to (6) above and Schedule 1 to this Measure shall apply in relation to a guild church designated and established under section 4 of the City of London (Guild Churches) Act 1952 as they apply in relation to a parish, but as if the references to a parochial church council of the parish were references to the guild church council of the guild church.

3(8) Subsections (1) to (6) above and Schedule 1 to this Measure shall apply in relation to a parish or place of worship in a team ministry established by virtue of a pastoral scheme pursuant to the Pastoral Measure 1986 or a church or place of worship established by virtue of a scheme made pursuant to the Church Representation Rules as they apply in relation to a parish but as if the reference to a parochial church council were references to the district church council of the church or place of worship. Where the district church council passes the resolution set out in Part I of Schedule 1, the bishop of the diocese shall make an amending scheme removing the district from the team ministry or parish as the case may be and assigning it to the Province.

3(9) The competent body of a religious community, school or other institution may consider and pass the resolutions set out in Parts I and II of Schedule 1 to this Measure with the necessary modifications.

3(10) Where a parochial church council or the appropriate body referred to in subsections (7) to (9) above has passed a resolution as set out in Parts I or II of Schedule 1 to this Measure and proceedings are pending or in progress in relation to a faculty application or under the Incumbents (Vacation of Benefices) Measure

1977, the resolution shall not come into force until the diocesan bishop or the relevant bishop of the Province as the case may be has signified in writing that the proceedings have been disposed of.

Priests and deacons of the Province

4(1) Where a parish is a constituent part of the Province by virtue of section 3(1) above, any priest who has been instituted to the benefice of which the parish forms part and any priest or deacon licensed in such a benefice shall be deemed to be a priest or deacon of the Province provided that any such priest or deacon may declare in writing before the appointed day that he wishes to remain in the Province of Canterbury or the Province of York as the case may be whereupon he shall execute a deed of resignation from any office in relation to the benefice held by him which deed shall become operative from such date as the diocesan bishop shall decide not being later than [nine] months after the appointed day.

4(2) Any priest or deacon who is beneficed, licensed or residing in the Province of Canterbury or the Province of York may declare in writing in the form set out in Part III of Schedule 1 to this Measure that he wishes to serve in the Province provided always that if he is beneficed or licensed to a parish which is not a constituent part of the Province in accordance with section 3(6) above, he shall resign any office held by him in relation to the benefice before being licensed to serve in the Province.

4(3) Subject to the provisions of Canon Law, no priest or deacon may officiate in the Province unless he is beneficed in the Province or holds a licence or permission to officiate issued by the presiding bishop.

4(4) Where a priest or deacon has made a declaration as set out in Parts III or IV of the said Schedule and proceedings are pending or in progress under the Incumbents (Vacation of Benefices) Measure 1977 or the Clergy Discipline Measure 2003, the application to serve in the Province or in the Province of Canterbury or the Province of York shall not be acted upon until the diocesan bishop or the presiding bishop as the case may be has signified in writing that the proceedings have been disposed of.

Ecclesiastical law

5(1) Subject to the provisions of this Measure, as from the appointed day the then existing ecclesiastical law and the then existing articles, doctrines, rites, rules, discipline and ordinances of the Church of England shall apply in the Province subject to such modification or alteration, if any, as after the passing of this Measure may be duly made therein by the Provincial Synod pursuant to the power contained in section 6(3) of this Measure.

5(2) The powers of the Provincial Synod under this Measure shall be so exercised as to ensure that the forms of service contained in the Book of Common Prayer continue to be available for use in the Province.

5(3) For the avoidance of doubt it is hereby declared that the Province is and shall continue to be a province of the Church of England for the purposes of charity law and of all other enactments unless the contrary intention appears.

Synods

6(1) Within three months of the appointed day the presiding bishop shall cause elections to the Provincial Synod to be held in accordance with the provisions set out in Schedule 2 to this Measure.

6(2) At the first meeting of the Synod canons shall be considered relating to the membership, elections and procedures of the Synod.

6(3) The Provincial Synod shall have power to modify or alter the then existing ecclesiastical law as referred to in section 5(1) above and to pass such Measures, canons and ordinances as are considered appropriate for the governance of the Province and to adopt by canon any Measure or other enactment passed by the General Synod after the passing of this Measure with such modifications as the Provincial Synod shall agree.

6(4) References in sections 3 and 4 of the Church of England Assembly (Powers) Act 1919 to the General Synod and its constitution and Legislative Committee shall, as from the appointed day, be construed as references to the General Synod and the synod of the Province and their respective constitutions and Legislative Committees.

6(5) The provisions of sections 1 and 3 of the Submission of the Clergy Act 1533 shall apply in like manner to the making, promulging and executing of canons by the synod of the Province.

6(6) Any cleric who is beneficed or licensed to serve in the Province following the making of the declaration set out in Part III of Schedule 1 to this Measure shall cease to be a proctor in Convocation or a member of the diocesan synod or the deanery synod as the case may be and, where applicable, his seat shall be filled as a casual vacancy.

6(7) Any lay person whose name is on the electoral roll of a parish which is a constituent part of the Province in accordance with section 3(6) above shall cease forthwith to be a member of the House of Laity of the General Synod, the diocesan synod or the deanery synod as the case may be and his seat shall be filled as a casual vacancy.

6(8) Subsections (6) and (7) above shall apply with the like effect to a cleric who makes the declaration set out in Part IV of the said Schedule and to a lay person who ceases to have his name on the electoral roll of a parish which is a constituent part of the Province.

Parishioners' rights

7(1) Where a parish is a constituent part of the Province in accordance with section 3(6) above, it shall not affect the right of parishioners to attend public worship in the parish church or their right to the occasional offices or to burial in the churchyard.

7(2) The relevant bishop of the Province shall have a duty under the Marriage Act 1949 to license churches for the solemnization of marriages and to grant common licences to marry.

Ecclesiastical offences

8 It shall be an offence against the laws ecclesiastical, for which proceedings may be taken under the Clergy Discipline Measure 2003 for any bishop, priest or deacon to act in contravention of any of the resolutions or declarations set out in Schedule 1 to this Measure.

Discriminatory discharge of certain functions

9 Without prejudice to section 19 of the Sex Discrimination Act 1975, nothing in Part II of that Act shall render unlawful sex discrimination against a person in respect of a Canon which –
(a) does not permit a woman priest to serve or officiate in the Province;
(b) does not permit a male priest ordained by a woman bishop to serve or officiate in the Province;
(c) does not permit a woman bishop to serve or officiate in the Province.

Pension provision

10 The Clergy Pensions Measures 1967 to 2002 and any regulations or rules made pursuant to such Measures and the Deacon-

esses and Lay Workers (Pensions) Measure 1980 shall extend to the Province.

Application of funds of Archbishops' Council

11 In considering and determining how to apply or distribute sums made available by the Church Commissioners in accordance with section 2 of the National Institutions Measure 1998, the Archbishops' Council shall consult the presiding bishop of the Province as to the sums, if any, to be made available to the Province or the parishes thereof.

Funds held on behalf of parishes

12(1) There shall be a board of finance for the Province constituted in accordance with the Diocesan Boards of Finance Measure 1925 with the necessary modifications.

12(2) On the appointed day in respect of a parish referred to in section 3(1) above or on such later date as a parish shall pass the resolution referred to in section 3(2) above, it shall be the duty of the diocesan board of finance to transfer to the board of finance of the Province all property, endowments, sums of money and all other interests whatsoever held in trust for or on behalf of that parish.

12(3) Where a parochial church council passes the resolution set out in Part II of Schedule 1 to this Measure, the board of finance of the Province shall transfer to the relevant diocesan board of finance all property, endowments, sums of money and all other interests whatsoever held in trust for or on behalf of that parish.

Exercise of patronage

13(1) Where an advowson of a benefice is vested in a diocesan bishop or a diocesan board of patronage and a parish of that benefice is a constituent part of the Province in accordance with section 3(6) above, the exercise of the patronage shall pass without any transfer or other assurance to the relevant bishop of the Province.

13(2) Registered patrons of all benefices where a parish is a constituent part of the Province in accordance with section 3(6) above may continue to exercise the patronage of the benefice in accordance with the provisions of the Patronage (Benefices) Measure 1986 and the presenting patron shall be under a duty to ensure that the presentee is a priest in good standing in the Province.

13(3) In section 16 of the Patronage (Benefices) Measure 1986 (presentation to benefices remaining vacant for nine months) references to the archbishop of the province shall be construed as references to the presiding bishop provided that, where the presiding bishop is the patron, the lapse provisions in section 16 shall not apply and he shall continue to be responsible for the filling of the vacancy.

13(4) In this section the expression 'a priest in good standing in the Province' means a cleric who has made a declaration in accordance with Part III of Schedule 1 to this Measure or who is either beneficed in the Province or holds a licence or permission to officiate from the presiding bishop or the relevant bishop of the Province.

Board of Education

14 The Province shall establish a Board of Education in accordance with the provisions of the Diocesan Boards of Education Measure 1991 and the Board shall have all the powers of a Board conferred by the said Measure including being responsible for any Church of England voluntary-aided or controlled school situate within, or largely within, a parish which is a constituent part of the Province in accordance with section 3(6) above and where the parochial church council of the parish appoints a member or members to the governing body of that school.

Pastoral reorganization

15(1) There shall be a pastoral committee for the Province constituted in accordance with Schedule 1 to the Pastoral Measure 1983 with the necessary modifications and there may be regional sub-committees as the presiding bishop shall determine.

15(2) Where, pursuant to the Pastoral Measure 1983, a diocesan pastoral committee is proposing that a parish church or other place of worship in the diocese should be declared redundant, the diocesan bishop shall first enquire of the relevant bishop of the Province whether the Province requires the building as a place of worship and, if it does, the building shall be transferred to the Province by pastoral scheme.

15(3) The provisions in subsection (2) above shall apply with the like effect where the pastoral committee of the Province is proposing that a place of worship be declared redundant.

15(4) Where a diocesan pastoral committee is of the opinion that a draft scheme is required which would affect parochial boundaries of a benefice in the Province, the provisions of section 12 of the Pastoral Measure 1983 shall apply with the necessary modifications.

Notices

16(1) A copy of any resolution passed by a parochial church council in accordance with section 3 above or of a declaration made by a bishop under section 2 above or by a priest or deacon under section 4 above, shall be sent to the following –
(a) the bishop of the diocese concerned or, being a declaration under section 2, the archbishop of the province concerned;
(b) the registrar of the diocese concerned or, being a declaration under section 2 above, the registrar of the province concerned;
(c) the diocesan secretary.

16(2) In addition to the notification in subsection (1) above, the secretary of the parochial church council which has passed a resolution in accordance with section 3 above shall notify -
(a) the rural dean of the deanery concerned; and
(b) the lay chairman of the deanery synod concerned.

Repeals

17 Section 3 (parishes), section 4 (cathedrals), section 6 (discriminatory discharge of certain functions) and Schedules 1 and 2 (parish and cathedral resolutions) of the Priests (Ordination of Women) Measure 1993 are hereby repealed with effect from the appointed day.

Interpretation

18(1) In relation to the Province, for any reference in an Act, Measure, Canon or other enactment to the archbishop of a province there shall be substituted a reference to the presiding bishop of the Province and for any reference to the diocese or the diocesan bishop there shall be substituted a reference to the Province and the relevant bishop of the Province.

18(2) Where there is a vacancy in the office of presiding bishop, the functions of the presiding bishop referred to in this Measure shall be carried out by such bishop serving in the Province as the chancellor of the Province shall appoint and different functions may be assigned to different bishops.

18(3) Where any Act, Measure, Canon or other enactment provides for a right of appeal to the archbishop of the province from the decision of the diocesan bishop, an appeal in the Province in respect of the decision of the presiding bishop acting in his capacity as the bishop of the diocese shall be to the senior bishop of the Province. For the purposes of this subsection the expression 'the senior bishop' means the bishop (other than the presiding bishop) who holds the licence of the presiding bishop and has been consecrated to the episcopate for the longest period, provided that if such bishop shall be unable or unwilling to act the next senior bishop who is able and willing shall act.

Amendment of this Measure

19 A motion tabled in the General Synod for the final approval of a Measure, Canon or other enactment which would amend or repeal any provision of this Measure or of any Canon promulged under the Measure shall not be deemed to be carried unless, before the motion is considered, a notice is included in the Synod's agenda or in a notice paper to the effect that the Synod of the Province has concurred in the motion being considered by the General Synod.

Short title, commencement and extent

20(1) This Measure may be cited as the Church of England (Additional Province) Measure 20__.

20(2) This Measure shall come into force in accordance with section 1 hereof.

20(3) This Measure shall extend to the whole of the Provinces of Canterbury and York except the Isle of Man and the Channel Islands.

20(4) Act of Tynwald may extend etc.

20(5) may be applied to the Channel Islands etc.

SCHEDULE 1
Resolutions and Declarations

Part I
Parish resolution to enter the Province

In accordance with the provisions of the Church of England (Additional Province) Measure 20__, this parochial church council resolves that the parish shall henceforth be a constituent part of the Province of [such title as shall be decided]

Dated this day of 20__

Chairman of the Meeting   PCC Secretary

Part II
Parish resolution to revert to a diocese in the Province of Canterbury or the Province of York

In accordance with the provisions of the Church of England (Additional Province) Measure 20__, this parochial church council resolves that the parish shall revert to the Diocese of   with effect from the date hereunder written.
[Either: The parish has been a constituent part of the Province of [such title as shall be decided] since the appointed day being more than five years before the resolution to revert was passed.]
[Or: The resolution to enter the Province of [such title as shall be decided] was taken on the day of 20__ being more than five years before the resolution to revert was passed.

Dated this day of   20__

Chairman of the Meeting   PCC Secretary

Part III

Cleric's declaration to serve in the Province

In accordance with the Church of England (Additional Province) Measure 20__, I, the [Right] Reverend AB, hereby declare that owing to my opposition to the promulgation of the Canon of the Church of England enabling women to be consecrated to the office of bishop, as from the date hereunder written, I apply to serve in the Province of [such title as shall be decided] [and I hereby resign from any office held by me at the date hereof].

Dated this   day of   20__

Witness to the signature of AB

Part IV

Cleric's declaration to serve in the Province of Canterbury or the Province of York

In accordance with the provisions of the Church of England (Additional Province) Measure 20__, I, the [Right] Reverend AB, hereby declare that, as from the date hereunder written, I apply to serve in the Diocese of   [and I hereby resign from any office held by me in the Province at the date hereof].

Dated this day of 20__

Witness to the signature of AB

SCHEDULE 2
Provincial Synod

1 The presiding bishop shall summon all bishops referred to in section 2(1) to 2(3) of this Measure to attend the Provincial Synod as members of the House of Bishops.

2 The presiding bishop shall instruct an appropriate person to conduct elections –

(a) among the priests and deacons who, on the day that nomination papers are posted, are either beneficed or licensed to serve in the Province. The election shall be conducted in accordance with such provisions of Canon H2 as are deemed relevant to the Province and the number of clergy to be elected shall be one proctor for every ten clergy or fraction of ten who are beneficed or licensed to serve in the Province and those elected shall form the House of Clergy of the Synod.

(b) among the churchwardens of all the parishes which, on the day that nomination papers are posted, are a constituent part of the Province in accordance with section 3(6) of this Measure. The election shall be conducted in accordance with such provisions of the Church Representation Rules as are deemed relevant to the Province and the number of laity to be elected shall be equal to the number of clergy to be elected in accordance with subparagraph (a) above and those elected shall form the House of Laity of the Synod.

SCHEDULE 3
Amendment and Repeal of Enactments

[Amendments of Acts and Measures – to be inserted at a later stage]

Draft Church of England (Additional Province) Measure Explanatory Memorandum

Introduction

1. It is anticipated that a Measure on the lines of this draft would be considered by the General Synod in tandem with a draft Measure making it lawful for women to be ordained to the episcopate. When the Measure to make it lawful for women to be ordained to the presbyterate was before the General Synod in the early 1990s, it was also considered necessary to have a Measure making financial provision for those unable to accept the legislation.

2. Under the Church of England Assembly (Powers) Act 1919 a Measure 'may relate to any matter concerning the Church of England' (section 3(6)). In view of the fact that this draft Measure provides for the additional Province to be a province of the Church of England with the 'then existing ecclesiastical law and the articles, doctrines, rites, rules, discipline and ordinances of the Church' being applied (clause 5(1)), the General Synod is competent to legislate in the matter.

Draft clauses

3. Clause 1 provides for the Province to be established on such day as the Archbishops of Canterbury and York shall appoint after consultation with the Provincial Episcopal Visitors (PEVs).

4. Clause 2(1) provides for the three PEVs to be the first bishops of the new Province with the proviso that any of the three can opt to remain in the Provinces of Canterbury and York.

5. Clause 2(2) provides for the Bishop of Fulham and any other bishop who has care of parishes which have opted for episcopal duties in accordance with the Act of Synod also to be bishops in the Province unless they declare in writing that they wish to remain in the Provinces of Canterbury and York.

6. Under clause 2(3) any other bishop – diocesan, suffragan or retired – residing in the Province of Canterbury or York may make the declaration set out in Schedule 1, Part III that he wishes to serve in the Province and, when accepted for service, any see held by him shall be vacated as shall membership of the House of Lords where applicable.

7. Clause 2(4) provides that stipends and expenses of office in accordance with the 1943 Measure shall continue to apply to the bishops referred to in subsections (1) and (2).

8. Clause 2(5) gives power to the bishops of the Province to choose one of their number to be the presiding bishop and clause 2(6) provides for the new Province to make Canons as to the manner in which future bishops are to be chosen and appointed.

9. Clause 2(7) prevents any bishop, other than those referred to in subsections (1) and (2), from officiating in the Province without a licence or permission to officiate issued by the presiding bishop. The presiding bishop shall also assign to such bishops the care of parishes. Clause 2(8) declares that no bishop of the province shall serve in the House of Lords.

10. Clause 3(1) provides that all parishes which have opted for episcopal duties in accordance with the Act of Synod shall automatically be parishes in the new Province unless the PCC has rescinded the resolutions under the women priests

legislation and the Act of Synod whereupon the parish will remain in the Province of Canterbury or York and will lose the power to prevent women priests and women bishops from officiating in the parish.

11. Clause 3(2) enables the PCC of any parish (which has not opted for episcopal duties in accordance with the Act of Synod) to pass the resolution in Schedule 1, Part I to enter and be part of the Province. Clause 3(3) gives power to the PCC of a parish which is part of the new Province to pass a resolution to revert to the relevant diocese in the Province of Canterbury or York. Clauses 3(4) and 3(5) deal with the procedures for passing resolutions and are based on similar provisions in the women priests legislation. Clause 3(6) declares which parishes are constituent parts of the new Province.

12. Clause 3(7) applies the legislation to guild church councils in the City of London, clause 3(8) applies the legislation to team ministries and clause 3(9) applies the legislation to religious communities, schools and other such institutions. Clause 3(10) prevents a parish entering the new Province where a faculty application or other proceedings are pending.

13. Clause 4(1) provides that where a parish is in the new Province on the appointed day, any priest or deacon beneficed or licensed to the parish shall automatically be a priest or deacon in the Province unless he declares in writing before the appointed day that he wishes to remain in the Provinces of Canterbury and York. Where he makes such a declaration, he shall be required to execute a deed of resignation in respect of any office held by him in relation to that parish but that shall not become operative for a period not exceeding nine months from the appointed day in order to enable the cleric to find a new post.

14. Clause 4(2) enables any priest or deacon in the Provinces of Canterbury and York to declare in writing in accordance with Schedule 1, Part III that he wishes to serve in the Province. Where the parish in which he serves is not part of the

Province he is required to resign any office held by him in relation to that parish.

15. Clause 4(3) prevents any priest or deacon officiating in the Province unless beneficed or holding the licence or permission to officiate of the presiding bishop. This provision is subject to paragraph 2 of Canon C8 which enables an incumbent or priest in charge to invite a priest or deacon to officiate in the parish church for a period of not more than seven days in a three-month period without the authority of the bishop. This would enable, for example, a parish priest of the Province to invite a priest serving in the Province of Canterbury or York to officiate at a wedding in the parish church.

16. Clause 4(4) prevents declarations taking effect if certain proceedings are pending.

17. Clause 5(1) provides for the ecclesiastical law of the Church of England on the appointed day to apply in the new Province. This is subject to such law being modified by the synod of the Province from time to time in accordance with the power contained in clause 6(3) below. However, there is a saving requiring the forms of service in the Book of Common Prayer 1662 always to be available for use in the Province (clause 5(2)).

18. Clause 5(3) declares the Province to be a province of the Church of England for the purposes of charity law.

19. Clause 6(1) provides for the Province to have a synod. The synod will have power to modify existing ecclesiastical law and power to adopt and modify by Canon future ecclesiastical law as may be passed by the General Synod for use in the Province. This follows the precedents for General Synod legislation being modified for use in the Channel Islands, the Isle of Man and the Diocese in Europe. There is also power for the synod of the Province to pass its own Measures, Canons and other ordinances for the

Province (clause 6(3)). Clause 6(4) applies the 1919 Act to Measures of the Provincial synod and clause 6(5) applies the 1533 Act to the making and promulging of Canons by that synod. Clause 6(6) removes a cleric serving in the Province from Convocation and diocesan and deanery synods in the Provinces of Canterbury and York and clause 6(7) removes laity whose names are on the electoral roll of a parish in the Province from synods in those provinces. Clause 6(8) has similar provisions for clergy and laity leaving the Province and returning to the Provinces of Canterbury and York.

20. Clause 7 preserves parishioners' rights to attend public worship in parish churches in the Province and with regard to their rights to the occasional offices – e.g. marriage, baptism and burial in the churchyard. Bishops of the Province are required to license churches for marriage under the 1949 Act (clause 7(2)).

21. Clause 8 makes it an ecclesiastical offence to contravene the declarations set out in the Schedule and clause 9 deals with the question of sexual discrimination. Both clauses are similar to clauses which were included in the women priests legislation.

22. Clause 10 provides for clergy serving in the Province to contribute to, participate in and benefit from the clergy pensions legislation.

23. Clause 11 makes it lawful for distributions under the National Institutions Measure 1998 to be made to the Province.

24. Clause 12(1) requires the Province to have a board of finance and imposes a duty on diocesan boards of finance to transfer to the board of finance of the Province all property, endowments etc. held on behalf of parishes which are in the new Province (clause 12(2)). A similar duty is imposed on the board of finance of the Province when a parish returns

to a diocese in the Provinces of Canterbury and York (clause 12(3)).

25. Clause 13(1) transfers the patronage of a benefice which is in the new Province from a diocesan bishop or a diocesan board of patronage to the relevant bishop of the Province. All other patrons continue to exercise their rights under the 1986 Measure subject to being under a duty to ensure that the priest appointed is a priest in good standing in the Province (clause 13(2)); that expression is defined in clause 13(4). Clause 13(3) modifies the lapse provisions in the 1986 Measure by providing that after nine months the patronage lapses to the presiding bishop rather than to the Archbishop of Canterbury or the Archbishop of York.

26. Clause 14 establishes a board of education for the Province and gives it the same powers as are conferred on a diocesan board of education by the 1991 Measure.

27. Clause 15(1) establishes a pastoral committee for the Province and gives the presiding bishop power to establish regional sub-committees. Clause 15(2) requires a diocesan pastoral committee which is declaring redundant a place of worship to enquire whether it is needed as a place of worship in the Province. Similar provisions apply in favour of a diocese where the pastoral committee of the Province declares a place of worship redundant (clause 15(3)). Clause 15(4) provides for the situation where it is proposed to change parochial boundaries involving a parish in a diocese and a parish in the Province.

28. Clause 16 sets out provisions concerning notices.

29. Clause 17 repeals provisions in the Priests (Ordination of Women) Measure 1993 so that it will no longer be possible for the PCC of a parish in the Provinces of Canterbury and York to pass or continue in force resolutions which prevent women priests from officiating in the parish.

30. Clause 18 deals with interpretation.

31. Clause 19 provides that this Measure may only be amended or repealed by the General Synod if, before the Final Approval motion is considered, the Synod has been informed that the Synod of the Province has concurred in the amendment or repeal.

32. Clause 20 deals with the short title of the Measure, commencement and extent.

33. Schedule 1 to the Measure sets out the various resolutions and declarations which may be made. Schedule 2 makes provision for the calling together of the first meeting of the Provincial synod. Schedule 3 will deal with the necessary amendments and repeals of enactments which will be required.

Part Three

Some Papers Submitted to the Working Party

I

The Bishop as
Bridegroom of His Church:
A Roman Catholic Contribution

AIDAN NICHOLS, OP

Introduction

In the predominant symbolism inherited from the New Testament and patristic period, we speak of the *motherhood* of the Church but the *fatherhood* of her ministers. This seems important background to the more specific theme of the bishop as bridegroom.[268]

1.   Henri de Lubac furnishes a convenient summary of the early testimony to the motherhood of the Church.[269] As Jerusalem was the mother city of Israel (cf. 2 Samuel 20.19; Matthew 23.27), so the heaven-born Jerusalem of the new *Aion* is the mother of Christians (Galatians 4.26). During the Donatist crisis, Augustine will portray the Church as a mother hen gathering her chicks to herself *(Contra Faustum* 14.9; *In Joannem,* tractate

---

[268] For an introduction to ministerial symbolics, consult J. Pascher, 'Die Hierarchie in sakramentaler Symbolik', in *Episcopus. Studien über das Bischofsamt. Festschrift Kardinal Michael von Faulhaber* (Regensburg, 1949), pp. 278–95. Pascher points out that a twofold symbolism for the episcopal office – the bishop as type both of Father and of Son – can occur even in the same text, as with Ignatius of Antioch's letter to the church at Tralles.

[269] See the essays collected under the general heading 'La maternité de l'Eglise', in H. de Lubac, SJ, *Les églises particulières dans l'Eglise universelle* (Paris, 1971).

15.4.7). Still in North Africa, the baptismal creed of the African church declares: 'Credo in . . . sanctam *matrem* Ecclesiam'. Such teaching concerns, evidently, the *Church universal*. This general theme of 'Mother Church' is well developed in the Ante-Nicene Fathers in East as well as West.[270]

2.   The same 'motherhood' can also be ascribed to a *particular* church, and is so ascribed in 2 John, addressed to 'the elect Lady and her children' (v. 1): that at least is how this text was understood in sub-apostolic Egypt and Africa, by Clement of Alexandria and Tertullian.[271]

3.   To the motherhood of the Church there corresponds the *fatherhood* of her ministers. It is true that Paul describes himself not only as a father to the church at Thessalonica (1 Thessalonians 2.11) and at Corinth (1 Corinthians 4.14–15), but also as a mother (RSV, 'nurse', *trophos*) to the Thessalonian church, and to the Church in Galatia (4.19). But the subsequent tradition treats the latter style as a Pauline flourish. In a stable formula the bishops (especially but by no means exclusively in Council) are referred to as 'the fathers'. Thus, for example, Athanasius declares the faith proclaimed at Nicaea to have reached the fathers from the fathers.[272] Such fatherhood is understood as rooted in the reality of apostolic succession. The bishops become fathers by succeeding to the apostles. As Augustine remarks in the *Enarrationes in psalmos*:

The apostles engendered you. They preached. They are the fathers.[273]

4.   This 'pair' – motherhood of Church, fatherhood of ministers – is, to de Lubac's eyes, the patristic equivalent of the couplet 'universal priesthood'/'hierarchical ministry' at the Second Vatican Council. On such ministers he writes:

---

[270] K. Delahaye, *Ecclesia Mater chez les Pères des trois premiers siècles* (Paris, 1964).

[271] Clement, *Adumbratio in Epistolam II Ioannis*; Tertullian, *Ad martyras* 1.

[272] Athanasius, *Oratio I contra Arianos* 8.

[273] Augustine, *Enarrationes in psalmos* 44.32.

These who are called to exercise this pastoral ministry share in the charge of Christ, the only Mediator. They are the normally indispensable instruments chosen to communicate the life of Christ and to support it in the interior of the Church – the Church who can then through each one of her children exercise in its totality her motherly function in regard to all those who have entered, or are destined to enter, her bosom.[274]

In other words, the fatherhood of the ordained ministry is at the service of the ecclesial motherhood to be exercised by women and other men.

These hierarchical ministers are given to the Church by the Father in a movement or mission that continues the movement or mission by which the Father gave the Son. So the ministry's origin is messianic not ecclesial. *Vis-à-vis* the people, these ministers are, in terms of theological symbolics, the Son coming from the Father to espouse himself to his Church. Here the 'nuptial' dimension enters for the first time into view. Theirs is, in de Lubac's terms, an 'instrumental' or 'vicarial' fatherhood,[275] making possible in all its immediacy the divine supernatural generativity of the Father in the Son through the Holy Spirit.

5. The *bridal* nature of the Church's motherhood has its New Testament charter in two main texts. First, there is the great mysteric linking of Christ and the Church in Ephesians 5.21–33 with its background in Genesis 2.24. The New Church–Eve is so one with her Spouse, the New Christ–Adam, that she is one flesh with him, his 'body'. But then we also have 2 Corinthians 11.4, where the Apostle speaks of the apostolic preaching as bringing about the nuptial union of neophytes with the Lord: 'I betrothed you to Christ as a pure bride to her one husband.'

The theme is emphasized in many patristic texts, and finds a privileged locus in the Fathers' use of the Song of Songs – beginning with Methodius of Olympus in *The Banquet*.[276] A typical

---

[274] de Lubac, *Les églises particulières*, p. 180.

[275] de Lubac, 'Paternité des ministres', in ibid., pp. 175–92.

[276] de Lubac, 'The Church and our Lady', in *The Splendour of the Church* (ET London and New York, 1956), pp 268–85; numerous patristic references are given in A. Feuillet, *Le Cantique des Cantiques. Etude de théologie biblique* (Paris, 1953).

witness is the Jerusalem Catecheses, whose author writes that
'Catholic Church'

> is the proper name of this holy Mother of us all; Bride of
> our Lord Jesus Christ, she bears the seal and likeness of the
> Jerusalem above; she began by being sterile but now she has
> numerous children.[277]

To sum up this material: the Church is the Mother of all reborn in the Spirit, teaching them the pure doctrine of Christ, at
once virginal and fecund.

6.   To the Church as Bride there corresponds *the bishop as
sacrament of the Bridegroom*. Exercising the Father's paternity
through Christ in the Holy Spirit, the hierarchical minister in the
episcopal order acts *vis-à-vis* Mother Church as bridegroom of
his particular church.

The evidence of the liturgy can be invoked here, on the principle, first stated by Prosper of Aquitaine, *Legem credendi statuat
lex supplicandi* ('The law of prayer must determine the law of
belief').[278] In the present Roman liturgy (to name only that),
the nuptial relation of the bishop to the Church is evoked at the
giving of the ring: one of the explicative ceremonies intended to
bring out the meaning of the prayer of consecration with laying
on of hands. In the version of the rites promulgated by Pope Paul
VI in 1968, the principal consecrator places the ring on the ring
finger of the new bishop's right hand, saying:

> Take this ring, the seal of your fidelity.
> With faith and love protect the bride of God, his holy
> Church.[279]

This formula is reflected in the text that accompanies the giving

---

[277] *Mystagogical Catecheses* 16.26.
[278] Prosper of Aquitaine, *Indiculus de gratia Dei*, prologue.
[279] *The Rites of the Catholic Church as Revised by Decree of the Second
Vatican Council and Published by Authority of Pope Paul VI* (ET New
York, 1976–80), vol. ii, p. 97.

of a ring by husband to wife in the rite of marriage as revised by authority of the same pontiff in the following year:

N., take this ring as a sign of my love and fidelity. [280]

The use of 1 Corinthians 7.27 to berate with a charge of adultery bishops who would leave their sees for others is presupposed in Athanasius' criticism of the translation to Constantinople of Eusebius of Nicomedia.[281] Gregory of Nyssa speaks of the episcopal ordination of Meletius at Antioch as 'spiritual marriage' (*pneumatikon gamon*).[282] Though the First Council of Nicaea's prohibition on transmigration and translation of bishops (in its 15th canon) does not turn on this principle (the canon applies equally to presbyters and deacons), soon after its discovery (perhaps by the Alexandrian exegetes?)[283] it entered the canonical tradition and is found in the Roman synod held for Gallican bishops under Pope Siricius (385–99).[284]

7. We can note *en passant* that if, as Augustine maintains, Peter 'bears the figure of the entire Church' (*totius Ecclesiae figuram gerens*),[285] then 'nuptial theological symbolics' can offer an explanation of this by way of the notion that the Roman bishop, as pastor of the only local church to carry a universal responsibility, acts as the *vicarial bridegroom of the Church universal* – a position maintained by Pius VI in his letter *Caritas illa* of 1777.[286] As such, it pertains to the Roman bishop to ensure the unity of the pastoral office as exercised by other hierarchical ministers in the episcopal order in their particular churches –

---

[280] Ibid., vol. i, p. 542.

[281] Athanasius, *Apologia secunda* 6.

[282] Gregory of Nyssa, *Oratio funebris in Meletium episcopum*.

[283] The thesis of L. Ober in his 'Die Translation der Bischöfe im Altertum', *Archiv für katholische Kirchenrecht* 88 (1908), pp. 209–29, 441–65, 625–48; ibid., 89 (1909), pp. 1–33.

[284] On this entire subject, see S. Schulz, *Transmigration und Translation. Studien zum Bischofswechsel in der Spätantike bis zum Hohen Mittelalter* (Cologne, Weimar, Vienna, 1992), pp. 1-24.

[285] Augustine, Letter 53, 1, 2 (cf *In Joannem*, tractate 124, 5; Sermon 295, 2).

[286] Cf. H. de Lubac, 'Ecclesia mater', in *The Splendour of the Church*, p. 199.

albeit in differing fashions within his own patriarchate and the patriarchal or quasi-patriarchal structures of the Oriental churches.

8. The notion of the bishop as paternally generative bridegroom for the particular church takes on enhanced importance in the context of *the celebration of the Holy Eucharist*. Although he acts as bridegroom in all the essential tasks of his office, his role as chief liturgist of his church makes him a unique case of the general principle that at the Mass the celebrant acts as sacramental sign of Christ the Bridegroom.

That general principle constitutes the principal theological illumination proposed for the central argumentative claim of the Roman magisterial interventions in this area during the pontificates of Paul VI and John Paul II.[287] The *claim* is that the precedent tradition is normative on the subject; the *proposed illumination* concerns the nuptial symbolism of the relationship between Christ the Bridegroom and his Church the Bride in the eucharistic action. Important elements in this 'illumination' are:

a. the ministerial priest can act *in persona Ecclesiae* to represent the union of the Church with Christ only because he first acts *in persona Christi*;

b. the sacramentality of the ministerial priest in this prior 'Christoform' configuration requires the natural resemblance of his gender to Christ the Bridegroom;

c. the complementary symbolism of Christ as Head of his Church body is best understood from within the nuptial symbolism of Christ as Bridegroom to his Bride and not the other way round since only the nuptial symbolic ordering guarantees a relational, rather than 'uni-personal' concept of the union of Christ and the Church. [288]

---

[287] See *Inter insigniores* (1976), n. 5; *Mulieris dignitatem* (1988), nn. 24–6; *Christifideles laici* (1988), n. 51.

[288] S. Butler, 'The Priest as Sacrament of Christ the Bridegroom', *Worship* 66 (1992), pp. 498–517. Sr Sara argues further that this is the position of classical Latin theology in St Bonaventure (see further J. Rezette, OFM, 'Le sacerdoce et la femme chez saint Bonaventure', *Antonianum* 51 (4) (1976), pp. 520–7), and that the counter-argument for which the congregation would then need a female representative confuses general symbolics with

If these considerations are valid for the ministerial priest in the order of presbyter, then they are so *a fortiori* for the same priest (*sacerdos*) in the order of bishop, since (as mentioned above) the bishop is the chief, not the delegated or auxiliary, liturgist in the particular church.

9.   A final question is, what sense can be made, in view of the above, of bishops without particular churches of their own? (In the Latin church, these would be coadjutor, auxiliary and titular bishops, as well as bishops emeritus of given sees.) Ordination to the episcopate qualifies a man to play his role in nuptial symbolics – both liturgically and in the exercise of the pastoral office. The active entering into that role and the carrying out of the duties it entails depends, however, on the determination of his ministry which is made by the head of the college of bishops – vicarial bridegroom of the Church universal – either explicitly, by (as in the Roman patriarchate) naming him bridegroom of this or that local church, or implicitly (in the Oriental churches) by concurring in the synodical procedures whereby this comes about.

---

specific sacramental symbolization and so falls to the ground. And she insinuates that an anthropological disaster has befallen those feminists who in rejecting this 'illumination' report that they 'fail to discover any positive symbolism in the imagery of masculine love', p. 506.

2

The Gender and Number of Bishops

JOHN HUNWICKE

Where to begin an enquiry about any aspect of Christian ministry? While St John would have us begin with the Father's sending of the Son and the symmetrical sending by the Son of his *Apostoloi, Shelihim*, the Synoptic tradition might urge us to begin with the calling of the Twelve (Matthew 10.1–4; Mark 3.13–19; Luke 6.12–16). All the commentaries on my shelves have no doubt that the duodecimality of the Twelve represents the dispositions of the pre-resurrection 'historical Jesus' (reasons are concisely summarized in Cranfield, *ad loc.*), and that he saw himself as thus gathering a New Israel, a new people of God corresponding to the Old Israel in its twelve tribes.

The Twelve were all male; any inferences drawn from this about the Lord's wishes for the gender of their successors in the later Church (if, of course, he intended there to *be* any later Church) are commonly disputed on the grounds that such an arrangement will lack theological content since it will have originated in his unthinking acceptance of the social mores of the day.

But if the Twelve correspond to the twelve patriarchs of Old Israel, it would have introduced an intolerable semiological confusion for any of the Twelve to have been female. Masculinity is not accidental, but logically inherent in the nature of the group. Among Christians for whom it is common ground that bishops are successors of the Apostles or even new members of the apostolic college, the burden of proof seems to rest upon those who argue that what was inherent to the Dominical structure of the group has ceased subsequently to be necessary. If the Twelve, like the Patriarchs, were fathers each of his family, bishops, as new aggregates, must share that ministry of paternity.

But perhaps we are mistaken to grub around in speculative might-have-beens. What is authoritative is not the speculative proto-history of the New Testament documents. Mgr Ronald Knox reminded us that I do not ask Blessed Q to bless the bed that I lie on, but the canon of Scripture that Holy Mother Church sets before us. Urmarkus and Protoluke are not our Scriptures; we owe no *obsequium* to the *magisterium* of the Jesus Seminar. Mark's longer ending, and the *Pericope de Adultera* are canonical even if they were not written by the authors of Mark and John. Ephesians, and the Pastoral Epistles, are canonical even if they are pseudonymous. And just as the apostolic *kerygma* coalesced authoritatively into the New Testament, so the apostolic ministry coalesced authoritatively into the form of ministry we have received from the same age. Speculations about the proto-history of that Threefold Ministry which is centred upon monepiscopacy do no harm; indeed Dom Gregory Dix demonstrated that Catholics can play these games with at least as great a show of erudition . . . and with distinctly more verve and wit . . . than Protestants and liberals. But, wherever they come from, such speculations are not the authoritative basis upon which the tradition may be messed around with. Those adaptations which each age calls for must develop organically from the normative tradition which Scripture, Fathers and the classical liturgical traditions witness.

It is well known among those who have taken an interest in the early history of the Christian ministry that nowhere in the New Testament are the three orders of bishop, priest and deacon all mentioned in the same breath, despite the claims made in that regard by the Preface to the Anglican Ordinal. A conclusion commonly drawn is that *episkopos* and *presbyteros* are two synonymous terms referring to the same 'order'. The better informed are also aware that where, in the 'Pastoral Epistles', *episkopos, presbyteroi* and *diakonoi* are referred to, *presbyteroi* and *diakonoi* tend to be plural, while the *episkopos* is singular.

The suggestion has been made that the (allegedly) pseudonymous writer may have been portraying an age when, as he was aware, the episcopate and the presbyterate had not yet become separate entities, but that he was 'really' writing at a time when the 'rule' of the single 'monarchical' bishop had become normal;

so he accidentally betrays this fact by anachronistically referring to the bishop in the singular (see especially Titus 1.5–7).

Little attention, however, is attracted by the fact that in 1 Timothy 3, where *dei . . . ton episkopon* is singular, this grammatical detail, far from being accidental, seems to be intrinsically related to the character of the ministry described. The bishop's duty is, as described, to be the *paterfamilias* of God's assembly; and a *paterfamilias* cannot be duplicated (Paul tells us that the *materfamilias* is to be *en pasei hypotagei* to him). There is an obvious, although not explicit, logic here relating this monistic paternal episcopal ministry to the unity of the one *oikos* of the Father. One God, one bishop, one flock of the redeemed.

A relationship between unity and the monicity of Fatherhood is also to be found in Ephesians 3—4, where the (allegedly) pseudonymous writer seals his plea for ecclesial unity with the coda: 'One God and Father of all, who is over all and through all and in all' (4.6). Earlier he has referred to the Father *ex hou pasa patria en ouranois kai epi ges onomazetai* (3.15), one of the most strangely translated verses in English Bibles. (Generations of the devout must have been mystified by the apparent assertion that every 'family' gets its 'name' from the Father.)

The Vulgate (and compare the Syriac) translators were not shy to be literal: *patria* is rendered *paternitas*, even though at Luke 2.4 it seemed more natural to render *patrias* by *familia* than by a word from the same root as *pater* (similarly the Syriac). Surely the point is that every created fatherhood is derived from and expressive of the one divine fatherhood. It is not easy to forget here the injunction of the Synoptic Christ (Matthew 23.9) that we should call no man on earth Father. This command seems never to have been taken literally: even anti-sacerdotalist Protestants who emphatically deny the style 'Father' to clergy do not deny it to their own begetters. We all have to call our progenitor – if we know who he is – something.

The Pauline refinement makes sense of it: genetic paternity; godfatherhood; stepfatherhood; spiritual fatherhood; all these derive their validity from, and are subject to the judgement of, the one Fatherhood of the one Father. And pre-eminent among these *paternitates* – indeed, qualitatively different from the rest of them – must be that of him who in the Father's name presides over his household, the *ekklesia* of the redeemed in any one place, the flock bought by his Son's blood. The probability that the tradition behind the Synoptic preoccupation with divine Fatherhood goes back to the incarnate Lord himself is confirmed (irrespective of ongoing debate between followers of Jeremias and of Vermes) by the evidence of his use of the Aramaic term *Abba*; and, most strikingly of all, by the convergent Johannine evidence. And here again we find the link between *Pater* and unity: *Pater hagie, tereson autous . . . hina osin hen . . .* (John 17.11).

From the Sarum Pontifical, through our respective Prayer Books down to *ASB*, the ordination rites of the Church of England have begun with the representative of the Church addressing the presiding bishop as *Father*. We are entitled to assume that this unbroken tradition in texts which for our community still stand as doctrinally normative is not merely a piece of late medieval deference or of Tudor legalese, but is doctrinally significant. Encouragement is offered by the conviction of St Ignatius that the bishop is *typon tou Patros* (*Trallians* 3.1; and see also *Smyrnaeans* 8.1; *Magnesians* 3; 6.1).

If the evidence we have examined is inhospitable to the notion of women bishops, it also provides problems for any scheme involving 'group' or 'team' or 'shared' episcopacy. The concept of the bishop as the one visible father of the one visible household of God creates problems for what Anglicans call 'suffragans' (compare Roman Catholic 'coadjutors'). While these gentlemen have been convenient since they were invented as confirming machines in over-large Victorian dioceses, they hardly provide theologically a pattern which calls for imitation. Sometimes we talk about them as 'extensions' of the *episcope* of *the* bishop; this receives formal and canonical confirmation from the fact that their every episcopal act is performed by virtue of commission from *the* (diocesan) bishop, and only thus. Rome and Byzantium get round the problem by legal fictions (bishops *in partibus infidelium*).

John Zizioulas – at least, in the days before he became Metropolitan of Pergamon – expressed misgivings about 'titular' bishops ('a contradiction between theory and practice in ecclesiology'; *Being as Communion*, 1985, p. 239). The fact that contortions have to be performed in order to reconcile such phenomena with

the perceived and inherited norm of monepiscopacy would seem
to disqualify them as precedents for any novel arrangements, at
least until any such radically new models for understanding episcopacy have been justified, debated ecumenically and received.
The same goes for other transient arrangements which have
emerged from particular problematic situations, such as the 'college episcopacy' of the Non-jurors. Radical novelties concerning
a ministry we claim to hold in common with the ancient and major Christian churches should not be pushed ruthlessly through
as immediate pragmatic responses to short-term problems in local ecclesiastical politics.

If sacraments, as 'efficacious signs', bear a natural resemblance to what they signify, it is of course difficult to see how a
woman can image or deliver the Fatherhood of God unless one
empties that notion of content or – contrary to the teaching of
Ephesians – maintains that God's Fatherhood is secondary to
human models. But the relationship between bishop and God the
Father provides, if anything, even greater problems for any ideas
of 'group' episcopacy. Trinitarian orthodoxy commits us to faith
in the Father as, alone, the principle without other principle, the
source and fount of the being of Son and Spirit (*arche anarchos;
pege; aitia; principium*). (It may be argued that this is the sense in
which one should use the term 'monarchy': singleness of origin
rather than singleness merely of rule or jurisdiction.)

The bishop expresses this role of monarchy in his church,
not least by being the fount of its sacramental grace in Baptism/
Confirmation and Order, the source of eucharistic liceity and the
sign of the synchronic and diachronic unities between his local
church in this place at this moment and the Church in other times
and places. It is one of the tragedies of history that *filioque* led
Byzantines to suspect that Westerners, apparently believing that
the Spirit has two *archai*, are guilty of ditheism – believing in two
Gods. A plurality of bishops and thus a plurality of *archai* (poly-
archy?) in a church would make its episcopal ministry an efficacious sign of plurality in the monarchic Fatherhood of the First
Person of the Holy and Undivided Trinity: in effect, we would be
committed to polytheism.

The Holy Trinity is a truth, I suspect, which many people have
no particular objections to leaving, as it were, on the statute

book as long as it does not get too much in the way of actual flesh-and-blood projects which may be dear to them in the 'real world'. The last paragraph will, to such a mind, look like playing around with a lot of old Greek and Latin terms in order to place difficulties in the way of Progress or of the Guidance of the Spirit or Whatever. But I rather think that 'group episcopacy', at least in our present English context, would lead to an effective cultural polytheism even in the 'real' world. Imagine a carefully balanced 'team' of bishops in some diocese or 'greater episcopal grouping' (or whatever stylish neologism is dreamed up). It will be carefully balanced to include at least one 'traditionalist', there to lure Catholics into believing that a place had been made to enable them to 'stay'. (Let us assume that he is an honest man and committed both doctrinally and practically to express that episcopal *patria*, imaging the Fatherhood of the First Person of the Trinity, which we have examined.) The 'team' will also include a woman; the first such ladies chosen will probably be selected carefully so as not to scare the horses, but before long they will have successors committed to maternal notions of Godhead. If the two models of Christian understanding which are alive among us now both continue to flourish and to diverge from each other, we *shall* have alternative deities on offer in different parishes which 'look to' alternative bishops on the diocesan menu.

3

Fatherhood, Headship and Tradition

GEOFFREY KIRK

1 *Paterfamilias*

It is a commonplace of the debate about women's ordination that Evangelical and Catholic opponents are coming from different corners. The Catholics, it is said, major on the priest as icon of Christ; the Evangelicals on the Pauline doctrine of headship. This distinction – the darling of those Liberals whose aspiration is to divide and rule – is expressed in the wording of the two Schedules to the 1993 Measure.

But is it the case that the Catholics and Evangelicals are using different, perhaps incompatible arguments? It has never seemed so to us. Evangelicals, of course, have often majored on issues of authority in the Church: what they delight to call 'leadership'. Catholics have been wary of such language as dangerously unscriptural (as any Cruden will tell you!).[289] So what is the argument from 'headship'; and what is the primary meaning of *kephale* in the relevant texts?

Because certain Evangelicals have allowed the idea of 'headship' to be subsumed into a notion of authority in the sense of 'dominance', it has proved difficult for them to discharge themselves honourably or acceptably in debate. They have, almost inevitably, fallen foul of the feminist identification of 'headship' and 'leadership' with a wholesale and perennial male 'conspiracy' to oppress women. Hierarchies in any form are to the proponents of women's ordination whatever is the feminist equivalent of a red rag to a bull.

---

[289] There is no entry under 'leadership' in the standard edition of Cruden.

More moderate proponents have meanwhile expended considerable ingenuity demonstrating that *kephale,* in many contexts, has no connotation of 'leadership' or 'authority', and simply means 'source' or 'origin'.

In the unpacking of the complex metaphor of 'the head', we suggest that both the supporters of women priests and the conservative Evangelicals have got it wrong.

To unravel a metaphor as rich as *kephale,* you must first identify its locus or 'core'. That, of course, is to be found within the wider (and primary) Pauline metaphor of 'the body'. (John Robinson's short book *The Body: A Study in Pauline Theology* (SCM Press, 1952) remains a broad and useful summary. Says Robinson in his preface: 'It is remarkable that there exists . . . no study which seeks to correlate all Paul's language on the Body.')[290]

Christ is 'the head of the Body, the Church' in various and interrelated senses. He is its source of reason, direction and will: members of the Body are conformed to the mind (*nous*) of Christ (1 Corinthians 2.16). He is its source, origin and progenitor: 'the firstborn [*prototokos*] from the dead', 'so that in all things he might take primacy [*proteuein*]' (Colossians 1.18). His headship of the Church, moreover, is related to headship within the Church and within the domestic church (the Christian family) in a way that only can be described as meta-analogical: the submission of wives to husbands (Ephesians 5.22–3) and the wearing of head-coverings by women (1 Corinthians 11.3–10ff.) are not merely expressions, but outworkings of this ultimate headship, which devolves upon the Son as the offspring of the Father.

The divine and the domestic (here so closely related) come together pre-eminently in the institution and continued celebration of the Eucharist. The Passover is a domestic rite in which the *paterfamilias* hands down the history of salvation to the youngest present. Though its principal participants are males (the most senior and the most junior), it includes, nevertheless, the entire family, both women and men.

The Last Supper is, in almost all respects, eccentric.[291] The

---

[290] Despite the passage of time this seems still to remain the case in 2004.

[291] I am assuming here, with Joachim Jeremias, that despite the witness of the Fourth Gospel, the Last Supper was a Passover meal.

thirteen at table are all men. They are a 'family' only in the sense that they represent the twelve patriarchs, 'the sons of Israel', and prefigure the universal Church, 'the household of faith'. There is no dialogue, moreover, by which the traduction of the saving history is effected. Instead the *berakah* becomes the *anticipation* ('which is given up for you') which is commended to the Church as an *anamnesis*: 'do this as the remembrance of me'.

The head of table at this eccentric Passover, moreover, is the Christ, the 'express image of the Father'. In Christ, God himself is rewriting salvation history. Henceforward the metanarrative which explicates all narratives will centre on him and be transmitted by those whom he has chosen: here a story is renewed and a people reconstituted. The Head of Table transmits the saving history to those who are to be heads of tables.

It is the tragedy of much Evangelical argumentation about 'headship' that it has adopted, for the most part, post-biblical imagery, and signally failed to see the Church as this extended *oikos*, the household of faith, constituted by the rites it celebrates (the Body of Christ confecting the Body of Christ in order to become the Body of Christ). Evangelicals have also failed to stress the biblical connection between headship in the domestic church (the family) and headship in the Church universal. That surely is a basic premise of Pauline ecclesiology. Nor have they grasped that this apostolic connection is faithfully represented, in the next generation, by Ignatius of Antioch and Clement of Rome, both of whom assume as axiomatic (i.e. as a tradition which they have received and are transmitting, not as their own opinion or perception) that there should be only one Eucharist in one location and that the bishop who presides at it does so as the image of the Father. The bishop is the bridegroom of his local church and the *paterfamilias* who heads its eucharistic table.

The *Pascha*, the Passover of God, the primary rite of the Catholic Church, is that at which the *Paterfamilias*, the Lord and Saviour, the *prototokos*, who has redeemed the body, presides over the gathering-in of the New Israel.

That authority in the Church ('headship') is directly related to table presidency at the *Pascha* of the New Israel, and that all this is related to the manner in which the *paterfamilias*, in home and Eucharist, is the icon of Christ (Ephesians 5.23–32) should be apparent to every unprejudiced reader. Arguments about Pauline 'headship' and iconic representation are not the separate and adversative arguments which Liberal proponents of women's ordination would love to proclaim, but essentially the same argument – the differing aspects of which give strength and coherence to the whole.

The head of the *oikos,* who is the *eikon* of the Father, establishes the table fellowship of the Eucharist – by which the *ekklesia* itself is established; order in the domestic church is affirmed; and the testimony of Scripture is vindicated by the *anamnesis* which reveals the coherence of the divine plan.

Evangelicals and Catholics in this matter are, or should be, at one. For to exercise 'headship' in the Body of Christ is to preside at the Eucharist as *paterfamilias* in the household of faith – nurturing his Body with his Body so that it may be his Body, and pledging oneself, like him, in sacrifice, so that the Church may truly be his Bride.

2   A word from the head

In its second report on the ordination of women (GS 829) the House of Bishops of the Church of England sought to address all the main texts of Scripture relevant to the issue. The treatment of an important (some would say *the most* important) passage in St Paul failed to take account of important work by Gerhard Dautzenberg and Reinhold Seeburg, which was easily available at the time in Manfred Hauke, *Women in the Priesthood? A Systematic Analysis in the Light of the Order of Creation and Redemption* (San Francisco, 1988, pp. 373–403).[292]

At the end of a lengthy passage on prophecy and speaking in tongues (and before he goes on to his great hymn on the resurrection of the body in 1 Corinthians 15) Paul gives his Corinthian correspondents specific directions about the conduct of public worship:

> As in all the churches of the saints, the women should keep silence in the churches. For they are not permitted to speak

---

[292] This section of this paper is indebted to the arguments set out there.

but should be subordinate, as even the law says. If there is anything that they desire to know, let them ask their husbands at home. For it is shameful for a woman to speak in church. What! Did the word of God originate with you, or are you the only ones it has reached? If anyone thinks he is a prophet, or spiritual, he should acknowledge that what I am writing to you is a command from the Lord. If anyone does not recognize this he is not recognized. So, my brethren, earnestly desire to prophesy, and do not forbid speaking in tongues; but all things should be done decently and in order. (1 Corinthians 14.33b–40)

It is easy, if one has the will, to make heavy weather of the interpretation of this passage;[293] but it is not the insoluble conundrum that some have hoped to make of it. Nor is it plausibly a later interpolation – a view which is losing ground among commentators. On the contrary, the argument here fits neatly into the developing pattern of Paul's thought, and has distinctly Pauline characteristics.

The key to understanding Paul's argument is the distinction he is making between two sorts of speaking: *lalein*[294] *glosse* (speaking in a tongue), which he associates closely with prophecy, and *lalein en ekklesia* (speaking in the assembly). The first, Paul has already made clear to his Corinthians (11.5ff.), is permitted to women. The second he forbids to women with as firm and categorical a series of injunctions as any in the Pauline corpus.

It is a commonplace among commentators that Paul's theology is occasional (that is to say, directed to a particular audience and need), rather than systematic. But the careful reader soon observes in Paul's habitual patterns of argument something which, while it is not systematic theology, certainly comes close.

---

[293] As do the bishops of the Church of England in GS 829, pp. 60–1.

[294] The use of *lalein*, a verb variously translated as *speak*, *chatter*, *gossip*, *natter*, has been commented on. Why should the Apostle so firmly forbid what was, in common usage, apparently so trivial? The answer seems to be that *lalein*, in this sense, refers to extempory speech under divine inspiration – *lalein glosse* is prophetic speech in tongues; *lalein en ekklesia* is the Spirit-inspired confection of the eucharistic prayer of praise and thanksgiving.

   Paul habitually argues on different levels of authority; and so a useful tool in understanding his pattern of thought is a list of those levels in ascending order of importance or seriousness. They are five:

1   The general moral code – patterns of behaviour which are thought, by society at large, to be 'natural' or unchallenge-able.
2   Paul's own authority as an Apostle and founder of churches.
3   The general practice of the Christian churches.
4   The principles of the Jewish Torah.
5   A command of the Lord Jesus Christ.

These levels of authority are sometimes invoked in isolation from each other. Sometimes, however, they are made to work together, as we see at 1 Corinthians 9.1–14, where Paul is demonstrating that he is entitled to financial support for his labours, and that he has freely renounced it.

   Paul begins by appealing to the common practice of other Christian communities (our level 3 – 'as the other Apostles, and the brothers of the Lord and Cephas' (v. 5)). He goes on to talk in more general terms (our level 1 – 'who serves as a soldier at his own expense, who plants a vineyard without eating any of its fruit?' (v. 7)). At a more serious level (our level 4) he appeals to the authority of the Torah ('does not the law say the same?' (v. 8)). His ultimate sanction (which for Paul and no doubt his readers settles the matter) is our level 5 – the claim to have a word from the Lord himself on the subject ('in the same way the Lord commanded' (v. 14)).

   The same levels of authority are used here to forbid women to 'speak in the assembly'.

   Paul has been giving a whole series of instructions about day-to-day church matters referred to him by the Corinthian PCC. In general they are directions made on apostolic authority alone (our level 2): 'Be imitators of me as I am of Christ.' The instructions about veils and hairdressing, numbers of speakers, and the availability of interpreters are all of this kind.

   Now he brings out his big guns. Not Paul's opinion alone, but the universal practice of the churches (level 3) 'as in all the

assemblies of the saints'; 'did the word of God originate with
you, or are you the only ones it has reached?'; the Torah itself
(level 4) – 'as even the law says'; and finally, the Lord in person
(level 5) – 'what I am writing to you is a command of the Lord'
– are the authority by which he speaks.

Then, as though this apparent authoritarian overkill were
not enough (and as an eloquent testimony to the intransigence
and wilfulness of the Corinthians), he adds the threat of
formal anathema – 'if anyone does not recognize this, he is not
recognized'. (The reference is to the saying we find recorded at
Matthew 7.21–3: 'Many will say to me in that day, Lord, Lord
. . . then I will say to them: I never knew you, depart from me you
workers of iniquity'; cf. 'if anyone has no love for the Lord, let
him be accursed' (1 Corinthians 16.22) with which, in his own
hand, Paul ends the present letter.)

There can be no reasonable doubt, considering the weight of
the language used, that Paul is absolutely serious in forbidding
women to 'speak in the assembly'. For faithful Christians, then,
it is then a matter of importance to decide what he means by that
phrase. Could 'speaking in the assembly' conceivably have been
a technical term familiar, no doubt, to Paul's readers but obscure
to us?

There are substantial reasons for supposing this to be the
case.

The distinction between *lalein glosse* and *lalein en ekklesia*
is between a charismatic and a formally ordered ministry. Such
a distinction the Jews had themselves already been making for
centuries.

- *Lalein glosse* (speaking in a tongue), like the wider category
  of 'prophecy', is a province open to women as well as men.
  'As even the law says', the Spirit moves whom it will, men and
  women, adults and children. Though Paul was of the opinion
  that in public such things should be ordered and regulated, he
  accepted all this as a matter of fact. A tradition extending from
  Miriam to Anna was one which a pupil of Gamaliel could be
  expected to take for granted.
- *Lalein en ekklesia* (speaking in the assembly) is obviously
  something quite different. We know that simply because Paul

can restrict it to men alone on the same principles ('as even the law says') which permitted women to prophesy. The entire liturgical activity of Israel, in both temple and synagogue, was restricted to males. But, in this particular context, what 'law' forbids what activity?

Fruitless hours of research have been expended trying to find a passage in the Pentateuch to which Paul could conceivably be referring. The truth seems to be that Paul is not using 'law' in the narrow sense of the canon of Scripture, but in the broader sense of holy tradition: Mishnah, not Old Testament. (Neither book, of course, existed in Paul's day in the form in which we know them.)

There are two relevant proscriptions in the rabbinic tradition. The first forbids women to take part in the public question-and-answer sessions which were the foundations of rabbinic discourse. A woman, says Rabbi Eliezer, had better do her arguing with her husband privately. ('If there is anything they desire to know, let them ask their husbands at home', says Paul, echoing him.)

The second forbids a woman to preside at the Passover meal. The Passover Haggadah includes questions asked of the eldest present by the youngest. Could a dowager, the eldest in her household, be the required respondent? The Rabbis held that she could not. She had better unite her household to that of her nearest male kinsman so that the obligations of the festival could be fulfilled by a male on her behalf.[295]

If we assume – and we have no reason *not* to assume – that the earliest churches borrowed the 'dialogue sermon' from Jewish custom, we have here two restrictions which cover neatly the role of the celebrant at the Christian Eucharist. He is, in Jewish terms, both the rabbi teaching formally (*dialegesthai* is the verb used in Acts 20.7) and the elder (*presbyteros*)[296] who heads the table at the paschal celebration (the role which Paul himself assumed after that near-fatal dialogue sermon in Troas).

---

[295] Mishnah, Second Division: *Moed Pesahim*, Ed. Danby, pp. 136–51, outlines these provisions. Commentaries in various versions of the Passover Haggadah have elaborated on them.

[296] Why is the minister of the Eucharist and *paterfamilias* of the Christian community, from the earliest times, called *presbyteros*? It cannot be from actual seniority (see 1 Timothy 5.1). It is surely because he is the one who makes the *berakah* at the paschal commemoration.

Precisely because the charismatic ministries of the Corinthian community were so lively as to be a cause for concern (and because women, as the law permitted, were active in them), Paul needed to use all the authority at his disposal to make the necessary distinction between such extraordinary gifts and the rather more mundane, formally sanctioned, ministry of the *presbyteroi*, from which he knew women to be excluded by a specific dictum of the Saviour.

It has been suggested that by 'a command of the Lord' Paul means some *word* of his own, speaking with the apostolic authority of an 'ambassador of the Lord Jesus Christ'. But this cannot be. Already (1 Corinthians 7.10–12) he has written: 'to the married I give charge, not I but the Lord . . . to the rest I say, not the Lord'. And again: 'Now concerning virgins I have no command from the Lord, but I give my opinion as one who by the Lord's mercy is trustworthy.'

Far from his being casual about the distinction, it would seem that, in Paul's opinion, confusion about the source and nature of spiritual authority is the real problem at Corinth. He is therefore assiduous in pointing it up. *Entole* (command), moreover, designates not a general principle, from which Paul might be thought to have adduced a particular directive of his own, but a specific 'precept', an actual 'word'.

Here, then, a specific command (*entole*) of the Lord Jesus is being used as evidence that the general principles of the Law, as they apply in the changed circumstances of Christian worship, still hold good. The teaching role and the table presidency of the Church are a male preserve. The Lord, Paul is telling a Corinthian community intoxicated with novelty, willed no change.

3.   A hidden tradition?

. . . women were active in the expansion and shaping of the Church in the first centuries: they were apostles, prophets, teachers, presbyters, enrolled widows, deacons, bishops and stewards. They preached, they spoke prophetically and in tongues, they went on mission, they prayed, they presided over the Lord's Supper, they broke the bread and gave the cup, they baptized, they taught, they created theology, they were active in the care of the poor and the sick, and they were managers and administrators of burial places.

So says Ute Eisen in the study *Women Officeholders in Early Christianity*.[297] The list is extensive, though repetitive. Two questions naturally arise: how early is early, and what hard evidence is there for the assertion that women ever presided at the Eucharist? It is clear, and agreed by all, that by the end of the fourth century the Church was already claiming the authority of the Apostle Paul to forbid celebrations by women. But is there hard and incontrovertible evidence for such eucharistic celebrations in the New Testament and the Apostolic period?

Despite the considerable efforts of Eisen (see above) and Karen Jo Torjesen (*When Women Were Priests*, New York, 1993), no indisputable evidence has been unearthed. The subordination of women which is part of the household teaching of Paul (Colossians 3.18ff.; Ephesians 5)[298] is extended to the household of faith particularly in its formal gatherings (1 Corinthians 14.35). There is no direct New Testament reference to the liturgical activity of women which does not condemn it. This, moreover, seems to have been determined in the Pauline communities, not by Graeco-Roman influence (as is sometimes claimed) but by Jewish precedent. Women were prophets (the precedent of Miriam herself ensured that continuing role); but they were not permitted to immolate the Paschal sacrifice or preside at the Paschal table (see Mishnah, *Pes.* 8.1 and 1 Corinthians 14.34: 'as even the law says').

'Paul's letters', says Torjesen, 'reflect an early Christian world in which women were well-known evangelists, apostles, leaders of congregations, and bearers of prophetic authority' (*When*

---

[297] Ute E. Eisen, *Women Officeholders in Early Christianity: Epigraphical and Literary Studies*, Liturgical Press, 2000.

[298] This is in line with current popular Stoic teaching, in which it is 'almost always the male adult freeman who is addressed as reader and instructed how he should behave in relation to women, children, and slaves. That women, children and slaves might also be able to do what is ethically "fitting" is hardly ever taken into account', says E. Schweizer, *Epistle to the Colossians*, Benziger, 1976, pp. 159ff.

Women Were Priests, New York, Harper Collins, 1993, p. 4) – which somewhat begs the question. Women have been most of those things continuously throughout the history of the Church. The assertion, however, that women celebrated the Eucharist (acting as *paterfamilias* in the *oikos* of faith – as Eisen claims) is quite another matter, and can only be made as a result of a number of doubtful inferences. For example, if Junia/s were a woman (see section 7.3 of the main report, above) and were s/he also an 'Apostle', it might also be inferred that s/he was a eucharistic celebrant. But that, as they say, is a long shot. The only account in Scripture of a eucharistic celebration is the event in Troas at which Paul was the celebrant and the liturgy of the word was interrupted by the unfortunate young man. In so far as such 'offices' can be identified in the New Testament and the apostolic age, there is, apart from the questionable Junia/s, no evidence whatever of women Apostles or bishops.

As part of the lively debate among feminist theologians as to whether Christianity is or is not a 'Good Thing' it is instructive to note deep divisions in assessing the early Christian period. Professors Karen Torjesen and Karen Armstrong (two doughty champions) are set against each other in a recent American book *Taking Sides: Clashing Views on Controversial Issues in World Civilizations* (McGraw-Hill, 1999):

> Professor of religion and associate of the Institute for Antiquity and Christianity, Karen Jo Torjesen, presents evidence of women deacons, priests, prophets, and bishops during the first millennium of Christianity – all roles that suggest both equality and liberation for women. Professor of religious studies Karen Armstrong finds in the early Christian Church examples of hostility toward women and fear of their sexual power which she contends led to the exclusion of women from full participation in a male-dominated church. (*Publisher's blurb*)

Beyond the Apostolic period there are the few pieces of inconclusive epigraphical evidence gathered by Professor Giorgio Otranto (in *Vetera Christianorum* 19 (1982), pp. 341–60) from the fourth and fifth centuries, and the very few other doubtful citations by Joan Morris in *Against God and Nature* (London, 1973, pp. 130–9).

Responding to this paucity of hard evidence, John Wijngaards (*No Women in Holy Orders?* (Canterbury Press, 2002), *The Ordination of Women in the Catholic Church: Unmasking a Cuckoo's Egg Tradition* (DLT, 2001)) has suggested that the reasons for an early discontinuance of female celebrations of the Lord's Supper were 'mainly the dominance of men and the fear of menstruation'.

Pressed further why these factors should have proved more significant in the third and fourth centuries than the first or second, Wijngaards appeals to the influence of Roman law, which firmly forbade women from holding any public office. This, he claims, was 'a principle that became part of Church law'. Bishop Christopher Hill has developed Wijngaards's thesis by pointing out that Roman secular law would only influence church law when celebrations of the Eucharist emerged from a domestic context into the public arena.

That is as it may be. But it will be granted that there is something rather topsy-turvy about a hypothesis intended to explain the demise of a practice for the existence of which there is no firm evidence.

One piece of alleged evidence, however, has provoked sustained interest and surfaced repeatedly. It demands special attention.

It is the claim that a fresco in the Capella Graeca of the Catacomb of Priscilla on the Via Salaria in Rome is a representation of a Eucharist celebrated by women.[299] The painting was first noted by Joan Morris (*Against God and Nature*), and was more recently referred to in a pamphlet by the Scottish Presbyterian theologian T. F. Torrance (*The Ministry of Women*, Edinburgh, 1992).[300]

---

[299] The fresco featured in a programme broadcast by the BBC on Sunday, 8 November 1992 (*Everyman: The Hidden Tradition*). The programme was made by Angela Tilby, who later became Vice-Principal of Westcott House, Cambridge.

[300] The fresco is in poor condition, and is deteriorating rapidly since the opening of the catacomb to public inspection. There is, however, a drawing made at the time of the discovery. Rather predictably, Dr Lavinia Byrne, echoing the conspiracy theory of Wijngaards, writes: '. . . when archaeologist Joseph Wilperts discovered this fresco in the nineteenth century he

Torrance seems to think (as does Morris) that the Catacomb of Priscilla has some connection with the wife of Aquila (Acts 18.1–3, 18–19; Romans 16.3–5; 1 Corinthians 16.19; 2 Timothy 4.19). Torrance even maintains that the fresco includes representations of Priscilla and her husband. Such is, of course, very far from probable. The catacomb itself dates from the end of the second century, and was excavated below a villa of the *gens Acilia*, fragments of which survive. It is not known when it received its present name, but a corruption of the original name of the property cannot be ruled out. The Capella Graeca is so-called on account of the Greek inscriptions over one of its niches, with dedications by a certain Obrinus (of whom nothing else is known), to his cousin and companion Palladius, and to his wife, Nestoriana. The fresco is dated by most authorities to the late third century.

The Capella Graeca painting is of seven figures seated at the opposite side of a table from the spectator. To either side, set on the ground, are six (or seven) containers, which appear to be either jars or baskets. Some may (or may not) contain bread. The condition of the fresco is poor, but it is certainly the case that at least one of the figures is female. The figure at the extreme left has arms extended and may (or may not) have a beard.

In one of the earliest [*sic*] catacomb paintings in Rome in the Capella Greca, within a century after the death and resurrection of Christ [*sic*], there is a remarkable mural depicting the breaking of bread at the celebration of the eucharist. Seven presbyters are seated in a semicircle behind the Holy Table, assisted by several deacons. This is known as the 'Catacomb of Priscilla', for Priscilla is seated to the right of the presiding presbyter (presumably her husband, Aquila, the *proestos* or

commissioned a watercolour reproduction of it. The artist who made a copy for the archives of the Pontifical Commission of Sacred Archaeology actually firmed up the evidence by adding manly thighs and a beard to the figure closest to us and made sure the others looked like real men – bar the veiled figure of the real/proper/natural woman.' Since Wilpert's drawing is the only evidence of the fresco in the condition in which it was found, Byrne simply cannot know this to be the case.

bishop), and is actively engaged with him in the eucharistic rite. (Torrance, *The Ministry of Women*, p. 1)

'. . . assisted', says Torrance, 'by several deacons'. It is a fatally compromising statement. For there are, and never were, any other figures in the painting apart from the seven at the table. Quite simply, Torrance was making extraordinary and specific claims about a painting he had never seen.

Mary Ann Rossi (who has written extensively on this and related subjects, and is the English translator of Professor Otranto) saw something else:

> It was most striking to me to realise that these were seven women sitting around the table. And it really strikes you when you see something you had not expected, and suddenly it is brought home. There is no doubt; I think you will agree when you have seen it, that they are seven women and not seven men . . . If you look at the shape of the people, these are not men. Women are not built the same! The presence, the aspect, the gestures! Ah, they seem to be self-assured, happy in their celebration. It's a look I have seen on the faces of women with whom I have been celebrating Mass in my country. It's a satisfaction, it's a happiness, it's a self-assured posture that I see in the seven women in the Priscilla painting. (Mary Ann Rossi, in *Everyman: The Hidden Tradition*)

Rossi's account, of course, is incompatible with Torrance's. The picture cannot, at one and the same time, represent seven concelebrating women and a mixed company (with deacons) in which a man (Aquila) and his wife (Priscilla) are concelebrating.

There are, however, further factors which render both readings of the picture improbable.

Torrance writes of a 'presiding presbyter . . . the *proestos* or bishop' (whom he identifies as 'presumably her husband Aquila') and of Priscilla (as he confidently claims) 'actively engaged with him in the eucharistic rite'. Rossi speaks of 'seven women concelebrating the eucharist'. But what precisely, in either case, is envisaged? Torrance's slippery phrase ('actively engaged with him in the eucharistic rite') goes to the heart of the problem.

Concelebration in the strict sense of a college of priests recit-ing the anaphora together is difficult to envisage at a time when the eucharistic prayer remained the extempore composition of the celebrant. 'Christian texts of this type', says Bouyer (meaning written prayers of thanksgiving at the Eucharist), 'become com-mon only after the great crisis of Arianism, i.e. after the second half of the fourth century' (*Eucharist*, Notre Dame University Press, 1968, p. 136) – which is to say: far beyond Torrance's incredible dating of the fresco to around AD 130, and well be-yond the generally agreed dating of around 290. The first firm evidence of concelebration in the modern sense relates to Papal masses in the seventh century. Not until the twelfth century (as St Thomas Aquinas attests) had it been exported from Rome and become common at ordinations elsewhere.[301]

A concelebration by seven women can, on these grounds alone, be ruled out. Nor is Torrance's husband-and-wife team any more probable. The hand gestures of the figures in the Cappella Grae-ca fresco are varied, random even. There does not seem to be any intention to exhibit a common liturgical posture, by which alone a shared celebration could be depicted.

The Capella Graeca picture, it must also be said, is not a stand-alone. There are four other similar frescoes in Roman catacombs of the period. These are conveniently to be found in black and white photographs in André Grabar's book *Christian Icono-graphy: A Study of its Origins* (London, 1969, plates 6–9).[302]

Grabar comments on them:

. . . in some cases the brevity [of the signs employed in cata-comb paintings] is certainly excessive, as when, for example, a scene that represents a meal of some kind has no detail that would distinguish between the Multiplication of Loaves, the Miracle of Cana, the Last Supper or the repast in paradise

---

[301] It is sometimes suggested that, in the immediately sub-apostolic period, 'concelebrating priests' stood beside their bishop raising their hands over the oblations in silence. But the evidence for such a practice is flimsy, and in any case it is not what is represented in the Capella Graeca. There the figures are clearly seated, and no common gesture defines them.

[302] The present author was involved in the television programme broad-cast on 8 November 1992 and lent a copy of the Grabar book to Tilby.

beyond the tomb. Those who planned the mural paintings in the catacombs were probably not entirely averse to a certain ambiguity in their image-signs, since the Multiplication of the Loaves, for example, was regarded as a symbol of the agape of paradise or a figuration of the Last Supper. (*Christian Iconography*, pp. 8–9)

While the exact significance of the Cappella Graeca fresco and its siblings may well remain a mystery, we can be sure that it is neither a representation of a eucharistic concelebration by women, nor a eucharistic snapshot of Priscilla and Aquila, those two dogged companions of St Paul.

From the evidence available to us one conclusion is inescapable: that if, peradventure, the Church ever did sanction the celebration of the Eucharist by women, it was a practice which, in the current parlance of the Church of England, was not 'received'.

4

Women as Members of 'Episcopal Teams'?

MARTIN WILLIAMS

What follows is as much an attempt to clarify my own mind as to contribute to a debate, which has yet to begin at all in Wales in any public way. I can only hope I have not missed the point entirely or indulged in dangerous or compromising fantasies – let alone be thought to be presuming to teach bishops their job!

'Team Episcopate': what would it mean? Would it serve the needs of the situation created by the ordination of women as bishops? If so, how would it work in practice? Can anything be learned from the (failed) proposal for an 'Ecumenical' bishop in Wales?

To address this question briefly first: it is ironical that a proposal which was intended to enlarge communion between previously divided Christians should be called in aid to suggest a model for Christians in impaired communion to move still further from unrestricted *communio in sacris*. Both situations, however – that of East Cardiff and that of the Church of England contemplating the ordination of women as bishops – demand an approach which will be both truthful and open to the creative power of the Spirit in maximizing the *potential* for communion and the eventual restoration of its full sacramental expression. In the words of the Apostolic Nuncio in his letter to Bishop Andrew Burnham of 6 November 2002: 'We must cultivate the spirituality of communion. We must incessantly feed the passion for unity.'[303]

It is arguable that the Welsh proposal failed because it began,

---

[303] See *New Directions* (January 2003), p. 6.

not from an agreed doctrine of the Church, nor from a common understanding and experience of what it is to be the Church, but from a desire to have a 'bishop' at all costs, as though this ministry was something to be superimposed on an existing organism. The proposal, in its final form, not surprisingly, suggested a 'bishop' who would indeed be a member of various 'teams' (local ministers, local church council, denominational committees, bishops' meetings, interdenominational structures), but would seem to lack either apostolic or local collegiality. He would be answerable, in the end, neither to the bishops who ordained him (he would not be a bishop of the Church in Wales), nor to the community which had asked for him, but to a bureaucratic body, the Enfys Commission, which was itself the creature of the Covenanted Churches.

Before trying to answer the question, 'What would be the meaning of the term "team bishop"?' it might be useful to set out what our expectations should be of the office of bishop *per se*.

1 It should serve God's purpose of communion, i.e. our common sharing in the divine life to be realized fully in his kingdom. Thus, at the 'horizontal' level, it serves 'the unity and peace of the holy churches of God'; at the 'vertical' or eschatological level, it holds before us the goal of communion, in his kingdom, with the triune God.

2 The Eucharist is not only the context of episcopal, as of all, ordination, but eucharistic presidency is the principal characteristic of episcopal office.

3 The bishop is the guardian of the deposit of faith and a 'walking sacrament' of the reality of the Incarnation. He may not be the most eloquent teacher of the faith in his community, but he should be prepared to 'banish erroneous and strange doctrines' and himself to refrain from promoting speculative ideas, however seemingly acceptable in current intellectual circles.

4 He should be a bishop-in-presbytery and a bishop-in-synod, that is to say, he will not act or teach apart from his college of presbyters, with whom his priestly solidarity will find regular expression in Chrism Eucharist, ordination and pastoral consultations. When the parish clergy meet with their bishop, they do so as representatives of the communities in which they

share the bishop's cure of souls and eucharistic presidency. (This is arguably more fundamental to a truly synodical church than the existence of *elected* lay representatives on diocesan synods.)

5 The bishop himself will be the 'face' or representative of the community for which he is ordained and at the same time a bishop of the universal Church in space and time. His solidarity with his departed predecessors in office is not, mercifully, affected by our unhappy divisions, but his collegiality with bishops elsewhere in this world will not only be restricted by schism but limited also by geographical, political and historical factors, such as the organization of the Anglican Churches in Britain and Ireland.

What might the term 'team bishop' mean in this context? There is presumably an analogy with team ministry at the parish level, where male and female presbyters form a ministerial team and seek to provide pastorally for congregations not all of which would accept the eucharistic presidency of a woman. A measure of unity can be maintained and diverse convictions be respected apart from those, of course, of militant feminizers. The team rector serves as the 'face' of this community, which he (or she?) would describe as rich in diversity rather than as simply divided. Would clergy regarding themselves as belonging to the college of priests of a Provincial Episcopal Visitor (PEV) or the Provincial Assistant Bishop (PAB) allow themselves to be members of such a team? (As far as I know there are no 'mixed' rectorial benefices in Wales which include clergy who relate to the PAB.) If so, episcopal ministrations in the parish have to be quite delicately organized, presumably. Indeed, a 'team episcopate' might enable such team ministries to exist where at present they do not. At present in Wales it could be argued that the PAB operates as a member of six episcopal 'teams', i.e. as Assistant Bishop in each diocese. (In many parishes he is regarded as the alternate of the Diocesan, or *vice versa*.) There are probably fewer parishes where he is the only episcopal president of the Eucharist or minister of confirmation. Credo Cymru, however, is clear that such a situation could not survive the ordination of women to the episcopate in Wales. A further degree of separation would be inevitable, unless, and this is the speculative drift of this paper, more traditionalist bishops were consecrated and mono-episcopal diocesan jurisdiction were abandoned.

How then would a team approach serve, if at all, the situation which would result from ordaining women as bishops? How might a 'team' episcopate meet the 'Five Tests' mentioned above, i.e. of serving the goal of Communion, of maintaining the Faith, of collegiality, and of maintaining and building Christian community?

1 An episcopate that is seen to be one rather than two manifests more adequately the communion of all the baptized in the mysteries of God, even if the stewards of those mysteries manifest some degree of impaired eucharistic communion.

2 The practice of non-communicating attendance at the Eucharist would have to be seen as a positive act of 'internal ecumenism' rather than as an act of protest or dissent. (There would be an inevitable separation of lines of succession were women to be ordained as bishops.)

3 Difficult as it is to see how an orthodox doctrine of the Incarnation can be implied in the ordination of women to the episcopate or presbyterate or in female presidency of the Eucharist, it is nevertheless arguable that an express desire to maintain orthodox faith and practice (e.g. as expressed in the Ordinal) should be respected, encouraged and supported by the close association in an episcopal team of traditionalist bishops.

4 How would a team of bishops relate to a college/colleges of priests? Either (a) all have to relate to all, even if they have to go their separate ways for Chrism Mass or ordination; or (b) traditionalist bishops would have to have their own college of priests, within the overall college, representing the parishes/communities of the episcopal area/diocese/province. The problem with (a) is the status of male priests ordained by female bishops.

5 Such an area/diocese/province will surely require a single, titular head. This could prove either an almost insuperable difficulty for such a scheme, or an opportunity to replace diocesan hegemony with a more collaborative model. The principal difficulty for traditionalists would arise if a woman became

the head of the team, but one cannot envisage an arrangement being acceptable to the other party which explicitly excluded women from the leadership of an episcopal team. The positive outcome would be that a 'diocesan' bishop would no longer have to have the same kind of control (or temptation to seek control) over what went on in the diocese/area without close collaboration with other bishops, who would not be his/her own appointees.

This means that an electoral/appointment system for all bishops would need to be devised which took account of the needs and desires of the local church rather than of the career ambitions of individual clergy – or their spouses! This would be an opportunity for bishops once again to become 'primarily leaders of communities' rather than 'having exclusive jurisdiction over a particular geographical area'.[304]

The communities of which a bishop would be leader would to a large extent be defined by their attitude to the ministry of women – for some, perhaps, a merely cultural, for others a theological issue. If traditionalist bishops were included in local teams, they would also inevitably (and rightly) form a network of what might be called a 'traditionalist rite' (where the matter of ordination is concerned). Such a network would have its separate identity for the purpose of ordination – of bishops, priests and deacons – while its bureaucratic structures would be minimal. The existing logistical infrastructure of the Church of England and of the Church in Wales may be crumbling somewhat, but some such structures are needed and a slimmed-down version of what we have, preferably less centralized, is probably preferable (and cheaper) than trying to reinvent it all. There are also strong historic and cultural ties to particular areas and centres, such as the ancient sees of England and Wales, which point to groupings of dioceses, each to be served by, say, five or six bishops, being the norm.

In Wales we might envisage a 'provincial' structure, with six or seven team bishops, including at least two traditionalists, working from 'diocesan' centres, as at present, but without

---

[304] William R. Crockett, in *Theology Wales* NS 1 (July 2002).

diocesan boundaries in any absolute sense. The senior bishop might have the title 'Archbishop of Wales' but there would need to be canonical recognition of the fact that he/she (?) did not preside at the ordination of a traditionalist bishop, but would request the senior bishop of the traditional bishops' conference to ordain Fr X for whatever see. Such a model might be adapted to comparable groupings of dioceses in the Church of England. Such an arrangement would obviously entail a large practical and legislative upheaval, but it would arguably be more practical and more charitable than to seek to divide the assets of the Church and set up two parallel jurisdictions.[305] It would mean traditionalist bishops being fully involved in the administrative life of the local church (which they may or may not welcome!), while playing a full part in the development of its eucharistic communities, including the nomination of clergy to parishes and the placing of deacons. The greatest upheaval, of course, would be in our whole experience of being the Church. It could be extraordinarily fruitful, although forced on us by a development which we ourselves would never have wished for. Whatever happens, we should also want to safeguard the possibility of the restoration of communion between traditionalist Anglicans and the Sees of Rome and Constantinople. We would want to be assured that any 'team episcopate' we entered into was recognizable by them as continuous, in intention, with the episcopate of the universal Church.

In such a scheme there would be two 'rites' or 'integrities', but only one administrative structure. At the inauguration of such a scheme, the clergy and the eucharistic communities over which they preside would need to opt for one or other rite and be assigned to the leadership of the appropriate team bishop. But, whereas, in the proposal for a free province, there would be a complete synodical separation and 'traditionalist' and 'modernist' provinces would grow apart, in this proposal there would be the opportunity to stay together, but with the clear understanding and *trust* that neither rite would seek to impose its will on the other. As an ecumenical bonus in such a scheme,

---

[305] This was written before I had seen Fr Geoffrey Kirk's article, 'A Pertinent Preposition', in the January 2003 edition of *New Directions*.

the local Roman Catholic bishop(s) would be invited to join the team, thus creating a third rite within each episcopal team. It may be thought that the internal divisions in Anglicanism and our mutual distrust now run so deep that separation rather than collaborative teams will be inevitable. There would certainly need to be further work done on the legitimacy from the canonical/ecumenical viewpoint of abandoning monoepiscopal diocesan jurisdiction, but such an abandonment does have its attractions, both for traditionalist Anglicans in the present climate and, of course, for those Christian communities, both Catholic and Protestant, who in the past have suffered most at the hands of the state church.

5

The London Plan
An Experiment in Episcopal Care

JOHN BROADHURST

Dr David Hope devised 'The London Plan' while he was still the bishop of that diocese. The final text, issued in May 1993, stated that 'The Bishop of Fulham would assume a non-geographical jurisdiction.' The term 'Fulham jurisdiction' is used many times.

The plan was a precursor to the Act of Synod. It was presented to the London diocese before the Manchester Bishops' meeting, which devised the Act of Synod. It was originally signed on 24 February 1994. The signatories were the diocesan bishop, the area bishops, the Bishop of Fulham and the Archbishop of Canterbury together with the diocesan and provincial registrars.

The scheme has been changed slightly since the original drafting, but it grants to the Bishop of Fulham considerably more than is granted by the Act of Synod.

> The Bishop of Fulham as of right shall be entitled to visit and enter those parishes and be responsible for confirmations, ordinations, presentation, institutions, licensings and permissions to officiate and the selection of candidates for ordination and such other Episcopal duties as shall be assigned to him by the ordinary.

In practice the Bishop of Fulham functions as the area bishop in petitioning parishes. In those parishes the duties of the ordinary are exercised by him. This arrangement is not without its complications, since many of the duties of the ordinary are already delegated to area bishops.

Because the London Plan is an agreement between six bishops, the original deeds stated that the declaration was intended to bind successors in title until rescinded by the Bishop of London and a majority of the suffragan bishops. In consequence the deed is redrafted and re-signed every time that there is a new episcopal appointment in the diocese. There has been some diminution of the original intent. The term 'Fulham Jurisdiction' appeared in the diocesan handbook and elsewhere. It has now been removed.

Other agreements have been signed between the Bishop of London and the Bishops of Southwark and Rochester. These deeds are contracts involving the Bishop of Fulham, who functions as a 'regional arrangement' under the Act of Synod in those dioceses. He is, however, a full member of the staff meetings of both dioceses and regularly attends them. He is also a member of the relevant diocesan synods, and participates fully in the life of those dioceses. In practice the situation in the two dioceses is rather different.

Rochester has been quite generous in the provision of title posts for new deacons, and there are two 'C' training parishes under the Bishop of Fulham's care. He has ordained both deacons and priests in the diocese. However, in this diocese, the Bishop of Fulham is only permitted to confirm in and for the petitioning parishes.

In Southwark, the Bishop of Fulham has a much wider ministry. Indeed he goes to three parishes regularly to confirm, even though these parishes have never petitioned under the Act of Synod. In Southwark, however, since 1995 there has not been a single title post for a new deacon. Only one candidate for ordination training has been sponsored.

In practice, the two dioceses work very differently. The Bishop of Fulham works with three diocesans and eight suffragans (seven of whom are area bishops) and in practice the relationships vary from bishop to bishop. The implications for local parishes are considerable.

What has developed in the Fulham Jurisdiction is a strong sense of ecclesial identity among clergy and laity and a real mutual commitment. The clergy meet regularly and support each other. The truth is that these parishes have developed a good common life and sense of mission. Because, in Rochester and Southwark, the Bishop of Fulham is a commissary for the diocesan bishop, *de jure* when he appears in a parish he appears as the diocesan bishop, in the same way that an ambassador appears for the monarch. Theologically and intellectually this could reflect a schizophrenic theology. Effectively, however, the Bishop of Fulham (and indeed a PEV) presents, as one might say, the orthodox face of a diocesan bishop whom many of the parishes consider to be heterodox. There are difficult problems for such a bishop in terms of communion and sacramental relationships within the diocese.

The present Bishop of Rochester is quite clear that if there is no impairment of communion between him and the Bishop of Fulham then there is absolutely no sense in parishes petitioning for extended episcopal care. The Bishop of Southwark, and some of the London suffragans, seem to find any impairment of communion very difficult. The problem here is that episcopacy is made to depend upon personal recognition. Bishops are properly bishops of the whole Church. Their relationship with each other should be mutual, equal and open. In reality, however, the relationships between the Bishop of Fulham and many of those with whom he works are lopsided. They work differently in one direction than the other, and this poses serious problems.

Has the Bishop of Fulham jurisdiction? Several of the bishops concerned have argued strongly that he has none. Though the 'Fulham Jurisdiction' has been removed from the London handbook, many of the legal deeds and documents for inductions, licensings and ordinations, in all three dioceses, still contain nonetheless the words 'within my Jurisdiction'. What does this imply?

In what sense is the Bishop of Fulham 'The Bishop'? Though he has varied jurisdiction, the clergy pray for him at Mass – either 'John our Bishop', or 'X Bishop of Y and John our Bishop'. He ordains and confirms for these parishes, and the clergy gather with him for the celebration of the Chrism Mass. He exercises *episcope* pastorally, sacramentally and didactically. The same is true of the PEVs, though they do not have the limited juridical *episcope*.

6

The Work of Provincial Episcopal Visitors

ANDREW BURNHAM

Provincial Episcopal Visitors (PEVs) were invented to offer 'extended episcopal care' under the terms of the Episcopal Ministry Act of Synod 1993, and the first were consecrated in 1994. A decade later they have an established, though not un-controversial, place in the life of the Church of England. Despite the extraordinary ability of ecclesiastical institutions and mechan-isms to outlive their usefulness, it is entirely unclear whether there will be such a thing as a PEV in 2024, or indeed 2014. It follows that this account, written in the first few years of the first decade of the twenty-first century, may soon enough be describing a quaint provision, a transitional phase, rapidly super-seded, in the process of ceasing to discriminate against women in ordained ministry. Meanwhile, as suffragan bishops of the metropolitan, PEVs extend their episcopal care in cooperation with diocesan bishops, whose episcopal care they also extend. Their main concern is for parishes which have successfully peti-tioned for 'extended episcopal care', for whom they perform what the Act of Synod calls 'appropriate duties', provided, that is, that the diocesan bishop has opted to make use of them. Where the diocesan bishop has opted instead to make 'diocesan' or 'regional', as against 'provincial', arrangements, the PEV none-theless has the background task which is his throughout the province, or the part of the province allocated to him. This task is to be ombudsman for all those within the province – whether resolutions under the Priests (Ordination of Women) Measure 1994 are in place or not – who have been uneasy about, or have had cause to complain about, the working of the Measure or the Act of Synod.

PEVs and impairment of communion

A frequent complaint against the PEV system has been that it is ecclesiologically illogical. It is not hard to see that if X is in communion with Y and Y is in communion with Z, X ought to be in communion with Z. If X is the diocesan bishop, Y is the PEV and Z is the congregation of a petitioning parish, it seems odd that, if Y will receive communion from X, and Z will receive communion from Y, Z – the petitioning parish – will not receive communion from X, the diocesan bishop. And yet communion is not a mathematical formula but an ecclesiological and spiritual relationship. Impairment of communion means that X, Y and Z are not out of communion with each other but are in 'impaired communion' with each other. There are circumstances, that is to say, when they are not able to be in full communion. Nor is impairment a very clear concept. There are different views and different approaches: different 'sticking points'.

We are not in entirely uncharted territory. In the Orthodox world there have been examples of 'mediate communion', such as existed between Constantinople and Bulgaria in the period 1872–1945. The churches were in impaired but not broken communion, in that each remained in full communion with the other Orthodox churches and patriarchates. Parallel jurisdictions have also been a feature of Christendom – four Patriarchs of Antioch simultaneously, for example – and in that land of much immigration, the United States of America, ethnic groups have continued to look to different hierarchies. Within the Roman obedience there have been different ritual churches – chiefly the Roman Rite and the Byzantine Rite – and, while impairment of communion is not the most helpful description, there have been limits placed on communion. Though the laity have been entitled to receive communion in either rite, presbyters have not been allowed to act in other ritual churches.

Anglicans have no doubt prided themselves on avoiding such complexities in the past, though the holding together of 'high', 'latitudinarian' and 'low' around the British Crown, the Book of Common Prayer, the 1662 Ordinal and the 39 Articles has sometimes concealed actual impairment of communion. The Kensitites and the Tractarians did not frequent each other's sacraments and what they gathered round separately would be, in one case, a table, and in the other, an altar. Fault-lines change and, amidst the fracture and uncertainty caused by the ordination of women, the advantage of the PEV system is that it restores something like the notion of sacramental objectivity, particularly amidst a whirlpool of unreliable emotions. PEVs as a matter of course receive Communion from bishops who belong to an all-male college of bishops. Petitioning parishes as a matter of course receive Communion from PEVs. Thus, it could be argued, PEVs are a means of integration, of keeping a fragmenting church together. Similar glue is provided by the laity, many of whom are content to receive Holy Communion from a variety of tables and altars, within and beyond the Church of England, often showing not the least inquisitiveness about whose Orders are whose.

The ecclesiology of the PEV system

One problem of the PEV system is that it does not come with its own already defined ecclesiology. A second problem, as remarked earlier, is that it is not hard to see that the PEV system itself could be easily overfaced by ecclesiological developments. This paper is an attempt to see how, first, the PEV system could evolve its own ecclesiology – *ex post facto*, admittedly, but that is sometimes a bearable consequence of pragmatism – and, second, whether conceivably it could be strengthened to cope with ecclesiological developments. Put bluntly, is there an intelligible and workable ecclesiology that would allow those unconvinced by the appropriateness of ordaining women priests and bishops, in some sense, to remain within the Anglican fellowship?

An early difficulty in examining the ecclesiology of the PEV system is that each of the three PEVs – the PEV for the Northern Province and the PEVs for the Southern Province – has a different job. The Northern PEV – the Bishop of Beverley – is the only PEV in his province, a province which includes 'diocesan' and 'regional' as well as 'provincial' arrangements under the Act of Synod. His area has included more than one diocese where the diocesan bishop himself does not ordain women to the priesthood. Successive Bishops of Beverley have worked – at least hitherto – with successive Archbishops of York who themselves have not ordained women to the priesthood.

The Southern PEVs work for an archbishop who himself does ordain women priests. One of the Southern PEVs – the Bishop of Richborough – has 'diocesan' and 'regional' as well as 'provincial' arrangements within his area. His area includes more than one diocese where the diocesan himself does not ordain women priests. The other Southern PEV – the Bishop of Ebbsfleet (the writer) – works in thirteen dioceses, all of which at present make a 'provincial' arrangement and none of which at prensent has another stipendiary bishop in the diocese who will not ordain women priests. He calls his area an 'apostolic district', a concept to which we shall return.

What the Church of England means by PEVs

Part of the ecclesiology of PEVs is explained by an outworking of what the Church of England would have them do – and that can be expressed by two phrases from the House of Bishops document *Bonds of Peace* (1994), 'extended episcopal care' and 'appropriate duties'. The Blackburn Report (2000), not endorsed by the House of Bishops, nor even 'taken note of' by the General Synod, recommended that PEVs were made assistant bishops in all the dioceses they covered.[306] The presumption of the Church of England bishops, then, would be that PEVs were in full communion with them but, because PEVs neither ordained nor received communion from women priests, they would be acceptable to 'traditionalists' as a 'safe pair of hands'.

Some of this understanding derived from a notion of 'taint' – an idea first mooted, it seems, by the then Archbishop of York, John Habgood, to whom must go the credit for the Act of Synod

---

[306] In Wales, 'the Provincial Assistant Bishop', as he is known, is by contrast a suffragan of all the Welsh dioceses. He was consecrated in 1996 for the task analogous to that of the English PEVs.

settlement and its early outworking. This was in spite of the fact that 'taint' had never been proposed as an argument by those leading the opposition to women priests. 'Taint' works something like this. Women 'taint' the sacraments and make them unsafe for men, especially men who are misogynists. At the deepest level, it is alleged, there may even be a muddle between menstrual blood and the blood of the Eucharist. Thus, the argument goes, PEVs act as a barrier against 'taint'. They at least have never had anything to do with women priests. 'Traditionalists' insulate themselves against 'taint' by a series of protocols that distance them from the problem, much as, for instance, 'travellers' have their own complicated cultural codes of purity and Orthodox Jews seek what is *kosher*.

Perhaps one cannot say that the notion of 'taint' is entirely wrong-headed. For instance, the symbolism associated with women and blood (childbirth) is very different from the symbolism associated with men and blood (battle). Is a woman priest standing at the altar and performing a ceremonial action with body and blood incontrovertibly miming the sacrificial death of the God-Man on Calvary?[307] Or might she not be miming the incarnation of a god, born from the womb of a god who is beyond gender or from a liaison with a sporting Zeus? What would an anthropologist, a visitor from Mars, without understanding of the rite, make of the ceremony? 'Taint' need not be fear of menstruation. It may be fear of a fatal muddle of symbol. The point is not that there are no women martyrs – far from it – but that martyrs of both sexes have usually been the victims of violent males, as was Jesus on the Cross.

What 'traditionalists' think about PEVs

Though the Church of England's own explanation of what it is doing by providing PEVs is undoubtedly germane, it does not do justice to what the 'traditionalists' themselves think about PEVs.

---

[307] It has been pointed out that this is very much a Western or Latin slant on what the priest in Christ symbolizes at the altar. A more Eastern view would be that at the altar the priest in Christ prays to the Father for the gift of the Spirit to come upon the worshippers and the elements.

'Taint' – as charged – is not a notion that 'traditionalists' accept. In their view, there are two categories of presbyters: those who are ordained within the Catholic understanding of priesthood and those who are not. It is important not to muddle up these categories. The first category includes all who have been duly ordained by a bishop in the apostolic succession. The second category includes those who cannot be 'duly' ordained – women, for instance – and those who have not been ordained by a bishop in the apostolic succession – Presbyterians, for instance. 'Traditionalists' would be as unhappy, intellectually, about receiving the sacraments from a Free Church minister as they would from an Anglican woman priest. The principle, quite simply, is the objectivity and certainty of Catholic sacraments. Yet it would be a bold man who would assert that neither a Free Church Eucharist nor the Eucharist of a woman priest conveys sacramental grace. 'The wind bloweth where it listeth . . .' But the Catholic would say with complete confidence that neither ordinance is a covenanted Catholic sacrament and, of course, many Anglicans have become Roman Catholic or Orthodox simply on the principle of the necessity of the objectivity and certainty of sacraments.

There is a mis-remembering of recent history. Many who now look to PEVs see them as the device which Cost of Conscience and Forward in Faith sought in the early 1990s. In truth the demand was for 'alternative episcopal oversight' and not 'extended episcopal care' and for bishops chosen by 'traditionalists' and episcopally ordained outside the normal Church of England framework of metropolitan consecrations. The provision of PEVs was initially problematic. These were men chosen by the Church of England and consecrated – in the South at least – by an archbishop who himself had ordained women priests. Only the Bishops of Beverley – consecrated by archbishops and bishops, none of whom had yet ordained women priests[308] – have been ordained before the ecclesiological rupture.

In fact the PEVs have been accepted, indeed been lionized –

---

[308] Both Bishops of Beverley in modern times were consecrated bishop in 1994. The first was consecrated for the See of Beverley. The second was consecrated for the See of Burnley and was translated to Beverley in 2000.

in more senses than one. The words 'alternative' and 'oversight' creep into people's discourse and are found, anyway, in the report of the Eames Commission. They are in much need of rehabilitation: 'alternative', after all, is how the Worship and Doctrine Measure describes services which are alongside but not subverting of the Book of Common Prayer; 'oversight' is the quintessential episcopal task. As it is, the Church of England speaks of the PEVs as providing 'extended episcopal care' and those in receipt of this 'care' regularly speak of the PEVs as providing 'alternative episcopal oversight'. The experience of PEVs is that some mean by 'alternative episcopal oversight' that the PEV is the 'Father in God' (to be prayed for as such in the Canon of the Mass) while the diocesan, as the joke goes, is the 'Father in Law'. Others – amidst a range of other emphases – mean that the PEV is the bishop who can be relied upon to celebrate 'with full Catholic privileges' while the diocesan remains the real bishop. Nothing new here: those who are old enough will remember Anglo-Catholic parishes which saved up their confirmations for colonial bishops on furlough. Bishop F. R. Barry (Southwell 1941–64), asked what he was going to do about a priest who celebrated the Sunday Mass in Latin, reputedly said, 'Let him die', thus demonstrating that episcopal oversight is a subtle affair or perhaps has more than one meaning.

There is indeed sometimes an ecclesiologically curious split between sacraments and pastoral care, on the one hand, and jurisdiction, on the other, and sometimes a no less ecclesiologically curious split between sacramental celebration, on the one hand, and pastoral and jurisdictional concerns on the other.

Episcopal vicars

So far there is clearly a victory of Anglican pragmatism over Catholic sacramental theology. Anglican pragmatism, as ever, is infuriating but effective. The principles of Catholic sacramental theology remain largely unavailable to Anglicans who, after all, cannot agree on how many sacraments there are, let alone whether baptism is truly regenerative or whether Christ is substantially present in the eucharistic elements. That is not to say, however, that there have not been efforts to introduce coherence to the PEV notion.

There are some Roman Catholic models for 'flying bishops'. Since there are quite frequent ecclesiological assaults on the notion of PEVs, there is something to be said for looking at Roman Catholic precedents to see if, indeed, the idea of PEVs is ecclesiologically defensible. After all, Anglicans and Roman Catholics share a good deal of the Western Canon Law tradition.

One Roman Catholic precedent is the non-episcopal convention of an 'episcopal vicar'.

Canon 476   As often as the good governance of the diocese requires it, the diocesan Bishop can also appoint one or more episcopal Vicars. These have the same ordinary power as the universal law gives to a Vicar general, in accordance with the following canons. The competence of an episcopal Vicar, however, is limited to a determined part of the diocese, or to a specific type of activity, or to the faithful of a particular rite, or to certain groups of people.

Certainly one of the understandings of PEVs – assistants who confirm and ordain but have no jurisdiction of their own – is not so very different from that of the 'episcopal vicar', a priest who assists the bishop run his diocese. The 'episcopal vicar' of, say, one of the counties that make up the Roman Catholic Archdiocese of Birmingham, will not ordain, but many of his other tasks are episcopal and he will confirm with the bishop's chrism. In my view, the earliest PEVs were viewed, by the Church of England, very much as 'episcopal vicars', though, of course, with much less jurisdictional power than 'episcopal vicars'. The first two PEVs[309] were experienced archdeacons, 60 or 61 years of age when they were consecrated, and it was the constituency not the Church of England that developed the job description well beyond that of an 'episcopal vicar'. But let us call Stage One the 'episcopal vicar' stage.

---

[309] The Bishop of Beverley and the Bishop of Ebbsfleet.

Personal prelatures

Well within the ministry of the first PEVs there were experiments
with what might be called the 'personal prelature' model, cham-
pioned by the first Bishop of Richborough. By the time of his
consecration (1995)[310] the argument was moving on. Some of the
relevant 'personal prelature' canons are as follows:

Canon 294   Personal prelatures may be established by the
Apostolic See after consultation with the Episcopal Conferences concerned. They are composed of deacons and priests of
the secular clergy. Their purpose is to promote an appropriate
distribution of priests, or to carry out special pastoral or mis-
sionary enterprises in different regions or for different social
groups.

Canon 295   A personal prelature is governed by statutes laid
down by the Apostolic See. It is presided over by a Prelate as its
proper Ordinary. He has the right to establish a national or an
international seminary, and to incardinate students and promote them to orders with the title of service of the prelature.

Canon 296   Lay people can dedicate themselves to the apostolic work of a personal prelature by way of agreements made
with the prelature. The manner . . . and the principal obligations . . . are to be duly defined in the statutes.

Here, then, is an 'ecclesiola' – a church in miniature – with
the Holy See in place, a prelate as ordinary, priests, deacons,
ordinands and lay people. The concept fitted the circumstances
of a breakaway Anglican group in the United States, reconciled
with the Holy See, and it might have fitted – might yet fit – a
residual Anglican group in the United Kingdom, reconciled with
the Holy See and fulfilling the venerable Anglican vocation of
forming a bridge between Catholic and Reformed communions.
'Personal prelature' has most recently (January 2002) fitted the

---

[310] The first Bishop of Richborough was also 60 when he was consecrated.

circumstances of a group of Roman Catholic 'traditionalists' in Brazil, for whom the Pope has appointed a bishop – a 'flying bishop', so to say.

Anglicanism is more relentlessly territorial in a Nicaean kind of way than the modern Roman Catholic Church, with its overlapping Eastern and Western Rites and 'personal prelatures', and no-one has yet conceded that there may be overlapping Anglican jurisdictions in England. We get close with the Bishop to the Armed Forces and the Bishop to the Prisons, not to mention the 'Royal Peculiars'. There are overlapping Anglican jurisdictions in Europe – the Bishop of Gibraltar-in-Europe and his ECUSA counterpart – and 'the Porvoo Communion' means that there are overlapping jurisdictions in Scandinavia.

There are two further problems with the 'personal prelature' notion as applied to PEVs and those who look to them. One is whether a 'personal prelature' can be separated from a relationship with the Holy See. In answer to the first, it is arguable that, in Anglican ecclesiology, the 'Royal Peculiars' have the same kind of direct relationship with the Crown that Roman Catholic 'personal prelatures' have with the Pope. The irony of this may well have escaped the Very Revd Wesley Carr, Dean of Westminster, no friend of the PEV structure,[311] or the various university college chaplains whose appointments also flourish under one extra-diocesan anomaly or another. Whether the irony is also lost on the Dean of Windsor, Bishop to the Armed Forces – arguably another 'prelature' – as well as one of Her Majesty's Domestic Prelates, is not clear. It may be that the Church of England, embarrassed by its Erastian shackles, would prefer not to have invented a new 'Peculiar'.

The second is whether a new 'personal prelature' is possible that is not in some sense 'a new religious movement'. This is a more telling objection. Anglo-Catholic 'traditionalists' do not see themselves as some sort of para-church – a Neo-Catechumenate or an Opus Dei – but as an authentic and well-anchored remnant within a larger church that is dangerously adrift from its moorings.

---

[311] In a public lecture in 2001 the Dean of Westminster attacked PEVs as an ecclesiological innovation.

Apostolic administrations

Undoubtedly the argument moves on as we see the work of the PEV developing. The third Bishop of Ebbsfleet,[312] the writer, inherited what the notepaper called 'The See of Ebbsfleet'. Here were the beginnings of strategic thinking about what would be needed if a jurisdiction were to evolve, as it certainly would if the ambitions of the supporters of women bishops or the rhetoric of Forward in Faith came to anything. The third Bishop of Ebbsfleet judged that a coherent 'See of Ebbsfleet' – provision for the 'traditionalists' from 13 contingent dioceses in the Southern Province – was not a diocese, nor indeed was it a jurisdiction. Yet it had some of the characteristics of what, for Roman Catholics in England before nineteenth-century Catholic Emancipation and the refounding of the Catholic hierarchy in England, was called an 'apostolic district'. Such a district – before Emancipation – would in law lack true jurisdiction (however much it was thought to have by its supporters) and – before the refounding of the hierarchy – would certainly not be a diocese. Indeed the shape of eventual dioceses and of the previous apostolic district would not need to be identical.

Such an 'apostolic district' is nowadays called by the Code of Canon Law an 'apostolic administration'. 'Apostolic administrations' were what the Rman Catholic dioceses in Russia were known as, before, notoriously, they were re-designated by the Vatican as 'dioceses', very early in the twenty-first century.[313]

> **Canon 371 ¶2**   An apostolic administration is a certain portion of the people of God which, for special and particularly serious reasons, is not yet established by the Supreme Pontiff as a diocese, and whose pastoral care is entrusted to an apostolic Administrator, who governs it in the name of the Supreme Pontiff.

---

[312] The second Bishop of Ebbsfleet, Michael Houghton, died in December 1999 after only a year in office.

[313] Notoriously because the Russian Orthodox viewed these new dioceses as an incursion upon its canonical territory.

Canon 372 ¶1 If however, in the judgment of the supreme authority in the Church, after consultation with the Episcopal Conferences concerned, it is thought to be helpful, there may be established in a given territory particular Churches distinguished by the rite of the faithful or by some other similar quality.

'Special and particularly serious reasons' certainly resonates with the ecclesiological difficulties of the Church of England in the 1990s. 'Particular Churches distinguished by the rite of the faithful or by some other similar quality' would not be the tendency for inner-urban use of the Roman Rite in Anglo-Catholic churches so much as the consistent orthodox theological position and remarkably uniform orthopraxis of congregations looking to the PEV for 'extended episcopal care'.

To call the 'sees' of the PEVs dioceses-in-waiting may be to overstate the case. The Church of England is committed to the process of 'reception' of the doctrine of women's ordination. Unless that means (as some think) 'waiting till people get used to the idea' or (as others think) an eschatological state for which we shall wait as long as we wait for the beating of swords into ploughshares, the point will come when PEVs will no longer be needed. 'Traditionalists' will see that they were sadly misguided or the Church of England will see the folly of the innovation of women's ordination. This all becomes more problematic with the ordination of women to the episcopate. At that point the 'sees' of the PEVs must become more like dioceses and the corporate life of 'traditionalists' more like that of a province of dioceses if there is to continue to be 'an honoured place' in the Church of England for 'traditionalists'. By then 'Episcopal Vicars' will have evolved into 'Apostolic Administrators' and the Church of England, with a new regional system of administration, replacing much of the present administrative structure of dioceses, will be content for these 'apostolic administrations' to be known as 'dioceses'.

Appendix 1

Membership of the Theological Working Party

The Reverend Jonathan Baker, MA, M.Phil.
Principal of Pusey House, Oxford

The Right Reverend John Broadhurst, DD, AKC, S.Th.
Bishop of Fulham

The Right Reverend Andrew Burnham, MA
Bishop of Ebbsfleet

The Reverend John Hunwicke, MA
sometime Head of Theology, Lancing College

The Reverend Dr Geoffrey Kirk, BA
Vicar of St Stephen and St Mark, Lewisham, Diocese of Southwark

Mrs Sara Low
Editor, *New Directions*

The Reverend Prebendary Sam Philpott
Vicar of St Peter, Plymouth; Priest in Charge of St Thomas, Keyham; Chairman of the House of Clergy, Diocese of Exeter (Convenor)

Ecumenical observers

Fr Aidan Nichols, OP
Prior, Dominican Priory of St Michael, Cambridge
(nominated by His Eminence the Cardinal Archbishop of Westminster)

The Right Reverend Bishop Kallistos of Diokleia
Assistant Bishop, Orthodox Archdiocese of Thyateira and Great Britain
(nominated by His Eminence Archbishop Gregorios of Thyateira and Great Britain)

In attendance

Dr Brian Hanson CBE, DCL, LL M, Solicitor and Ecclesiastical Notary
sometime Registrar and Legal Adviser to the General Synod of the Church of England; Chairman of the House of Laity, Diocese of Chichester (Legal Assessor)

Mr Stephen Parkinson
Director of Forward in Faith

Assessors to the Theological Working Party

Mr Oswald Clark, CBE, BA, BD, LL M
sometime Chairman of the House of Laity, General Synod of the Church of England

Dr Mary Tanner
sometime Secretary of the Council for Christian Unity

Those who gave evidence to the Theological Working Party

The Most Reverend the Archbishop of York

The Right Reverend the Bishop of Chichester

The Right Reverend the Bishop of Beverley

The Right Reverend the Bishop of Edmonton

The Right Reverend the Bishop of Horsham

The Right Reverend the Bishop of Lewes

The Right Reverend the Bishop of Pontefract

The Right Reverend the Bishop of Richborough

The Right Reverend the Bishop of Whitby

The Reverend Prebendary David Houlding
Vicar of St Stephen with All Hallows, Hampstead, Diocese of London; Chairman, Catholic Group in General Synod

The Reverend Canon Arthur Middleton
sometime Acting Principal, St Chad's College, Durham

The Reverend John Richardson
Senior Assistant Minister, United Benefice of Henham, Elsenham and Ugley, Diocese of Chelmsford

The Venerable Martin Williams
Archdeacon of Morgannwg, Diocese of Llandaff

Membership of the Legal Working Party

The Reverend Paul J. Benfield, LL B, B.Th., of Lincoln's Inn, Barrister
Vicar of St Nicholas, Fleetwood, Diocese of Blackburn

The Reverend Canon Beaumont L. Brandie, BD, AKC
Team Rector of the Parish of the Resurrection, Brighton, Diocese of Chichester (Convenor)

Dr Brian Hanson CBE, DCL, LL M, Solicitor and Ecclesiastical Notary
sometime Registrar and Legal Adviser to the General Synod of the Church of England; Chairman of the House of Laity, Diocese of Chichester

The Reverend James Patrick, LL B, of the Inner Temple, Barrister
Honorary Assistant Curate of All Saints with St John, Clifton, Diocese of Bristol

Mr Clifford Payton, BCL, MA, of the Inner Temple, Barrister
Churchwarden of the Parish of St Giles in Reading, Diocese of Oxford

The Reverend Jonathan Redvers Harris, LL B, LL M, Solicitor
Vicar of All Saints, Ryde, Diocese of Portsmouth

In attendance

Mr Stephen Parkinson
Director of Forward in Faith

Assessors to the Legal Working Party

Mr Oswald Clark, CBE, BA, LL M
sometime Chairman of the House of Laity, General Synod of the Church of England

The Reverend Robin Ellis, BCL, MA
sometime Archdeacon of Plymouth

Appendix 2

Forward in Faith's Submission to the Rochester Commission on the Theology of the Ordination of Women to the Episcopate

Take heed then to have but one Eucharist. For there is but one flesh of our Lord Jesus Christ and one cup to show forth the unity of his blood; one altar; as there is one bishop, along with the presbytery and deacons my fellow servants: so that whatever you do you may do according to the will of God.

(Ignatius, *To the Philadelphians* 4)

A   Premises

A1 It is in the nature of Orders in the Church that they are equivalent and interchangeable – that is to say that they are received and respected everywhere and by all. The Church of England expresses this understanding in its Canon A4:

> A4 Of THE FORM AND MANNER OF MAK- ING, ORDAINING, AND CONSECRATING OF BISHOPS, PRIESTS, AND DEACONS
>
> The Form and Manner of Making, Ordaining, and Con- secrating of Bishops, Priests, and Deacons, annexed to the Book of Common Prayer and commonly known as the Ordinal, is not repugnant to the Word of God; and those who are so made, ordained, or consecrated bishops, priests, or deacons, according to the said Ordinal, are lawfully made, ordained, or consecrated, and ought to

be accounted, both by themselves and others, to be truly bishops, priests, or deacons.

A2 This mutuality of Orders derives from the role of the diocesan bishop as fount of Orders and focus of unity in the diocese (and we would add, between dioceses – though this notion, always implicit in the Church of England's synodical structures, is less clearly expressed in its formularies). The Church of England expresses this understanding in its Canon C18:

C18   Of DIOCESAN BISHOPS

1.   Every bishop is the chief pastor of all that are within his diocese, as well laity as clergy, and their father in God; it appertains to his office to teach and to uphold sound and wholesome doctrine, and to banish and drive away all erroneous and strange opinions; and, himself an example of righteous and godly living, it is his duty to set forward and maintain quietness, love, and peace among all men . . .

4.   Every bishop is, within his diocese, the principal minister, and to him belongs the right, save in places and over persons exempt by law or custom, of celebrating the rites of ordination and confirmation; of conducting, ordering, controlling, and authorising all services in churches, chapels, churchyards and consecrated burial grounds; of granting a faculty or licence for all alterations, additions, removals, or repairs to the walls, fabric, ornaments, or furniture of the same; of consecrating new churches, churchyards, and burial grounds; of instituting to all vacant benefices, whether of his own collation or of the presentation of others; of admitting by licence to all other vacant ecclesiastical offices; of holding visitations at times limited by law or custom to the end that he may get some good knowledge of the state, sufficiency, and ability of the clergy and other persons whom he is to visit; of being president of the diocesan synod.

A3 From Canon A4 we conclude that the mutual acceptability and recognition of Orders is a primary and indispensable expression of *koinonia* and fellowship within the Church. But Orders are much more. In considering 'The Status of the Question' in its Second Report on the Ordination of Women to the Priesthood (GS 829) the House of Bishops of the Church of England put the matter succinctly:

> 33   As we considered the arguments for and against the ordination of women we found ourselves asking, what is the status of the question of the ordination of women to the priesthood? It is sometimes argued that this is a 'second order' question, such as obligatory clerical celibacy, not impinging directly upon 'first order' questions, such as the doctrine of the Trinity, or of the Person of Christ, or of the Atonement, where the central tenets of the Christian faith are plainly at stake. However, we have come to doubt whether in this context such a distinction is useful. This for two reasons:
>
> (a)   For many of those who favour the ordination of women, as well as for many of those who do not, the question is not one of comparative doctrinal indifference. It is seen as closely bound up with what is believed about the nature of God, about Christ and about the Church and about creation. It is thus intimately related to the 'centre' of the faith.
>
> (b)   The distinction is also unhelpful insofar as it may appear to imply a distinction between matters of faith as primary and matters of order as secondary. But it is an article of faith that the Church is a communion of saints. The ordained ministry is a principal instrument given by God for the maintenance of true communion. In this way questions of church order touch upon matters of faith.

We note that the House of Bishops' statement accords with views widely held across the entire theological spectrum and across the centuries. So *The Catechism of the Catholic Church* (1994) maintains:

1120 The ordained ministry or ministerial priesthood is at the service of the baptismal priesthood. The ordained priesthood guarantees that it really is Christ who acts in the sacraments through the Holy Spirit for the Church. The saving mission entrusted by the Father to his incarnate Son was committed to the apostles and through them to their successors: they receive the Spirit of Jesus to act in his name and in his person. The ordained minister is the sacramental bond that ties the liturgical action to what the apostles said and did and, through them, to the words and actions of Christ, the source and foundation of the sacraments. (cf. also *Lumen Gentium* 10, para. 2)

In the *Institutes*, 1536 (Book 4, Chapter 3, Section 2), Calvin writes:

[St Paul] shows that the ministry of men, which God employs in governing the Church, is a principal bond by which believers are kept together in one body . . . in this way, the renewal of the saints is accomplished, and the body of Christ is edified . . . Whoever, therefore, studies to abolish this order and kind of government of which we speak, or disparages it as of minor importance, plots the devastation, or rather the ruin or destruction of the Church. For neither are the light and heat of the sun, nor meat and drink so necessary to sustain and cherish the present life, as is the apostolical and pastoral office to preserve a Church on earth.

A4 We hold that, with regard to such an innovation – one which, because it affects 'a principal instrument given by God for the maintenance of true communion', inevitably increases divisions in the Body of Christ – the onus of proof (proof 'beyond reasonable doubt') rests with those who seek to innovate. The consequences of the innovation, foreseeable and unforeseeable, are the sole responsibility of the innovators.

A5 We hold that the threshold of proof or demonstration for changes in the Sacred Ministry (which is required to be received by all; and which touches upon matters of faith) is and ought to be that set out in Article VI of the Articles of Religion appended to the Book of Common Prayer of 1662:

> VI Of the Sufficiency of the holy Scriptures for Salvation.

> HOLY Scripture containeth all things necessary to salvation: so that whatsoever is not read therein, nor may be proved thereby, is not required of any man, that it should be believed as an article of the Faith, or be thought requisite or necessary to salvation.

B Scripture and tradition

B1 Proposing the Measure for the ordination of women to the priesthood in 1992, Bishop Michael Adie described the development 'as consonant with scripture and required by tradition' (*The Ordination of Women to the Priesthood: The Synod Debate, 11 November 1992: The Verbatim Record*, Church House Publishing, 1993, p. 9).[314] We

---

[314] Adie's claim, which seems at first sight bold and definitive, proves on closer examination to be strangely tentative. Did the proposer of the Measure suppose that the tradition equally required the ordination of women as bishops? And if he did, why did he not propose it? We cannot tell. The bishop described women's ordination as a 'requirement'. (Those who heard him no doubt recalled the unwise words of Dr Carey that those who claim that only a man can represent Christ at the altar are guilty of 'a most serious heresy'.) But it was obviously a requirement that Adie was either unwilling or unable to press. He affirmed that 'different views and *different theologies* will still have a respected and *secure* place in the Church' (italics ours). Two questions (perhaps unenvisaged in the heat of debate) inevitably arise:

a) If women's ordination is in any sense a 'requirement' why, in terms of the legislation, was it introduced as permissive and optional? (Schedules A and B).

b) Following the precedent of the 1992 Measure, would the present permissive and optional status of women in the presbyterate consequentially apply to women in the episcopate?

reflect that, with regard to Holy Scripture, he did not seek to show that it could be 'read therein' or 'proved thereby'.

We believe that it cannot, and that the tradition (as expressed in the writings of the Fathers and the Schoolmen) has consistently appealed to Scripture as ruling out any such development.[315]

B2 There are numbers of famous Pauline texts which have hitherto been taken to exclude the headship, or liturgical action, of women (1 Corinthians 11.2–16; 14.33–8;[316] 2 Corinthians 11.3; 1 Timothy 2.11-15; Ephesians 5.21; 1 Corinthians 7; Galatians 3.27–8).

---

[315] The most salient, but by no means all, the relevant texts are cited on pages 4–8 of the official *Commentary* (CTS Do 494) on the declaration *Inter Insigniores* (CTS Do 493) by the Sacred Congregation for the Doctrine of the Faith, and detailed in the footnotes accompanying it. We note, moreover, that the tradition makes frequent reference to two other factors which emerge from the scriptural record: the choice of only male Apostles and the role of Mary in the economy of salvation.

It has been said that it is difficult, perhaps impossible, to judge from what motive – symbolic intent, practical logistics, mere expediency, etc. – the Lord admitted only men to the Twelve. On the contrary, we believe that his failure to include women in a group so richly significant (both in its allusions to the past and its promise for the future) is eloquent. If the cultic and social equivalence of women and men was indeed (as has sometimes been alleged) an intrinsic part of his gospel, Jesus could have found no more powerful means of expressing that fact than by the appointment of one or more female Apostles. He did not do so. The Mother of God both in the New Testament and the Apostolic and sub-Apostolic period, is accorded the utmost reverence and respect; but never is she assigned the role of an Apostle. She is *with* the Apostles (Acts 1.14) and by tradition was part of the group on Pentecost Day; but she is not *of* them. It is Matthias, not Mary, who makes up the number (Acts 1.26). It is Peter 'and the Eleven' who make the first apostolic proclamation in the power of the Spirit (very pointedly indeed if the group mentioned at 2.1 is the same mixed company mentioned at 1.14).

[316] A serious omission from the consideration of the biblical evidence in GS 829 occurred in the treatment of 1 Corinthians 14.33–8. The bishops appeared to be unaware of the work done by Dauztenburg and Seeberg. This is usefully summarized in Manfred Hauke, *Women in the Priesthood?*, Ignatius Press, 1988, pp. 363–90.

Much exegetical ingenuity has been expended to demonstrate that these passages are either impertinent or irrelevant. They have been said to be later interpolations. They
have been claimed to be occasional admonitions, relevant to
a particular pastoral crisis (usual of Gnostic origin), but of
no importance to a modern audience. They have even been
portrayed as pre- or after-thoughts of the Apostle, contrary
to the main sense of Paul's proclamation. (Thus transgress-
ing the classic principle of exegesis that one passage should
not be interpreted so that it is 'repugnant' to another, and
consequently attributing to the Apostle a remarkable degree
of intellectual incoherence.) [317]

We believe that to sloganize Galatians 3.28 as an appeal for
the liturgical and social equivalence of women and men, and
to interpret it (as many have done) apart from the rich meta-
phorical pattern of headship and 'the Body' in which it is set,
is to abandon any real attempt at exegesis.

---

[317] We are not impressed by any of these attempts, which seem to us,
in nearly every case, to rob the text of subtlety and paradox. Let the most
flagrant example – the attempt to maintain that *kephale* in some contexts
means not 'head' (implying hierarchy, authority and primacy) but 'source'
(meaning root or origin) – stand for them all. To separate out in this way the
various elements of a complex and ruling metaphor – one which, in terms
of the wider metaphor of the Body of Christ, is central to Paul's Christology and ecclesiology – is to demonstrate a tragic failure to appreciate the
texture of Pauline thinking. Much – indeed undue – stress has been placed
on Galatians 3.28. This is a reference to the baptismal covenant, and finds
its place in the Pauline corpus in the company of two other similar passages
(neither of which refers to 'male and female' (1 Corinthians 12.13; Colossians 3.11; see also 1 Corinthians 11.11 and Romans 10.12). The passage
which governs the trio is 1 Corinthians 12.13ff., which moves seamlessly
into the great metaphor of the Body. That metaphor lies at the heart of the
paradox by which Paul reconciles the concepts of hierarchy and authority
within his Christology and ecclesiology. There is no question of equality
meaning equivalence. Paul teases out the implications of this great paradox
in other places: the relationship of Jew and Gentile (and so the significance
of the saving work of Jesus the Jew) in Romans 9—11; the relationship of
slave and master (and thus of Paul to his master, the Lord Jesus) in the letter
to Philemon; the relationship of man and woman as husband and wife (and
so of the *mysterion* of Christ and the Church) in Ephesians 5.

B3 Bishop Adie was also vague about what he took the traditional requirement to be.

His argument seemed to be that God in Christ took upon
himself full humanity and that humanity to be full had
obviously to be either male or female. It did not much
matter, thought Adie, in which sex God was incarnate. (As
the received phrase has it, 'the maleness of Jesus was not
soteriologically significant'.) A male priesthood had seemed
reasonable in previous ages when women had been accorded
only a subordinate role in society; but, once women in our
own day had gained full social equality, the full humanity of
Jesus could best be expressed and upheld by a priesthood of
both women and men.[318] Such an argument begs more questions than it settles.

Adie, moreover, gave little help to his hearers as to how such
a development, which had been consistently rejected by the
tradition, could now be held to be *required* by it. Members
of the Commission will remember that this very fact was

---

[318] The Green Paper of the Scottish Episcopal Church on the consecration
of women to the episcopate argues similarly, and in doing so exposes a
common misunderstanding.

The threefold basis of Anglicanism has long been held to be Scripture,
Tradition and Reason, the last of these being understood in its contemporary context. In the modern world there are few functions and offices
to which women cannot aspire. In our context therefore, there would
appear to be no rational grounds for maintaining a prohibition on women
bishops.

Reason is here taken to mean 'reflection on contemporary experience'.
But that is not what was originally intended. The original intention was that
'reason' – the human faculty of rational analysis – should be employed to
illuminate and reconcile passages of Scripture and aspects of the tradition,
so that their coherence could be affirmed and their relevance to present conditions explained. Paul Avis has put the matter thus in a letter to the present
author:

Hooker has Scripture, Reason, Church/Tradition. However, his understanding of reason is far from that of the Enlightenment or of modern
individualism. It seems to make sense to think of reason as an indispensable instrument for interpreting Scripture and Tradition, rather than as a
separate source of truth

pointed out by the then Chairman of the Church of England Doctrine Commission, Alec Graham, who described Adie's assertion as 'really quite a claim' (General Synod, *11 November 1992: Verbatim Record*, p. 40). [319]

B4 In our view it has not been demonstrated that women's ordination is 'consonant with Scripture and required by tradition'; but even were it possible so to do, we hold that such a demonstration would fall short of the fundamental requirement that a doctrinal innovation of this serious kind (in a matter which the House of Bishops has described as 'intimately related to the "centre" of the faith') should be directly answerable to the word of God written (that is to say: 'read therein' or 'proved thereby').

---

[319] Underlying Adie's argument – and the more sophisticated version of it advanced by the American patristics scholar Richard Norris ('The Ordination of Women and the "Maleness" of Christ', *Anglican Theological Review* Supplementary Series 6 (June 1976), pp. 69–80) – is probably the further assertion (as the feminist theologian Daphne Hampson has put it) that 'were the maleness (or Jewishness) of Jesus to be brought into play, Christ would not be the saviour of all'. Hampson goes on to deny '. . . that differences of sex, as also of race, are of significance Christologically' (*Theology and Feminism*, Blackwell, 1990, p. 55). The problem is that the Fathers and the Schoolmen were unanimously agreed (against Adie, Norris and Hampson) that the maleness of Jesus *is* Christologically significant. They affirmed that he was the Messiah, the Son of David; and that he was the Son of the Father. They rightly understood those categories to be male and to be located in the Jewishness of the chosen culture of our redemption (John 4.22; Rom. 11.11–12). They affirmed the saving particularity of the divine revelation and of the Incarnation. They thus denied the very premise upon which Adie's argument was built.

Richard Norris placed emphasis on a phrase of Gregory Nazianzen 'not taken not healed'. Gregory was countering the assertion of Apollinarius that the humanity assumed at the Incarnation was in some sense special or tailor-made. Had Gregory maintained, with Norris, that Jesus' humanity in some sense 'included' femaleness as well as maleness, in a way in which the humanity of other men (for example, male priests) does not, he would obviously have conceded the very point he was striving to defend. Norris is simply misrepresenting Gregory.

C   The consequences of the ordination of women to the priesthood

C1   The ecumenical consequences of the ordination of women to the priesthood were spelt out in a remarkable and unprecedented series of letters between Pope Paul VI and Archbishop Coggan, and Pope John Paul II and Archbishop Runcie. Similar admonitions have been addressed to Archbishops of Canterbury by Ecumenical Patriarchs.[320] That the consequences, in respect of the ancient churches of East and West, have been as predicted, the Commission will be aware. What in our view, however, has not been sufficiently noted is the consequent change in the position of the Church of England *vis-à-vis* those ancient churches.

Defending the authenticity of the orders of the Church of England against the condemnation of Pope Leo XIII (*Apostolicae Curae*, 1887), the Archbishops of Canterbury and York appealed to the practice of the early Church and of the Orthodox Churches in more recent times (*Saepius Officio*, Church Union edition, 1977, XX, pp. 36–8). The claim was that Rome (and in this case Leo himself) was the innovator.

The ordination of women signals an end to that traditional defence of the authenticity of the sacred ministry in the Church of England and throughout the Anglican Communion. Anglicans are henceforward obliged to conduct ecumenical relations with the Vatican and the Phanar, in respect of the reconciliation of ministries, with reference to the authority not of the ancient Church, but of their own provincial synods.[321]

---

[320] *The Ordination of Women*, CTS Do 493, pp. 24–8; GS 829, pp. 125–37.

[321] This is frankly admitted by the Green Paper of the Scottish Episcopal Church, which baldly states, '. . . for which there is no precedent before modern times'.

C2 In the debate in November 1992, Bishop Mark Santer referred to wider ecumenical considerations than those with
Rome or Constantinople:

> The fact that Roman Catholics should be so deeply con-
> cerned by our Anglican debate is itself a sign of our growth
> in love and communion in recent years. If they did not feel
> a close bond with us, they would not bother to express
> their concern. This makes it all the more painful to ex-
> press a contrary view. The fact is that we are concerned
> for communion with all our fellow Christians, including
> our fellow Anglicans who do ordain women, and not only
> for communion with Rome.

It is clear that the decision to ordain women in the Church
of England removed an impairment of communion (not of
the Church of England's making) with Anglican provinces
which had already ordained women. (The same decision, of
course, introduced a *new* impairment of communion with
those provinces who do *not* ordain women.) What is not
altogether clear, however, is how any of this has helped
relations with other churches overall.

The doctrine of provincial autonomy – strengthened, if not
invented for the purpose – has resulted in a position whereby orders are no longer interchangeable between Anglican
provinces or within them. By the express will of participating churches (enacted by due synodical process) orders are
no longer 'a principal instrument given by God for the maintenance of true communion' (GS 829, para. 33). As a direct
consequence of this, Anglicans can no longer properly seek
with other churches a degree of *koinonia* which they themselves no longer possess. The *Anglican–Moravian Conversations* (GS 1202, pp. 14–15) include in the requirements for
'full visible unity' the service of 'a reconciled common ministry'.[322] This vision of visible unity was specifically welcomed
by the General Synod (*Report of Proceedings*, vol. 27,

---

[322] GS 1202, p. 15.

p. 365). However, by the ordination of women on a provincial and (in some provinces, diocesan) basis, Anglicans have lowered the aspirations of ecumenical dialogue. A fully reconciled ministry is precisely what they can no longer deliver.

C3   The acknowledged 'impairment of communion' resulting from the ordination of women on a provincial or diocesan basis has also affected the authority and credibility of what have come to be called the 'instruments of unity' of the Anglican Communion.

• The Lambeth Conference – once a conference of bishops – is now a conference of church leaders who may or may not regard each other as bishops (see also *E1* below).
• The Anglican Consultative Council, which at the first meeting after its inauguration sanctioned unilateral action by the Diocese of Hong Kong, seems therefore to be committed to a view of 'our Anglican ecclesiology' (Archbishop Carey in a recent letter to the Primates of South-East Asia and Rwanda) which many provinces of the Communion (and many faithful Anglicans in other provinces) do not share.
• The failure of the recommendations of the Eames Commission to be taken seriously by the very provinces to which they were addressed (in particular the resistance to any form of Extended Episcopal Care in the United States) has rendered suspect the authority of other such 'Archbishop of Canterbury's Commissions' (for example, the recently appointed Sykes Commission). Their writ clearly does not run.

C4   Underlying the Reports of the Eames Commission (and used as a basis of the Episcopal Ministry Act of Synod in the Church of England) a doctrine of 'open reception' has been developed and deployed. There has even been talk (logically indefensible) of 'two integrities'. It was said that to the orders of women ordained in the Anglican Communion there remained 'a degree of provisionality'.

In our view (and that of the Church of England hereto-fore [see *A1* above] orders exist to assure the faithful of the apostolicity of doctrine and the authenticity of sacraments received. We hold that 'The ordained priesthood guarantees that it really is Christ who acts in the sacraments through the Holy Spirit for the Church' (*The Catechism of the Catholic Church*, 1102). (Or, in the words of the evangelical theologian J. L. Packer, through the ordained ministry we are encouraged 'to realise and remember that Christ in person is ministering' (in James Tolhurst (ed.), *Man, Woman and Priesthood*, Gracewing, 1989, p. xii). It is a denial of the very nature and purpose of the sacred ministry in the economy of salvation for an ecclesial body to suppose that it can properly authorize a ministry in which it admits that it cannot itself place wholehearted confidence.

D   The ordination of women to the episcopate

D1 In general, of course, we hold that the arguments against the ordination of women to the priesthood apply *a fortiori* to the episcopate. Our Lord's admission of only men to the Twelve is, as we have argued, eloquent of his will and purpose. It is the more telling in the case of bishops, the successors of the Apostles, whose authority in the Church rests upon their relationship, through the Apostles, with him. So Clement of Rome writes to the Corinthians:

> The apostles received the Gospel for us from the Lord Jesus Christ; Jesus Christ was God's ambassador. Thus Christ is sent from God and the apostles from Christ; both these dispositions originated in an orderly way from God's will. (Clement, *1 Corinthians* 42, in *Ante-Nicene Fathers*, vol. i, p. 16)

We note that it is precisely a sense of this orderly continuity which informs the conviction of the Holy See that it has no authority to admit women to the priesthood or the episcopate.

Could the Church today depart from the attitude of Jesus and the Apostles, which has been considered as normative by the whole of tradition up to our own day? . . .

The priestly ministry is not just a pastoral service; it ensures the continuity of the functions entrusted by Christ to the Apostles and the continuity of the powers related to those functions. Adaptation to civilizations and times therefore cannot abolish, on essential points, the sacramental reference to the constitutive events of Christianity and to Christ Himself. (*Inter Insigniores*, 4)[323]

D2 As we have shown (see *A2* above), the bishop's role as the focus of unity of his diocese is central to the Church of England's understanding of the episcopate. Furthermore, the Church of England's synodical structures have always, in the Upper Houses of the Convocations and more recently in the House of Bishops of the General Synod, given the episcopate a corporate identity and role at the provincial and national levels. The Church of England has also retained ordination by bishops in the historic episcopate as an effective sign of its continuity with the Church through the ages.

D3 The Cameron Report (the Report of the Archbishops' Group on the Episcopate, 1990) speaks of the local church, the Church throughout the world and the Church through the ages as the three 'planes' of the Church's life (p. 21 and *passim*), and shows how the ministry of the bishop is crucial to each. It summarizes the episcopal role in each 'plane' as follows:

In the local church the bishop focuses and nurtures the

---

[323] The argument has often been advanced that the Lord's choice of male Apostles, and the replication by them of that choice, was inspired by prudence alone (because they did not wish to compromise the wider mission by going against social prejudices). Against this view we must weigh the fact that sacraments are a memorial of saving events. Their signs are linked to those very events. They are necessarily relative to one culture and one civilization; but they are destined to be reproduced everywhere until the end of time.

unity of his people; in his sharing in the collegiality of bishops the local church is bound together with other local churches; and, through the succession of bishops the local community is related to the Church through the ages. Thus the bishop in his own person in his diocese; and in his collegial relations in the wider church; and through his place in the succession of bishops in their communities in faithfulness to the Gospel, is a sign and focus of the unity of the Church. (p. 160, para. 351)[324]

D 4 If this understanding of the role of the diocesan bishop is to be upheld within the Church of England we believe that the Rochester Commission needs to ask itself

- whether, at the present time or for the foreseeable future, a woman appointed to a diocesan bishopric would be able to focus and nurture the unity of the local church;
- whether, given the known views of the churches which

---

[324] We note that the current Green Paper of the Scottish Episcopal Church on the ordination of women to the episcopate uses the description or definition of the bishop's office set out in the Mission and Ministry section of the Lambeth Conference Report 1988:

(a) A symbol of the unity of the Church in its mission.
(b) A teacher and defender of the faith.
(c) Pastor of the pastors and of the laity.
(d) An enabler in the preaching of the word and in the administration of the sacraments.
(e) A leader in mission and an initiator of outreach to the world surrounding the community of the faithful.
(f) A shepherd who nurtures and cares for the flock of God.
(g) A physician to whom are brought the wounds of society.
(h) A voice of conscience within the society in which the local Church is placed.
(i) A prophet who proclaims the justice of God in the context of the gospel of loving redemption.
(j) A head of the family in its wholeness, its misery and its joy. The bishop is the family's centre of life and love.

While we do not reject this rather sentimental description, we find it lacking in any ecclesiological rigour and of little practical use in the present debate.

make up the great majority of the Church throughout the
world, a woman bishop could ever be the bond of unity
between her diocese and the rest of the Church; and

• whether, given that the episcopate has always been male, a
woman bishop could ever be a recognizable link between
her diocese and the Church throughout the ages?

In short, would a woman appointed to the episcopate in the
Church of England now or in the foreseeable future be 'a
sign and focus of the unity of the Church'?

D5   In our view, the answer to all these questions and considerations is, patently and unequivocally, 'no'. Indeed, we go
as far as to say that a woman bishop would inevitably be a
sign of the Church of England's separation from the Church
through the ages and the Church throughout the world, and
a focus not of unity but of division.

It is clear to us that the answers to these questions will affect,
for future generations, the Church of England's own self-
understanding, and consequently its relations with other
ecclesial bodies both within the Anglican Communion and
beyond it. The questions, moreover, can only be answered
from the position in which the Church of England finds itself. The answers to those questions will necessarily, where
appropriate, take account of the terms of the 1992 Measure
to ordain women to the priesthood and the rationale behind
that legislation.

We can illustrate this by looking at the three questions separately:

D6   *Would a woman appointed to a diocesan bishopric be able
to focus and nurture the unity of the local church?*

It is the case that in every diocese of the Church of England
there are, and for the foreseeable future will be, those who
could not in conscience receive or affirm the ministry of a
woman bishop. Those bishops, priests and lay people have

an acknowledged and *secure* place within the Church.[325] It is hard to see how a woman bishop could focus or nurture unity between those bishops, clergy and lay people and others of the contrary opinion. At present, while there is a significant degree of impairment of communion, and straining of pastoral relationships, within the dioceses of the Church of England, those dioceses continue to function as dioceses and the communion between one diocese and another is unimpaired. This is because, as the Episcopal Ministry Act of Synod makes clear, all the clergy continue to recognize the diocesan bishop as the Ordinary by whom (or on whose behalf) they are instituted or licensed and to whom they owe canonical obedience, and all bishops recognize their fellow bishops as fellow members of the college of bishops.

If women were ordained to the episcopate, all of this would cease to apply.[326] A significant minority of clergy and lay

---

[325] 'There must be provisions which ensure that those who do not agree with the ordination of women still have room and space in the Church of England. Hence the provisions for bishops, clergy and parishes. These ensure that people with different views and different theologies will still have a respected and secure place in the Church . . . As has been said, "The opposite of a correct statement is a false statement, but the opposite of a profound truth may well be another profound truth." Those of us who believe that it is right to take the decision to ordain women to the priesthood are determined to keep space for those of a different view' (Bishop Michael Adie, in General Synod, *11 November 1992: Verbatim Record*, p. 9).

[326] This situation seems to have been anticipated by the principal author of the Act of Synod 1993. In an interview in *File on Four*, broadcast on 7 October 1997 on BBC Radio 4, Dr Habgood was asked whether the notion of two integrities (and so the practical as well as theoretical reversibility of the legislation) was compatible with women bishops:

Liz Carney:	So while the two integrities exists, is there any possibility that a woman will be consecrated bishop?
John Habgood:	I think that I'm probably out of line here and I'm not in any case in any position to do anything about it, but I would have argued against it.
Liz Carney:	So, in the end, hasn't the Act of Synod set a precedent

people would be unable to recognize a woman as being the diocesan bishop or to make oaths of canonical obedience to her. Such clergy would be able to accept neither institution or licensing by a woman bishop nor institution or licensing undertaken by a male bishop on her behalf. Not only would such clergy and lay people be unable to receive her own sacramental ministrations; they would also be unable to receive those of priests ordained by her, whether male or female.

It has been suggested that, by a division of the office of a bishop into its sacramental and juridical parts, it might be possible for the diocesan bishop (were she a woman) to continue as the 'ordinary' of a diocese, while another (male) bishop, appointed for the purpose, could act sacramentally for her among those who refused her ministry. In our view, the sacramental and juridical aspects of a bishop's ministry cannot be separated in this way. As we have demonstrated in section A above, canon law expresses the theology and ecclesiology of the Church. The bishop's role as ordinary is not a matter of mere bureaucracy, but fundamental to the Anglican, and catholic, understanding of the episcopate. Such a division would, moreover, be offensive to women bishops, and probably unacceptable to them. Forward in Faith rejects such a solution as both sexist and deconstructive of the episcopal office.

D7 *Given the known views of the churches which make up the great majority of the Church throughout the world, could a*

---

	which means that women won't be able to fulfil their ministry?
John Habgood:	There are lots of ways you can fulfil your ministry without being a bishop.
Liz Carney:	But isn't this natural justice? If you allow women to be ordained as priests, in the course of events some women could be ordained as bishops: hasn't this system denied them that right?
John Habgood:	Well, perhaps it has, but this is a part of what has to be paid for maintaining the unity of the Church.

*woman bishop ever be the bond of unity between her dio-
cese and the rest of the Church?*

In our view women bishops would seriously and deleteri-
ously affect what the Cameron Report refers to as 'collegial
relations in the wider church'. Many, in the debate preceding the 1992 vote, pointed out that the Roman Church
continues to refuse the validity of Anglican orders.[327] But
parallel to that, and mitigating the severity of *Apostolicae
Curae*, was the fraternal concern of two Popes. In letters of
unprecedented warmth and affection, they saw the ordination of women as a greater impediment to unity than the
defects of rite and intention alleged by Leo XIII. The Sacred
Congregation for the Doctrine of the Faith made the position of the Roman Church clear in its commentary on *Inter
Insigniores*:

> ... The question of the ordination of women impinges too
> directly on the nature of the ministerial priesthood for one
> to agree that it should be resolved within the framework
> of legitimate pluralism between churches.[328]

That is the whole meaning of the letter of Pope Paul VI to
the Archbishop of Canterbury (CTS Do 493, p. 11).

Tragically the further impairment of communion occasioned
by women bishops would not be confined to relations with
the Roman Church. It would extend to other churches of
the Anglican Communion and to ecclesial bodies both Eastern and Western. From the Missouri Synod of the Lutheran
Church (now active in Eastern Europe) to the Syrians,
Armenians and Copts, the adoption of a female episcopate

---

[327] Michael Adie himself alluded to this in this opening speech: 'we must
bear in mind that in formal terms, whatever the local reality, the Roman
Catholic Communion does not accept the validity of Anglican orders'
(General Synod, *11 November 1992: Verbatim Record*, p. 11).

[328] The Commission will be aware of the subtlety and ambiguity, in such
a context, of the use of the term 'churches' by the CDF.

in the Church of England would finally signal the reception of an irreconcilable ministry and ecclesiology.

D8 *Given that the episcopate has always been male, could a woman bishop ever be a recognizable link between her own diocese today and the Church through the ages?*

Opinions clearly differ – and will continue to differ – as to whether a man can ever adequately represent a woman; whether a male priesthood can represent and include women. Christians have even diverged (though it is hard to see how with integrity they could do so) about whether a male incarnation can include and represent women. What, in our view, cannot be in doubt is that a female episcopate is unprecedented[329] and in no sense continuous with the practice of the Christian millennia. To claim that our forebears would have behaved as we do, had they shared our wisdom and perspicacity, is unpardonably to patronize those from whom we received the faith and without whom we would be ignorant of it.

D9 Thus, we conclude, there are additional ecclesiological reasons, above and beyond those which apply also to the ordination of women to the priesthood, which mean that the ordination of women to the episcopate would actually be contrary to the very nature and purpose of the episcopate itself.

E The consequences of the ordination of women as bishops

E1 Should the Church of England, nonetheless, now proceed to the ordination of women to the episcopate it will need to take into account a number of factors. Some of these factors

---

[329] We note that even Professor Giorgio Otranto, who has advanced what he takes to be evidence of women presbyters in Apulia and elsewhere in the fifth to ninth centuries, has not offered support, archaeological or otherwise, for women bishops.

arise naturally and inevitably from such a controversial decision. Others are of its own making (see *D5* above).

In the event of such ordinations there will be a significant minority in the Church of England which will find itself unable to accept (for the reasons outlined above) the ministry of women as bishops or the ministry of bishops who continue in communion or 'full visible unity' with those women.[330] This will include bishops, priests and lay people. In particular, bishops who could not endorse the ordination of women to the episcopate would be unable to recognize women bishops as members of the college of bishops, and the House of Bishops would therefore become a church leaders' meeting rather than an episcopal college.[331]

Ecclesiologically speaking, the situation would be much graver even than that which already exists as a consequence of the ordination of women to the priesthood. It is even questionable whether a church in which such a situation was allowed to exist (indeed deliberately brought into being) could properly be termed a church at all, at least as that word has hitherto normally been understood.

E2 In its *First Report on the Ordination of Women to the Priesthood* the House of Bishops of the Church of England wrestled with the tension between the role of the bishop as a 'focus of unity' both within the diocese and between dioceses, and the persisting diversity of opinion on women's ordination. The House at that time suggested that once a province had proceeded to the ordination of women to the priesthood it would be anomalous to appoint as a diocesan bishop one who was at variance with the mind of the House.

The House of Bishops later revised this opinion, and in its wholehearted endorsement of the Act of Synod proposed that all offices in the Church should be equally open to

---

[330] See Forward in Faith, *Agreed Statement on Communion*, 1993, http://www.forwardinfaith.com/about/uk_com_statement.html.
[331] See *C3* above.

opponents. Five appointments have since been made of diocesans who cannot in conscience ordain women to the priesthood. (However, two of the five appointments were of the same individual, and another of the five was already a diocesan bishop in 1992; in the same period 28 appointments were made of diocesans who do ordain women to the priesthood.)

E3   We can see that the House of Bishops might now wish to reconsider its generosity of 1993. Deep internal divisions about who were legitimately its members would obviously undermine the authority of the House. There could be no appeal to 'collegiality' among those who did not properly constitute a college. Nor would there seem to be any reason for the Church, or the nation at large, to heed a House of Bishops which could not even agree about its own constitution and membership.

E4   But it will not be easy to go back on rights conceded in the Schedules of the 1992 Measure, and in the assurances given to opponents of the innovation in the Act of Synod, 1993. Those assurances were based on a 'doctrine of reception' whose basic concepts were borrowed from the world of ecumenical dialogue. No-one could maintain that the ordination of women to the priesthood has yet been received by a consensus even within the Church of England, let alone within the Universal Church, which the Act of Synod and its supporting documents make clear is to be regarded as the proper locus of such reception.[332] Bad faith in such a matter would surely raise questions about the general trustworthiness of the Church of England in the wider ecumenical arena also.

The provision of Schedules A and B and the assurances given in the Act of Synod were, moreover, the ground upon which

---

[332] See the verbatim account of the relevant meeting of the Ecclesiastical Committee, which includes *Bonds of Peace* and the draft Act of Synod. HMSO.

individuals took decisions profoundly affecting their own lives and the lives of their dependents (whether, for example, to remain in the Church of England, and whether to continue in, or be ordained to, its ministry). It would be profoundly shocking were such assurances summarily to be withdrawn.

E5 The Church of England, its General Synod and its House of Bishops are, we believe, obliged by their own existing undertakings and understandings to provide a place, and an acceptable form of episcopal ministry, for those conscientiously opposed to women priests and bishops. We acknowledge, at the same time, that the Church may wish to be seen to keep faith with the women it has already ordained by proceeding, at some stage, to their ordination as bishops. We understand that it will also need, so far as possible, to avoid the anomalous absurdity of consecrating 'alternative' bishops precisely to be out of communion with other bishops which it consecrates.

E6 In our view the Rochester Commission and the House of Bishops will need now to consider what the requirements would be for maintaining the openness of the period of reception to which, by formal undertakings, the Church of England is committed. A document such as this is not the place to spell out such requirements *in extenso*; but it may be as well for us to comment on certain possibilities which have been mooted, and to give some indication of what seem to us to be the irreducible *minima*.

It has been suggested that the ordination of women to suffragan bishoprics might allow women an *entrée* into the college of bishops while maintaining the unity of the diocese (and unity between dioceses), where the diocesans would remain men. There are serious objections to such a scheme:

- It would, no doubt, be unacceptable to the women who were to be consecrated, who are not seeking the replacement of one 'glass ceiling' by another.

- It would raise serious questions about the episcopal credentials of suffragan bishops. Suffragans presently belong to the order of bishops no less than diocesans (indeed suffragans are only suffragans by analogy with the relationship of diocesans to metropolitans). A suffragan who could not in principle be preferred as a diocesan would arguably (cf. a priest who could not, in principle, be allowed to exercise the cure of souls) not be a bishop at all.

Nor is it the case that a male diocesan, in full and unimpaired communion with a female suffragan, could be a sign of unity to those who could not receive her ministry. They would need to subsist in the college of priests of a bishop who had no such collegial relationship with a woman suffragan. That alternative bishop would need to exercise among them the full rights and pastoral obligations of a diocesan (see Canon C18, section A2 above). He would need to have the right to select candidates for ordination, to ordain them and to supervise appointments to all ecclesiastical offices and benefices under his jurisdiction.

E7 The Church of England (as a church which does not yet consecrate women to the episcopate) already enjoys a degree of communion (impaired but real) with other churches which do. Some of those churches (members of the Anglican Communion) have taken the step unilaterally (thus further impairing the 'full visible unity' which once existed). Others are churches into deeper communion with which, after lengthy negotiation and theological reflection, the Church of England has more recently entered. This new and exciting pattern of relationships, we believe, offers a very real way forward in the present difficulty.

There is, on the one hand, a considerable pressure to secure the consecration of women as bishops and, on the other, a determined and structured opposition. Reconciliation between these two positions is not realistically to be envisaged. Both, we believe, deserve space in which to develop, in freedom and integrity, their distinctive visions of the future church.[333]

E8   In the passage which we quoted at the outset, St Ignatius of Antioch exhorted the Philadelphians 'to have but one Eucharist . . . as there is one bishop'. It is the special calling of the episcopate to guard the unity of the Church, and we continue to hope that the House of Bishops of the Church of England, who have set up the Rochester Commission and to whom it will report, will live up to this calling, and resist a step which would inevitably destroy the unity of the Church of England's episcopate.

However, should the House of Bishops nonetheless allow this step to be taken, we have proposed the establishment of a free province of the Church of England, one which would exist in that degree of communion (impaired but real) which the Church of England has recently embraced in the Porvoo Communion and which it shares with many other provinces of the Anglican Communion.

The Church of England, for the sake of unity, has recently embraced, across the seas, sister churches with polities and sacramental arrangements which differ from its own on important matters, and come into fuller communion with them. We trust that it will now work to accommodate, with a similar openness and generosity of heart, the passionately held beliefs and sacramental practices of those of its own members who continue to adhere to the faith and practice of the universal Church through the ages.

Geoffrey Kirk
for and on behalf of the Council of Forward in Faith
17 October 2001
The Feast of Ignatius of Antioch, bishop and martyr

---

[333] The so-called 'Gamaliel argument' (Acts 5.34–40) was much used in the campaign to secure the ordination of women to the priesthood. It can be no less valid now than it was then.

Appendix 3

RECEPTION AND COMMUNION

A Paper Written for the Rochester Commission, June 2003

DAVID HOULDING

What is a Bishop? **What is he for?** **What does he do?**

In the Ordinal, bishops, priests and deacons are all asked:

> Do you believe the doctrine of the Christian faith as the Church of England has received it?

Reception is not a doctrine of itself; rather, it is a process by which doctrine or dogma is taken up in the life and practice of the Christian community. It reflects the local to the universal and vice versa.

A definition of reception

The *Oxford Dictionary of the Christian Church* (3rd edn) gives this definition for the understanding of the concept (as opposed to doctrine) of reception.

The informal process by which the whole Church gives subsequent assent to a conciliar or Papal decision in the light of its conformity with Scripture and tradition. Decisions of the early Oecumenical Councils were accepted partly because they corresponded to the *sensus fidelium*. While the development of Papal authority (esp. the definition of Papal infallibility) has led reception to be comparatively neglected in the RC Church, Anglicans and Orthodox have emphasised it in modern times. Recently the idea has been used within the Anglican Communion to support experimentation, e.g. with the ordination of women to the priesthood in some provinces, in the expectation that such innovations might come to be 'received'. (p. 1371)

The distinguished Roman Catholic scholar, Fr Adrian Hastings, has sought to set out a meaning and context for reception. Citing the second Vatican Council, Hastings has argued that the authority of an official teaching of the Church is not determined solely by its source but also by the way in which the teaching has actually transformed the self understanding and pastoral practice of the Church as a whole. This, he claims, is what is meant by reception.

Development and continuity

We can see from this that reception and authority are corollaries; one flows into the other, always as a dynamic process. This is consistent with Newman's understanding of the development of doctrine. For development there has to be continuity. The question then rests on the understanding of the whole in relation to the particular, for any development to gain the authority it needs for its implication.

The Eames Commission, in its first report, states,

in the wider ecumenical debate Anglicans ought not to suggest that such restrictions result in their being 'out of communion' with one another. Much more unites them within the one Anglican fellowship than divides. The way in which those on different sides of the debate, who follow different practices over the ordination of women, live with this diversity, entering one another's pain, may itself be an important experience of, and witness to, the communion that exists. Those who witness on different sides of the debate need each other within a single fellowship. To take the step of declaring that communion is broken, or to describe the position as no longer being 'in communion', would be to do less than justice to the concept of communion as we now understand and experience it. (Paragraph 40)

Once a synodical decision has been made then that necessarily must be respected on all sides as a considered judgement of that particular representative gathering. However, it has always been recognised that councils not only may, but have, erred. Conciliar and synodical decisions would still have to be received and owned by the whole people of God as consonant with the faith of the Church throughout the ages professed and lived today. (Paragraph 42)

Authority in the Church

It is clear from these two quotations that the concept of authority and reception are intrinsically linked; that which is pronounced on by the Church needs to be believed by the people; what may be presented as an intrinsic part of the Christian faith in any one part of the Church needs the authority of the whole Church. Otherwise, in the end, it cannot be part of the faith.

This is true of salvation history itself. In Genesis 3 we have the first example of authority not being received. The divine logos which has created the world is rejected by Adam and Eve. A price is paid: this results in the Fall.

The biblical model

In the covenantal history of the Old Testament we see numerous examples of how the pilgrim Israelites fail to receive authority in a variety of different ways. This is in direct contrast to the revelation of God, which comes to its fulfilment in the person of

Christ (cf. Hebrews 1.1–2). The Ten Commandments themselves are not received as Moses first presents them to the people. This leads to the community being destabilized. The Old Testament story of the non-reception of the covenant paves the way for the need for God to introduce an alternative way by which he may be reconnected with his people. The 'Fiat' of Mary, who is the prototype and the image of the Church, is the ultimate example of the process of reception being given authority. Salvation is located at a particular moment in time, but also needs the cooperation of humanity. Mary's reception *literally* of the divine logos is the result of her choice to 'receive' from God. Mary's 'Yes' is an example that conscious (i.e. free) will and obedience are two different sides of the same coin. Salvation is wrought because it is received first, so that it may be incarnated in the life of Christ and therefore of the Church. Mary is the 'model' of reception.

Heresy or orthodoxy

In the life of the early Church during the second century, the deposit of the canon of Scripture, brought about through struggle and debate, was finally settled when the Church was able to come to a common mind as to the authority that certain writings held. Until the corpus of authoritative books was completed this was itself a process of reception. This reminds us that often in the process of reception, heresy in its proper sense (opinion contrary to established doctrine) is important for the determination of the truth. This is the birth of the process that we describe today as the search for the *consensus fidelium*.

The Marcionite heresy is the classic controversy about the bounds of the New Testament canon. It illustrates how untidy, divisive and contentious the life of the Church can become. The process of reception throughout the history of the Church is not necessarily the choice between two options of right and wrong. Often it is about searching for an acceptance which is shrouded in confusion and doubt.

Theological formation

The nature and substance of the first four ecumenical councils confirms this difficulty with reception in the formulation of the catholic creed of Nicaea (325) and of its later adoption at Constantinople (381). To answer the Arian heresy, it was reiterated at Ephesus (431) and later at Chalcedon (451). The first thousand years of Christianity are a powerful reminder of the place of reception in the theological formation of the emergent Church. From the first schism between East and West, through to each and every subsequent splinter within the Universal Church since, the root of the problem could be explained by the refusal of one group to accede to the inclusion of doctrinal or moral teaching.

Reformation and the liturgy

In the theological melée of the Reformation 'reception' is not only a question of doctrinal purity and clarity, but also becomes a matter of social and political significance. An obvious example of this is in the compilation of the Prayer Books of 1549 and 1552 – where we know from historical commentary that the first becomes popular and is widely used because of its more traditional associations with the past, whereas the 1552 book with its much stronger Calvinist influence is not popular and therefore not received by the people of England. By the reign of Queen Elizabeth I it becomes politically expedient for a settlement to be imposed on the English church by the Crown for the stability of society and supremacy of the state. It takes another hundred years for a Prayer Book to be issued which restores some of the more catholic traditions of 1549 expunged in 1552. During this time, of course, the Laudians had had their influence and there was a natural rejection of Puritanism. The book of 1662 is received and becomes normative for 300 years.

'Reception' of a liturgy, however, cannot be put on the same level as faith or order, but in Anglican terms it has to be remembered that due to lack of any other documental evidence or theological expression, the liturgy is the one place where we find doctrine expressed, in terms both of the text and of its accompanying ritual.

Infallibility of the Church

A primary challenge to reception comes in the work of the First Vatican Council in its defining of papal infallibility. The *Oxford Dictionary of the Christian Church* describes this teaching as follows:

> While many Christians maintain that the Church is infallible, upon the basis of such texts as Jn 16: 13, Acts 15: 28, various beliefs have been held as to the seat where such infallibility resides. It has sometimes been sought in those doctrines and truths of revelation which have been accepted by all the historic branches of the Church; at other times in the definitions of such councils of the Church as have been generally accepted as Oecumenical. At the First Vatican Council (1870) the RC Church declared that the Pope was infallible when he defined that a doctrine concerning faith or morals was part of the deposit of the divine revelation handed down from apostolic tradition and was therefore to be believed by the whole Church. In RC doctrine such a definition is infallible even antecedently to its acceptance by the Church. The RC Church also teaches that the same infallibility attaches to whatever is taught as part of the deposit of revelation by the entire body of RC bishops in union with the Pope, whether inside or outside an Oecumenical Council; this point, made in the First Vatican Council, was stressed at the Second Vatican Council. (p. 831)

The principle of conscience

To what extent is this new doctrine imposed on the Church? Often misunderstood, it still appears to many that the teaching office of the Church overrides the principle of conscience in the process of reception. However, conscience is never abrogated; rather, it remains part of the consensus of the understanding of the doctrine or the teaching in the magisterium of the whole Church. The definition of papal infallibility caused the Roman Catholic Church in the nineteenth century considerable difficulty in that the Church reached a position whereby its infallible teaching became antecedent to its reception by the Church. In other words, it does not become binding because the faithful receive it; it becomes binding because it is! The faith must be true because it is believed, not simply because the Church requires it to be true. Hence, the importance of conscience.

This can be demonstrated in the way that Paul VI's teaching on contraception has been viewed by the faithful over the past generation. All evidence suggests that although this teaching has the weight of papal encyclical, it is still yet to be received by the faithful. It may be widely enjoined upon the faithful as the teaching of the Church, but at the same time it still must permit the right of conscience to allow the possibility of holding back from it. Equally, it could be argued this is not a good example as this teaching was never infallible in the first place; although 'conscience' does play a very significant part in the faithful's adherence to it.

A Church of England problem

In the current debate over the ordination of women both as presbyters and as bishops, we recognize that their ministry is still to be received within the Church of England. This does not mean to say that there are not many excellent women exercising a valued ministry in a whole variety of different ways. It does mean that their orders are not accepted by all. Holy Order is given to the universal Church to be a sign of its sacramental unity. Despite the Church of England's claims to valid orders, stemming from the correspondence between Rome and Canterbury in the 1890s, there is still the problem of division within the universal Church which raises the question of authority. How can the Church of England initiate such a change without destroying its claims to catholicity?

The price that the Church of England pays at the present time is an 'impairment' of communion for its two stances on the question of women's priestly ordination. As the Eames Commission puts it: 'Both positions the church claims may be held with equal integrity' (by those in favour and by those opposed). This is not the same as being 'out of communion', which would necessitate an alternative church, but it is to say that there are sacramental acts performed which are not recognized by everyone. Hence the significance of paragraph 40 quoted above about the need to maintain the highest degree of communion within the present contradictory positions regarding women priests. The Church must always seek to minimize division and to maximize unity.

The guiding principle

Unity must always be more than a mere concept; it should be one of the hallmarks of the Church in its universal manifestations. As the Common Declaration, signed by Pope John Paul II and the Archbishop of Canterbury in 1989, put it:

> . . . Against the background of human disunity the arduous journey to Christian unity must be pursued with determination and vigour whatever obstacles are perceived to block the path.

> We here solemnly re-commit ourselves and those we represent to the restoration of full ecclesial communion in the confidence that to seek anything less would be to betray our Lord's intention for the unity of his people.

Unity is both a gift and a goal. In seeking the goal the Church must always nourish the gift that is already present within Christ's body. The divine command is there from the outset. Decisions taken by one part of the body inevitably affect the whole. When unity is threatened is it not justified to ask by what authority does one branch of the Church proceed down a particular route?

The nature of change

If there is an element of dubiety over women's priestly ordination then that can only be exacerbated by proceeding with their episcopal ordination. It is certainly difficult to see how one period of reception can be initiated before the other has been concluded. It is precisely because such a move to ordain women as bishops is so far from being received even within the Church of England that it can be stated that such an innovation would change the nature of the episcopate itself. Who decides when one period of reception is over and another begins, especially while the initial decision still lacks acceptance by the greater part of the universal whole?

A change too far

A recent survey suggests that women bishops are far from being accepted by the faithful of the Church of England (*The Mind of Anglicans*, a survey by Christian Research and Cost of Conscience, 2003). The details of this survey need to be carefully studied and an analysis is given in *New Directions* in the editions of July and August 2002; this evidence is not to be lightly dismissed.

The Church of Rome continues to state the position that such a development is not possible. It claims that the Church does not have authority to make this change as part of the ordinary magisterium, and that such a change is indeed not within its competence. That is to say, the Church has authority to proclaim 'only such doctrine as coheres with scripture as interpreted by the tradition'. The Church too must make the theological case to justify its course of action. In other words it embraces the notion that there are some things that cannot be *received* because they cannot be proposed in the first place. From this we can see how the admission of women as bishops, despite the order remaining, would nonetheless also change it.

A focus for unity

Since Apostolic times the bishop has always been *the focus of unity* for the local church. He relates the local to the universal and the universal to the local; it is difficult to understand how a woman ordained can be such for the Church of England in the present situation. If the period of reception of the ordination of women to the priesthood has not been terminated (and presumably if alone for the sake of conscience cannot be for the foreseeable future), it is impossible for the Church to proceed with the admission of women as bishops without stifling 'conscience' and imposing its doctrine. In this situation, although a woman bishop may hold juridical and ecclesiastical authority, if any of the parishes within the diocese (or the episcopal area over which she exercises her episcopate) do not receive her ministry, she cannot be said to be the focus of sacramental unity. Therefore, down the line, the bishop may exercise a ministry of pastoral administration but no longer can she be able to exemplify the *plene bene esse* (the fullness of life) of the Church. That inevitably changes the nature of the episcopate.

At present the Church of England lives with a somewhat contradictory situation in that its orders are no longer 'interchangeable'. With the admission of women to the episcopate, then episcopal orders too will no longer be 'interchangeable'. Nor, then, would the orders of both men and women whom they would purport to ordain; hence the compounding of the current situation. What of male bishops in whose consecration women bishops have taken part? Communion between those bishops and some of their presbyters would be broken (not simply 'impaired' as at present) and communion between bishops themselves – more significantly – would also be broken.

'Ruptured communion'

Where the bishop is, there is the Church. When bishops are no longer in communion with one another, where is the Church? Can the Church exist when its episcopal orders are no longer interchangeable? It will no longer be a question of impaired communion, but communion will be ruptured at its source. It will simply no longer be possible to talk about the bishop as the focus of unity, for that very unity itself will not exist. The bishop will *de facto* become something different from what he is at present.

The sacramental life

There is further the question of whether 'reception' can apply to changes in *order*. Once an opinion has been incarnated in the persons of an order, reception is no longer applicable. If dubiety exists in the priesthood, then the certainty of the sacraments, duly celebrated, is also called into question. One cannot – as the Catholic Church is saying and as the Church of England has also previously said – 'try out' sacraments. They are not experimental! It is of their very nature that they are trustworthy and authoritative. They are to be guaranteed signs of Christ's presence and activity in the world. If they are not that, then they are of little worth.

Bishop Kenneth Kirk enunciated this principle in a paper for the Church Assembly in 1947, where he stated that 'where sacraments are concerned the Church is always obliged to take the least doubtful course'. Through the ordination of women as bishops the level of confusion is increased by the possibility that the orders conferred on men as well as women would also now be in doubt. That in turn, as time goes on, would be a situation that could only increase and not be lessened. *Communion, Koinonia,* becomes impossible and division will be inevitable at all levels of the Church's life.

The law as it is

Even if all the parishes and individual clergy and lay people in a diocese do accept the ministry of a woman bishop, there comes the problem of that ministry being recognized by a fellow bishop. Collegial unity must be expressed both universally and locally.

Only when the Church declares that there is no alternative but to proceed and to receive women bishops, can the period of reception be deemed to be concluded. The Church of England has specifically declared that this is not the current position. The Priests (Ordination of Women) Measure states the opposite. For the sake of those who remain unable to accept the General Synod's decision, their view is safeguarded in law. We can see from this that *reception* and *justice* are closely linked. If it were to be forced, then it would be unjust and the community of the Church would change, becoming unrecognizable from the past. If it is perceived by countless numbers of the faithful to be unjust, women themselves will come off worse and not better. Conscience will be squeezed out altogether. Enforced reception can only result ultimately in legalized tokenism. Has the Church reached that point?

Provisionality of the Church

In conclusion we recognize the untidiness of the present situation. It is always a mistake to believe that any ecclesiology can be perfect. Even the Church is provisional and denominations within the universal Church of Jesus Christ even more so. Perfection can only be achieved in the eschatological vision of the Church triumphant, when 'sacraments shall cease and all shall be one'. In the meantime the work for unity is always ongoing. As Henri de Lubac writes:

> The concrete and living unity of the church is not a uniformity. It is, if we can say it like this, a pluriformity, it is a concert, a harmony . . . to realise this all diversity must be taken up into the essential movement towards unity.

Anything that hinders that process must be in conflict with the tradition and not consonant with it. The search for unity is not an optional extra, but of the very essence of the Church's life.

Truth received and declared

It is difficult to see how the ordination of women bishops fits these criteria. For the process of reception is not only dependent on the local, but, in the end, principally on the universal. In the documents of the Second Vatican Council the matter of 'received tradition' is given greater prominence as a balance to the promulgation of infallible teaching. The Assumption of the Blessed Virgin Mary is the clearest example. The teaching given in 1950 was not defining something new; rather, it was the reworking of an earlier theme which has been believed since Apostolic times and has widely been held to be true by the faithful over countless generations.

Unanswered questions

The Eames Commission makes an honourable attempt to provide the right conditions for the Church to maximize its unity. Equally, if further periods of reception are to be introduced in the matter of Holy Order before one has been settled, then one can only conclude that it is a mechanism for increasing experimentation. The question has to be as to who can initiate a process of reception. Eames would suggest that a province of the Communion might do so by decision of its synod. But where does that end? What might a diocese do, or even a parish? Where does authority rest? Who decides and how when a period of reception is over?

Reception versus experimentation

Is this again a matter for an autonomous decision by a local synod? Anglicans have borrowed this theological concept to justify experimentation. It must be questioned as to how relevant or even honest this is in light of the definition given at the outset. Is it not just a means to justify the ends? Provision for conscience is crucial, if the concept of *reception* is to carry any weight. As a consequence, Anglicans struggle with ecclesiology, which is inevitable all the time that there is the issue of *communion* with

the universal Church to be resolved. It is the price we continue
to pay for the Reformation. The ministry of Peter continues to
hold the Church together in 'one communion of love'. Further
departure from Apostolic tradition can only lead to disintegra-
tion. Reception, in my view, is only an intelligible concept within
a coherent ecclesiology. The rest is mere chaos!

Conclusion

As the Bishop of Chichester has said:

> In a fully rounded ecclesiology, catholicity is a criterion for
> apostolicity, and the instruments which serve the catholic com-
> munion of the church belong to the *heart* and not the periphery
> of Christian faith.

The Church of England believes that from the Apostles' time there
have been these orders of ministers in Christ's Church: bishops,
priests and deacons; and in the Church of England 'these orders
continue, and are used reverently and esteemed' (Preface to the
Ordinal). All ministry finds its focus in the person of the bishop.
He is the guardian of the faith and the source of authority in
accordance with Scripture and tradition. As the 1938 Doctrine
Report puts it:

> [within this apostolic order] the Episcopate symbolizes and
> secures, in an abiding form, the apostolic mission and author-
> ity within the church; historically the Episcopate became the
> organ of this mission and authority.

In the divided state of the Church, the episcopate is intended to
be (and in principle so far remains) one of the shared instruments
of unity. In the admission of women to this Holy Order, we reach
the point of 'no return'. The question remains: can it be right for
a particular church or denomination to make a unilateral change
of this sort? In relation to women bishops various questions arise
which I believe need answering before any decision is taken.

1 Can we define a period of reception? If so, who can initiate
   it? By what authority can it be terminated?

2 Does not the ordination of women as bishops introduce greater confusion into the life of the Church? Will not a
   further element of doubt be introduced within its male orders
   as well? Can this ever be rectified?

3 Is not *communion* further impaired – even 'disrupted' altogether – should part of the local church proceed in this way?
   Even if we can live provisionally with the present situation,
   would not further innovation not only change the order of
   bishops but also thereby change the nature of the Church?

4 If proceeding to the ordination of women as bishops can
   be held to be contrary to both Scripture and the tradition,
   can it therefore be received by the Church? – let alone by the
   Church of England?

5 Is the concept of *reception* helpful or even honest in this debate? Can apostolic succession be preserved by autonomous
   decision-making? How is apostolicity dependent on catholicity?

6 What is driving this debate? Is it being driven by imperatives
   from within or from outside the tradition? Does equality
   mean interchangeability? Of role or function?

7 At what price unity? How seriously do we take the texts in
   John's Gospel especially in chapter 17? Are they an add-on?
   Something we assent to as an ideal? Or do they regulate the
   Church's life at the present time?

8 Is there a distinction to be made between bishop and priest?
   What insights are to be gained from the Eastern tradition as
   well as from the Latin West?

9 What is a bishop?   What is he for?   What does he do?

Bibliography

Church of England sources

Church Assembly Documents (in order of publication)

Committee appointed by His Grace the Archbishop of Canterbury, 1919, *The Ministry of Women*, London: SPCK

Archbishops' Commission on Christian Doctrine, 1938, *Doctrine in the Church of England*, London: SPCK

Central Advisory Council on Training and Ministry, 1962, *Gender and Ministry*, London: Church Information Office

Commission Appointed by the Archbishops of Canterbury and York, 1966, *Women and Holy Orders*, London: Church Information Office

Advisory Council for the Church's Ministry/Council for Women's Ministry in the Church, 1968, *Women in Ministry: A Study*, London: Church Information Office

General Synod Documents (in order of publication)

GS104, 1972, *The Ordination of Women to the Priesthood*, London: Church Information Office*

GS252, 1973, *The Ordination of Women: Report of the Standing Committee on the Reference to the Dioceses*, London: Church Information Office

GS Misc 88, 1978, *Ordination of Women: A Supplement to the Consultative Document GS 104 (Prepared at the request of the Standing Committee by Miss Christian Howard)*, London: Church Information Office*

GS Misc 198, 1984, Ordination of Women to the Priesthood: Further Report. A Background Paper by Christian Howard, London: Church Information Office*

GS 694, 1986, *The Priesthood of the Ordained Ministry*, London: General Synod Board for Mission and Unity

GS 738, 1986, *The Ordination of Women to the Priesthood: The Scope of the Legislation*, London: General Synod of the Church of England

GS Misc 246, 1986, *The Ordination of Women to the Priesthood: The Scope of the Legislation (GS 738). Memorandum by the House of Bishops*, London: General Synod of the Church of England

GS 764, 1987, *The Ordination of Women to the Priesthood: First Report by the House of Bishops*, London: General Synod of the Church of England

GS 829, 1988, *The Ordination of Women to the Priesthood: A Second Report by the House of Bishops*, London: General Synod of the Church of England

GS 944, 1990, *Episcopal Ministry* [The Cameron Report], London: Church House Publishing

GS 830Y, 1992, *Draft Priests (Ordination of Women) Measure, Draft Canon C4B and Draft Amending Canon No. 13. Revision Committee Report*, London: General Synod of the Church of England

GS 996, 1992, *The Ordination of Women to the Priesthood: Reference of the Legislation to the Dioceses. Voting Figures*, London: General Synod of the Church of England

GS 1019, 1992, *Senior Church Appointments: A Review of the Methods of Appointment of Area and Suffragan Bishops, Deans, Provosts, Archdeacons and Residentiary Canons*, London: Church House Publishing

GS 1202, 1996, *Anglican–Moravian Conversations*, London: Council for Christian Unity

GS 1248, 1997, *Eucharistic Presidency: A Theological Statement by the House of Bishops of the Church of England*, London: Church House Publishing

GS 1395, 2000, *Episcopal Ministry Act of Synod: Report of a Working Party of the House of Bishops* [The Blackburn Report], London: General Synod of the Church of England

GS Misc 580, 2000, *Bishops in Communion: Collegiality in the Service of the* Koinonia *of the Church*, London: Church House Publishing

GS Misc 632, 2001, *The Eucharist: Sacrament of Unity. An Occasional Paper of the House of Bishops of the Church of England*, London: Church House Publishing

GS 1457, 2002, *Working Party on Women in the Episcopate: A Progress Report from the House of Bishops*, London: General Synod of the Church of England

*These reports were the work of Dame Christian Howard.

Other material

Church of England, 2000, *The Canons of the Church of England* (6th edn), London: Church House Publishing

Church of England, 2004, *Church of England Year Book 2004*, London: Church House Publishing

Forward in Faith, 1993, *Agreed Statement on Communion*, London: FiF

General Synod, 1993, *The Ordination of Women to the Priesthood: The*

Synod Debate 11 November 1992 [The Verbatim Record], London: Church House Publishing

Other Anglican sources

Anglican Consultative Council, 1971, *The Time Is Now: Report of the ACC Meeting at Limuru, Kenya, 23 February–5 March 1971*, London: SPCK
Anglican Mission in America, 2003, *Report of the Study concerning the Ordination of Women*, Pawleys Island, South Carolina: AMiA
Eames Commission, 1994, *The Archbishop of Canterbury's Commission on Communion and Women in the Episcopate: The Official Reports*, Toronto: Anglican Book Centre
Faith and Order Board, Scottish Episcopal Church, 2001, *Green Paper – A Paper for Discussion within the Scottish Episcopal Church*, Edinburgh: Scottish Episcopal Church
General Synod Working Group on Women in the Episcopate, 2003, *Episcopal Ministry and Women: A Draft Issues Paper*, Sydney, New South Wales: Anglican Church of Australia

Ecumenical sources

Roman Catholic

Catholic Church, 1976–1980, *The Rites of the Catholic Church as Revised by Decree of the Second Vatican Council and Published by Authority of Pope Paul VI*, New York: Pueblo Publishing
Catholic Church, 1983, *The Code of Canon Law (in English Translation)*, London: Harper Collins
Catholic Church, 1994, *Catechism of the Catholic Church*, Dublin: Veritas
John Paul II, 1988, *Mulieris Dignitatem, Apostolic Letter on the Dignity and Vocation of Women*, London: Catholic Truth Society
John Paul II, 1989, *Christifideles Laici*, London: Catholic Truth Society
John Paul II, 1994, *Ordinatio Sacerdotalis* in *Acta Apostolicae Sedis, 86, 545–548*, Vatican City
Leo XIII, 1887, *Apostolicae Curae*, London: Catholic Truth Society
Sacred Congregation for the Doctrine of the Faith, 1976, *Inter Insigniores, (Declaration on the Question of Admission of Women to the Ministerial Priesthood)*, Vatican City
Sacred Congregation for the Doctrine of the Faith, 1977, *The Ordination of Women: Official Commentary from the Sacred Congregation for the Doctrine of the Faith on Its Declaration Inter Insigniores of 15th October 1976, together with the Exchange of Correspondence in 1975 and 1976 between His Grace the Most Reverend Dr Frederick Donald Coggan,*

Archibishop of Canterbury and His Holiness Pope Paul VI, London: Catholic Truth Society

Sacred Congregation for the Doctrine of the Faith, 2004, *Letter to the Bishops of the Catholic Church on the Collaboration of Men and Women in the Church and in the World*, Vatican City

Vatican II, 1964, *Dogmatic Constitution on the Church [Lumen Gentium]*, Boston, Massachusetts: Pauline Books

Orthodox

Inter-Orthodox Consultation on the Place of the Woman in the Orthodox Church and the Question of the Ordination of Women, 1990, *Conclusions of the Inter Orthodox Consultation on the Place of the Woman in the Orthodox Church and the Question of the Ordination of Women (Rhodes, Greece, 30 Oct.–7 Nov. 1988)*, Minneapolis: Light and Life Publishing

Other

Anglican–Methodist Commission on Women and Holy Orders, 1968, *Women and the Ordained Ministry: Report of an Anglican-Methodist Commission on Women and Holy Orders*, London: SPCK/Epworth Press

Anglican–Roman Catholic International Commission, 1982, *ARCIC I Final Report*, London: CTS/SPCK

Anglican–Roman Catholic International Commission, 1999, *The Gift of Authority: Authority in the Church III*, London: Catholic Truth Society

World Council of Churches, 1964, *Concerning the Ordination of Women: A Symposium* Geneva: World Council of Churches

World Council of Churches, 1982, *Baptism, Eucharist and Ministry*, Geneva: World Council of Churches

Books and articles

Armstrong, Karen, 1993, *The End of Silence: Women and Priesthood*, London: Fourth Estate

Avis, Paul, 1999, *Anglican Orders and the Priesting of Women*, London: Darton Longman & Todd

Avis, Paul (ed.), 2003, *Seeking the Truth of Change in the Church: Reception, Communion and the Ordination of Women*, London: T & T Clark

Baker, John Austin, 1981, *The Right Time*, London: Movement for the Ordination of Women

Bam, Brigalia,1971, *What Is Ordination Coming to? Report of a Consultation on the Ordination of Women Held in Cartigny, Geneva, Switzerland, 21st–26th September 1970*, Geneva: World Council of Churches

Barber, Paul, 'What Is a Peculiar?', *3 Ecc LJ* 299

Barker, M., 2003, *The Great High Priest*, Edinburgh: T & T Clark

Barker, M., 2004, *Temple Theology: An Introduction*, London: SPCK

Baron-Cohen, Simon, 2003, *The Essential Difference: Men, Women and the Extreme Male Brain*, London: Allen Lane

Barr, Liz, and Barr, Andrew, 2001, *Jobs for the Boys? Women Who Became Priests*, London: Hodder and Stoughton

Behr-Sigel, Elisabeth, 1990, *The Ministry of Women in the Church*, Redondo Beach, California: Oakwood Publications

Behr-Sigel, Elisabeth, and Ware, Kallistos, 2000, *The Ordination of Women in the Orthodox Church*, Geneva: World Council of Churches

Bennett, Joyce Mary, 1992, *Hasten Slowly* (2nd edn), Chichester, West Sussex: Little London Associates

Blomfield, F. C., 1995, *Wonderful Order*, London: SPCK

Bogle, Joanna, 1987, *Women and the Priesthood: Looking Ahead*, London: Vox

Bouyer, Louis, 1968, *Eucharist*, Notre Dame, Indiana: Notre Dame University Press

Bouyer, Louis, 1979, *Woman in the Church*, San Francisco: Ignatius Press

Bradley, I. C., 1995, *The Power of Sacrifice*, London: Darton, Longman and Todd

Bray, G., 2002, 'Bishops, Presbyters and Women', *The Theologian – the Internet Journal for Integrated Theology*, www.theologian.org.uk

Brent, A., 1992, *Cultural Episcopacy & Ecumenism*, Leiden: EJ Brill

Bridge, G. R., 1997, *Women and the Apostolic Ministry?*, Halifax, Novia Scotia: The Convent Society

Brierley, P., 2003, *The Mind of Anglicans*, London: Christian Research/ Cost of Conscience

Broadhurst, John (ed.), 1996, *Quo Vaditis? The State Churches of Northern Europe*, Leominster: Gracewing

Brown, Raymond E., 1979, 'Roles of Women in the Fourth Gospel', *The Community of the Beloved Disciple*, Mahwah, New Jersey: Paulist Press

Butler, S., 1992, 'The Priest as Sacrament of Christ the Bridegroom', *Worship 66*

Byrne, Lavinia, 1994, *Woman at the Altar: The Ordination of Women in the Roman Catholic Church*, London: Mowbray

Canham, Elizabeth, 1983, *Pilgrimage to Priesthood*, London: SPCK

Carter, Douglas, 1974, *Debating the Ordination of Women*, London: Church Literature Association

Clark, Gillian, 1993, *Women in Late Antiquity: Pagan and Christian Lifestyles*, Oxford: OUP

Clark, Stephen B., 1980, *Man and Woman in Christ: An Examination of the Roles of Men and Women in the Light of Scripture and the Social Sciences*, Ann Arbor, Michigan: Servant Books

Craston, Colin, 1986, *Biblical Headship and the Ordination of Women*, Bramcote, Nottingham: Grove Books

Craston, Colin., Baldwin, Joyce, and Packer, J. I., 1973, *Evangelicals and the Ordination of Women*, Bramcote, Nottingham: Grove Books

Cross, F. L., and Livingstone, E. A. (eds), 1997, *Oxford Dictionary of the Christian Church* (3rd edn), Oxford: OUP

Daniélou, Jean, 1961, *The Minstry of Women in the Early Church*, London: Faith Press

Delahaye, K, 1964, *Ecclesia mater chez les Pères des trois premiers siècles*, Paris: Cerf

de Lubac, H, 1956, *The Splendour of the Church*, London and New York: Sheed & Ward

de Lubac, H., 1971, *Les églises particulières dans l'Eglise universelle*, Paris: Aubier

de Lubac, H., 1982, *The Motherhood of the Church*, San Francisco: Ignatius Press

Demant, Vigo Auguste, 1977, *Why the Christian Priesthood Is Male* (2nd edn), London: Church Literature Association

Denny, E., and. Lacey, T. A, 1895, *De Hierarchia Anglicana*, London

Dicken, Hélène, 1978, *Women and the Apostolic Ministry*, London: Church Literature Association

Doe, N., 1996, *The Legal Framework of the Church of England: A Critical Study in a Comparative Context*, Oxford: Clarendon Press

Donovan, Mary S., 1988, *Women Priests in the Episcopal Church: The Experience of the First Decade*, Cincinnati, Ohio: Forward Movement Publications

Dowell, Susan, and Williams, Jane Welch, 1994, *Bread, Wine & Women: The Ordination Debate in the Church of England*, London: Virago Press

Draper, J. (ed.), 1988, *Communion and Episcopacy: Essays to Mark the Centenary of the Chicago–Lambeth Quadrilateral*, Oxford: Ripon College, Cuddesdon

Edwards, Ruth B., 1989, *The Case for Women's Ministry*, London: SPCK

Edwards, Ruth B., 1992, *Christian Priesthood* (2nd edn), Edinburgh: Movement for Whole Ministry in the Scottish Episcopal Church

Eisen, Ute E., 2000, *Women Officeholders in Early Christianity: Epigraphical and Literary Studies*, Wilmington, Delaware: Michael Glazier

Elwes, Teresa (ed.), 1992, *Women's Voices: Essays in Contemporary Feminist Theology*, London: Marshall Pickering

Field, Barbara, 1989, *Fit for This Office: Women and Ordination*, Melbourne: Collins Dove

Feuillet, A., 1953, *Le Cantique des Cantiques: Étude de théologie biblique et réflexions sur une méthode d'exégèse*, Paris: Les Editions du Cerf

Fiorenza, Elisabeth Schüssler, 1983, *In Memory of Her: A Feminist Theological Reconstruction of Christian Origins*, London: SCM

Fiorenza, Elisabeth Schüssler, and Häring, Hermann, 1999, *The Non-Ordination of Women and the Politics of Power*, London: SCM Press

France, R. T., 1995, *Women in the Church's Ministry: A Test-Case for Biblical Hermeneutics*, Carlisle: Paternoster Press

Francis, Leslie J., and Robbins, Mandy, 1999, *The Long Diaconate, 1987–1994: Women Deacons and the Delayed Journey to Priesthood*, Leominster: Gracewing

Franklin, Margaret Ann, (ed.), 1986, *The Force of the Feminine: Women, Men and the Church*, Sydney/London: Allen & Unwin

Franklin, Margaret Ann, and Jones, Ruth Sturmey (eds), 1987, *Opening the Cage: Stories of Church and Gender*, Sydney/London: Allen & Unwin

Franklin, R. William (ed.), 1996, *Anglican Orders: Essays on the Centenary of Apostolicæ Curae 1896–1996*, London: Mowbray

Furlong, Monica, 1984, *Feminine in the Church*, London: SPCK

Furlong, Monica, 1991, *A Dangerous Delight: Women and Power in the Church*, London: SPCK

Furlong, Monica, 1998, *Act of Synod – Act of Folly?*, London: SCM Press

Gilchrist, Michael, 1991, *The Destabilisation of the Anglican Church: Women Priests and the Feminist Campaign to Replace Christianity*, North Melbourne, Victoria: AD2000 Publications

Gill, Sean, 1994, *Women and the Church of England from the Eighteenth Century to the Present*, London: SPCK

Goldberg, Steven, 1977, *The Inevitability of Patriarchy*, London: Temple Smith

Grabar, André, 1969, *Christian Iconography: A Study of Its Origins*, London: Routledge & Kegan Paul

Grieger, Vernon S., 1988, *Earthly Images of the Heavenly Bride: Women and the Church*, Doncaster, Victoria: Luther Rose Publications

Gumbley, K. F. W. 'Church Legislation in the Isle of Man', *3 Ecc LJ* 240

Guthrie, Harvey H., Borsch, Frederick Houk, Marshall, Michael, and Leonard, Graham, 1970, *The Ordination of Women: An Exchange*, Atlanta: Catacomb Cassettes

Habgood, John, 2004, 'Thoughts on GRAS', *New Directions 7* No. 106

Hailsham of St Marylebone, Lord (ed.), 1973, *Halsbury's Laws of England, 4th edition*, London: Butterworth

Hampson, M. D., 1990, *Theology and Feminism*, Oxford: Blackwell

Harper, Michael, 1994, *Equal and Different*, London: Hodder and Stoughton

Harris, Barbara C., Hiatt, Suzanne R., Wu, Rose, and Katahweire, Mabel,

2000, *Women's Ordination in the Episcopal Church Twenty-Five Years Later*, Cambridge, Massachusetts: Episcopal Divinity School

Hauke, M., 1988, *Women in the Priesthood? A Systematic Analysis in the Light of the Order of Creation and Redemption*, San Francisco: Ignatius Press

Hayter, Mary, 1987, *The New Eve in Christ: The Use and Abuse of the Bible in the Debate about Women in the Church*, Grand Rapids, Michigan: Eerdmans

Hennecke, E., 1965, *New Testament Apocrypha*, London: Lutterworth

Heyward, Carter, 1999, *A Priest Forever: One Woman's Controversial Ordination in the Episcopal Church*, Cleveland, Ohio: Pilgrim Press

Hill, C., and Yarnold, E. (eds), 1994, *Anglicans and Roman Catholics: The Search for Unity*, London: SPCK

Hill, M., 2001, *Ecclesiastical Law* (2nd edn), Oxford: OUP

Hodgson, Leonard, 1967, *Theological Objections to the Admission of Women to Holy Orders*, London: Anglican Group for the Ordination of Women

Holloway, Richard (ed.), 1991, *Who Needs Feminism? Men Respond to Sexism in the Church*, London: SPCK

Hook, Norman, 1977, *A Command of the Lord: The Theological Implications of Women in the Priesthood* (2nd edn), London: Church Literature Association

Hooker, R., 1593 fol., *Laws of Ecclesiastical Polity*, London

Hope, David, 2004, 'Sermon preached at S. Bartholomew's, Armley on 3rd March 2004', *New Directions* 7 No. 107

Hopko, Thomas (ed.), 1983, *Women and the Priesthood*, New York: St. Vladimir's Seminary Press

Hunwicke, John, 2002, 'Pope Philogynes', *New Directions* 5 No. 90

Jones, Ian, 2004, *Women and Priesthood in the Church of England: Ten Years On*, London: Church House Publishing

Kassian, Mary A., 1992, *The Feminist Gospel*, Wheaton, Illinois: Crossway

Kimel, Alvin F. (ed.), 1992, *Speaking the Christian God: The Holy Trinity and the Challenge of Feminism*, Grand Rapids, Michigan: Eerdmanns

Kirk, Geoffrey, 2003, 'A Pertinent Preposition', *New Directions* 6 No. 92

Leahy, B., 2000, *The Marian Profile in the Ecclesiology of Hans Urs von Balthasar*, London: New City Press

Leeder, L., 1997, *Ecclesiastical Law Handbook*, London: Sweet and Maxwell

Lewis, C. S., 1948, 'Priestesses in the Church?', *Time and Tide* xxix

Lewis, C. S., 1971, *Undeceptions: Essays on Theology and Ethics*, London: Geoffrey Bles

Low, Robbie, 2002, 'The Mind of Anglicans', *New Directions* 5 Nos 86 and 87

Macquarrie, J., 1986, *Theology, Church and Ministry*, London: SCM Press

Maitland, Sara, 1983, *A Map of the New Country: Women and Christianity*, London: Routledge & Kegan Paul

Marshall, Rob, 1993, *Never the Same Again – a Journey through Women's Ordination with the Bishop of London*, London: Darton, Longman and Todd

Martimort, A. G., 1986, *Deaconesses: An Historical Study*, San Francisco: Ignatius Press

Mascall, E. L., 1972, *Women Priests?*, London: Church Literature Association

Mason, Kenneth, 1998, *Mothers in God – a Catholic Perspective on Women as Bishops*, Edinburgh: Movement for Whole Ministry in the Scottish Episcopal Church

McAddo, H. R., 1997, *Anglicans and Tradition and the Ordination of Women*, Norwich: Canterbury Press

McGovern, Thomas J., 2001, *Priestly Identity: A Study in the Theology of Priesthood*, Dublin: Four Courts Press

McLoughlin, W., and Pinnock, J. (eds), 1997, *Mary Is for Everyone: Essays on Mary and Ecumenism*, Leominster: Gracewing

Mitchell, J., and Mitchell, H. B. (eds), 1999, *Taking Sides: Clashing Views on Controversial Issues in Word Civilizations*, New York: McGraw-Hill

Moll, Helmut (ed.), 1988, *Church and Women: A Compendium*, San Francisco: Ignatius Press

Montefiore, Hugh, 1978, *Yes to Women Priests*, Great Wakering, Essex: Mayhew-McCrimmon; Oxford: Mowbray

Moore, Paul, 1979, *Take a Bishop like Me*, New York: Harper & Row

Moore, Peter (ed.), 1978, *Man Woman and Priesthood*, London: SPCK

Moore, Peter (ed.), 1982, *Bishops: But What Kind? Reflections on Episcopacy*, London: SPCK

Morris, J., 1973, *Against God and Nature*, London and Oxford: Mowbrays

Morris, Leon, Gaden, John, and Thiering, Barbara, 1976, *A Woman's Place [Documents of the Doctrine Commission of the General Synod of the Church of England in Australia]*, Sydney: Anglican Information Office

Müller, G., 2000, *Priesthood and Diaconate*, San Francisco: Ignatius Press

Nairne, Penny, 1990, *Women Priests: Which Way Will You Vote?*, London: SPCK

Neave, Rosemary, 1990, *The Journey and the Vision: A Report on Ordained Anglican Women in the Church of the Province of New Zealand: Comprising Historical Material, a Report on the 1989 Ordained Anglican Women's Conference, Stories of the Experience of Ordained Anglican Women, and Results of a Questionnaire on How Their Ministry Has Been Received*, Newmarket, Aotearoa, New Zealand: Women's Resource Centre

Nichols, A., 1990, *Holy Order*, Dublin: Veritas

Norman, E., *Ecclesiastical Law Society Lecture, 'Authority in the Anglican Communion'*, 5 *Ecc LJ* 172

Norris, R., 1976, 'The Ordination of Women and the "Maleness" of Christ', *Anglican Theological Review*, Supplementary Series 6

Ober, L., 1908, 'Die Translation der Bischöfe im Altertum', *Archiv für katholische Kirchenrecht* 88

Oddie, William, 1984, *What Will Happen to God? Feminism and the Reconstruction of Christian Belief*, London: SPCK

Otranto, G., 1982, 'Note sul sacerdozio femminile nell'antichita in margine a una testimonianza di Gelasio I', *Vetera Christianorum* 19

Pascher, J., 1949, 'Die Hierarchie in sakramentaler Symbolik', *Episcopus: Studien über das Bischofsamt. Festschrift Kardinal Michael von Faulhaber*, Regensburg

Petre, Jonathan, 1994, *By Sex Divided: The Church of England and Women Priests*, London: Fount

Piper, John, and Grudem, Wayne (eds), 1991, *Recovering Biblical Manhood and Womanhood: A Response to Evangelical Feminism*, Wheaton, Illinois: Crossway

Podmore, C. (ed.), 1998, *Community – Unity – Communion: Essays in Honour of Mary Tanner*, London: Church House Publishing

Porter, Muriel, 1989, *Women in the Church: The Great Ordination Debate in Australia*, Ringwood, Victoria; New York: Penguin

Puente, Pablo, 2002, Letter of 6 November to Andrew Burnham in *New Directions* 6 No. 92

Quick, O. C., 1927, *The Christian Sacraments*, London: Nisbet

Ratzinger, J., 1987, *Principles of Catholic Theology: Building Stones for a Fundamental Theology*, San Francisco: Ignatius Press

Ratzinger, J., 1996, *Called to Communion: Understanding the Church Today*, San Francisco: Ignatius Press

Rezette, J., 1976, 'Le sacerdoce et la femme chez Saint Bonaventure', *Antonianum* 51

Rhoads, Steven E., 2004, *Taking Sex Differences Seriously*, San Francisco: Encounter Books

Robinson, J. A. T., 1952, *The Body: A Study in Pauline Theology*, London: SCM Press

Routley, E., 1955, *Hymns and the Faith*, London: John Murray

Ruether, Rosemary Radford, 1988, *Full Incorporation of Women Into the Ministry of the Church*, Mahwah, New Jersey: Paulist Press

Ruether, Rosemary Radford, 2000, *Women and Roman Catholic Christianity*, Washington, D.C.: Catholics for a Free Choice

Rutler, G. W., 2003, *Priest and Priestess*, Rosemont, Philadelphia: Good Shepherd Press

Saward, John, 1977, *Christ and His Bride: The Ordination of Women*, London: Church Literature Association

Saward, John, 1978, *The Case against the Ordination of Women* (3rd rev. edn), London: The Church Literature Association

Schiess, Betty Bone, 2003, *Why Me, Lord? One Woman's Ordination to the Priesthood with Commentary and Complaint*, New York: Syracuse University Press

Schönborn, C., 1994, *God's Human Face: The Christ Icon*, San Francisco: Ignatius Press

Schulz, S., 1992, *Transmigration und Translation: Studien zum Bischofswechsel in der Spätantike bis zum Hohen Mittelalter*, Cologne: Böhlau

Schweizer, E., 1976, *Der Brief an die Kolosser*, Zurich: Benzinger Verlag

Smail, T. A., 1987, *Forgotten Father: Rediscovering the Heart of the Christian Gospel*, London: Hodder and Stoughton

Steichen, Donna, 1991, *Ungodly Rage: The Hidden Face of Catholic Feminism*, San Francisco: Ignatius Press

Stevenson, Kenneth, 1994, *Covenant of Grace Renewed*, London: Darton, Longman and Todd

Stewart, H. F. (tr.), 1977, *Saepius Officio*, London: Church Literature Association

Sykes, S., 1995, *Unashamed Anglicanism*, London: Darton, Longman & Todd

Tanner, M., 1997, 'The Anglican Position on Apostolic Continuity and Apostolic Succession in the Porvoo Common Statement', in *Visible Unity and the Ministry of Oversight: The Second Theological Conference held under the Meissen Agreement between the Church of England and the Evangelical Church in Germany*, London: Church House Publishing

Thorne, Helen, 2000, *Journey to Priesthood: An In-depth Study of the First Women Priests in the Church of England*, Bristol: Centre for Comparative Studies in Religion and Gender, University of Bristol

Thrall, M. E., 1958, *The Ordination of Women to the Priesthood*, London: SCM Press

Tolhurst, J. (ed.), 1989, *Man, Woman and Priesthood*, Leominster: Gracewing

Toon, Peter, 1990, *Let Wo[Men] Be Wo[Men]: Equality, Ministry and Ordination*, Leominster: Gracewing

Torjesen, K. J., 1993, *When Women Were Priests*, New York: Harper Collins

Torrance, T. F., 1992, *The Ministry of Women*, Edinburgh: Handsel Press

Von Balthasar, H. U., 1986, *The Office of Peter and the Structure of the Church*, San Francisco: Ignatius Press

Wakeman, Hilary, 1996, *Women Priests: The First Years*, London: Darton, Longman and Todd

Walrond-Skinner, Sue, 1994, *Crossing the Boundary: What Will Women Priests Mean?*, London: Mowbray

Watts, Michael (ed.), 1993, *Through a Glass Darkly: A Crisis Considered*, Leominster: Gracewing

Webster, Margaret, 1994, *A New Strength, a New Song: The Journey to Women's Priesthood*, London: Mowbray

Weinandy, T. G., 1985, *Does God Change?*, Still River, Massachusets: St Bede's Publications

Wetherell, David, 1987, *Women Priests in Australia? The Anglican Crisis*, Melbourne: Spectrum

Wijngaards, J. N. M., 1986, *Did Christ Rule Out Women Priests?*, Great Wakering, Essex: McCrimmon's

Wijngaards, J. N. M., 2001, *The Ordination of Women in the Catholic Church: Unmasking a Cuckoo's Egg Tradition*, London: Darton, Longman and Todd

Wijngaards, J. N. M., 2002, *No Women in Holy Orders?*, Norwich: Canterbury Press

Williams, Rowan, 2003, 'The Structures of Unity', *New Directions* 6 No. 100

Wilson, Harold, 1975, *Women Priests? Yes, Now!*, Nutfield: Denholm House Press

Wilson, W. Gilbert, 198, *Why No Women Priests?*, Worthing: Churchman

Young, F. M., 1994, *Presbyteral Ministry in the Catholic Tradition or Why Shouldn't Women Be Priests?*, Exeter: Methodist Sacramental Fellowship

Zizioulas, John D., 1997, *Being as Communion*, New York: St. Vladimir's Seminary Press

Zizioulas, John D., 2001, *Eucharist, Bishop, Church: The Unity of the Church in the Divine Eucharist and the Bishop during the First Three Centuries*, Brookline, Massachusetts: Holy Cross Orthodox Press

Index of Biblical Texts

Index of Proper Names

Biblical names are to be found in the Index of Subjects

Index of Subjects

Index of Statutes, Measures, Acts and Canons

Canons of the Roman Catholic Church